A PRECIOUS TREASURE:

JONATHAN EDWARDS'S PREACHING AND TEACHING BASED ON BIBLICAL KNOWLEDGE AND PURITAN EDUCATION

A PRECIOUS TREASURE:

JONATHAN EDWARDS'S PREACHING AND TEACHING BASED ON BIBLICAL KNOWLEDGE AND PURITAN EDUCATION

John L. Inman III

Preface by Thomas Kidd

Volume 7

A Series of Treatises on Jonathan Edwards

JESociety Press

WWW.JESOCIETY.ORG

Special Edition Hardcover March 19, 2026

A publication of JESociety Press
Visit https://www.jesociety.org

For permission requests and inquiries,
Email: rob@jesociety.org
Web: www.jesociety.org

Cover: Stockbridge mission house adapted from https://commons.wikimedia.org/wiki/File:Mission_House_(Stockbridge,_Massachusetts).JPG

PRAISE FOR THIS VOLUME

"Edwards' Stockbridge sermons are finally gaining due attention, as is Edwards' identity as a pastor-theologian. Inman builds on these trends and shows his subject at work as a contextually-sensitive, psychologically-brilliant preacher and teacher of theology through Scripture. He even offers application for ministers today. His sensitive portrayal of this eighteenth-century educator deserves a wide reading."

Douglas A. Sweeney
Dean and Professor of Divinity
Beeson Divinity School

"John Inman's *A Precious Treasure* makes a new and helpful contribution to how historians and theologians understand how Edwards adapted his preaching in light of his perception of his audience's biblical literacy. Specifically, he looks at how Edwards not only used the homiletical tradition he inherited and deployed to a Colonial audience, but also how he advanced theology through preaching for a Native American audience by deploying a new pedagogy. I am thankful to see this in print."

Jason G. Duesing
Provost and Professor of Historical Theology
Midwestern Baptist Theological Seminary

"Rich with historical detail and pedagogical insight, Inman's volume takes readers deep into the vision Edwards had for creating and maintaining biblical literacy among those to whom he ministered. Inman interestingly demonstrates how Edwards accomplished this task not merely with his scripturally aware Northampton congregation, but also with the more biblically illiterate native peoples he ministered to in Stockbridge. Parents, Christian educators, pastors, and Edwards readers will highly benefit from this unique study of Edwards who was constantly finding ways to get the Bible into the hearts and minds of his contemporaries."

Robert Caldwell
Professor of Church History
Southwestern Baptist Theological Seminary

"In this very valuable contribution to Edwardsean studies, Dr. Inman has sought to help us understand the background of Edwards' preaching content in Northampton and Stockbridge. What Inman has shown very clearly, is that Edwards was well aware of the varying degrees of Biblical knowledge held by his hearers, and that that appreciation led Edwards to tailor his sermons appropriately. Dr. Inman, while clearly recognizing there has recently been a renaissance in Edwardsean scholarship, he has at the same time, also appreciated the need to account for the principles that influenced the content of Edwards' messages in two very different contexts. The result is a well-documented, scholarly interpretation that fills the gap in our knowledge of what drove Edwards to preach the content he did. While exposition of the Bible remained central to Edwards' ministry, Inman also proves that it was the degree to how well the Bible was known and believed which led Edwards to tailor those messages in Colonial New England."

Dr. Michael McMullen
Lee and Tammy Roberson Endowed Chair of Church History
Professor of Church History
Editor, Midwestern Journal of Theology
Midwestern Baptist Theological Seminary

She is of a wonderful sweetness, calmness and universal benevolence of mind; especially after those times in which this great God has manifested himself to her mind. She will sometimes go about, singing sweetly, from place to [place]; and seems to be always full of joy and pleasure; and no one knows for what. She loves to be alone, and to wander in the fields and on the mountains, and seems to have someone invisible always conversing with her.

–Jonathan Edwards on his wife Sarah Pierpont Edwards

The same can be said of my dear wife Megan. Here's to wandering through fields and forests, and across mountains and rivers as we journey together to bring Him glory,

With love to my sweet Goldberry, your grateful Bombadil

ABSTRACT

This book is concerned with showing the biblical, pedagogical principles Jonathan Edwards utilized in advancing theology through sermons in light of his his audience's biblical knowledge, shown in the format and delivery of his sermons to a colonial audience and Native American audience with different biblical knowledge. While there are many works on Edwards's ministry, philosophy, theology, and preaching, this work combines Edwards's biblical instruction and how he utilized it in his sermons for a Native American audience at Stockbridge maintaining a high exposition of Scripture.

Contents

Preface

For evangelicals, the Bible is the indispensable source for preaching. This statement is both obvious and urgent, as the watching world and a preacher's imagination will always suggest endless topics that sermons might cover besides the biblical text. But the sufficiency of Scripture does not give the preacher a license to exegete in a vacuum, without attending to the needs of his people. A given congregation could be rich or poor; old or young; struggling with manifest sins or subtle complacency. The good shepherd knows the state of his flock, and that knowledge shapes his preaching of the all-sufficient Word.

One of the most pressing questions that a pastor should ask about his church is how well they know the Bible. Of course, there will be a range of familiarity depending on a member's age, or their time spent in a Bible-preaching church. But there are also deep cultural patterns that affect biblical literacy among different peoples, including the availability of the Bible in the vernacular language, and the relative centrality of the Bible to a society's educational and media culture.

As John Inman's *A Precious Treasure* shows, the great pastor-theologian Jonathan Edwards worked in two highly disparate ministry contexts during his career: the Bible-saturated town of Northampton, Massachusetts, and the Bible-lacking Mohican missionary frontier of Stockbridge, Massachusetts. Virtually any topic in Edwards' career is worth studying, but understanding the ways that Edwards modulated his preaching depending on the audience's biblical literacy is particularly rewarding, as seen in Inman's work. Few pastors had ever operated in such different contexts as Edwards did when he shifted from Northampton to Stockbridge, after being dismissed from his Northampton pastorate in 1750.

The New England colonies had exceptionally high rates of literacy, as the Puritan founders insisted that widespread understanding of Scripture was essential to the health of a godly commonwealth. As historian Harry Stout has noted, New England churchgoers would conventionally hear sermons three times a week (twice on Sundays and once midweek), each of which was deeply biblical and doctrinal, and typically lasted at least an hour. Stout estimates that the average New England churchgoer probably heard about seven thousand sermons in a lifetime. Though these churchgoers were usually farmers with little formal education, their level of biblical literacy probably exceeded that of most evangelical church members today.[1]

Of course, access to the Bible is more pervasive in today's internet age than it was in Edwards's Northampton. Most obviously, Bible apps and widespread smartphone ownership have put the Bible at the fingertips of much of the world's population, while owning a household copy of the Bible remained somewhat rare in pre-Revolutionary America. But ubiquity of Bible access certainly does not ensure that the Bible is read or applied. Evidence would suggest that the percentage of American adults who regularly read the Bible has dropped significantly in recent years, even though Bible engagement in modern America has never approached the high levels among colonial New Englanders.[2]

But more subtle differences in western information and educational culture also account for the profound difference in Bible literacy between colonial America and today. Preaching input among the colonists was not only consistent and profoundly biblical, but preaching then had an exclusive influence that we simply can't imagine in the streaming media era. For the average colonist in the 1740s, preaching often wielded a singular intellectual impact in a time when other media (newspapers, books, etc.) were typically in short supply, especially outside of major towns like Boston.

Most importantly for our chronological comparison of the Bible and media, there was *no electronic media at all* until the advent of the telegraph in the mid-1800s. Imagine your typical evangelical churchgoer today: he or she likely hears a more-or-less biblically grounded sermon on Sunday morning, lasting maybe thirty minutes. Maybe he or she occasionally delves into a daily Bible reading plan too. But this Bible-based content may be just a small piece of flotsam amidst a raging flood of other content: social

[1] Harry S. Stout, *The New England Soul: Preaching and Religious Culture in Colonial New England* (New York: Oxford University Press, 1986), 3–4.

[2] "State of the Bible," American Bible Society https://sotb.americanbible.org/ [accessed 1/13/2026].

media and news sites, podcasts, Netflix, Spotify, and much more. Even if this churchgoer does hear three hours of sermons a week (maybe via podcasts), the sermons stand beside many other intakes, from NFL games to pop music to a favorite show on a streaming service. Some of this media may be anti-biblical, some not, but the point is that evangelical churchgoers live in a much noisier mental world today than people did in the 1740s. One reason why the West is post-Christian today is that it is easier than ever to imbibe phenomenal amounts of information and entertainment, none of which necessarily has anything to do with the Bible. Secular people rarely find that algorithms on Facebook or YouTube push them to think about eternal things.

The Mohicans of Stockbridge lived in a media culture that was even more narrow and local than that of the colonial farmer in Northampton. Most notably for preaching and Bible literacy, traditional Mohicans had no written language, and no translated Bible. (John Eliot's "Indian Bible" of 1663 was a translation into Massachusett, an Algonquian dialect related to Mohican.) Thus their tribal culture and traditions, including religious practices, were transmitted orally. This orality synced with a pastor's sermonic method, but there was no biblical text for the Mohicans to follow visually as Edwards preached sermons via Mohican or Mohawk translators. Scholars have noted that translating Christian concepts such as sin or the one supreme God into Indian vernacular presented special challenges, because Native Americans often had no equivalent terms or beliefs for Christian categories. However, Edwards also used Christian doctrines such as original sin to emphasize the common humanity, and common moral debility, of whites and Indians. He was not inclined to accuse the Indians of stubborn cultural savagery, as some other colonial observers did.

Admirers of Jonathan Edwards sometimes say that the church would be better off if pastors preached just like him. I agree with this point, if we mean that our preaching should be biblically rigorous, and passionate about the truth revealed in Scripture. But I would also remind such admirers that Edwards was speaking, as Inman demonstrates, into not just one but two distinctive cultures of biblical literacy. Moreover, the cultures of Northampton and Stockbridge were starkly different from the media environment of contemporary America. Preachers now can't assume the level of biblical or doctrinal literacy that Edwards could in 1740s Northampton. Perhaps our contemporary situation is closer to preaching in 1750s Stockbridge, where some audience members literally knew nothing about the biblical texts on which he was preaching.

Perhaps what most sets a modern congregation apart from both Northampton and Stockbridge, however, is the intense competition pastors today face from other voices and media. Before and after service (and sometimes during a sermon!) congregants will be taking in other messages (texts, websites, articles, social media, etc.), which will at a minimum distract them from internalizing the Word of God. Thankfully, a pastor does not depend on his rhetorical talents alone to make the Word pierce a distracted heart. Throughout the generations and across media cultures, the church has trusted the Holy Spirit to do an enduring work in believers' lives, via the preached Word. I recommend John Inman's *A Precious Treasure* as a worthy examination of Edwards, an unusually brilliant expositor, and his efforts to convey the truths of the Word to his generation.

Thomas S. Kidd
Midwestern Baptist Theological Seminary

INTRODUCTION

> But till the Bible was sent abroad in the world, all the world lay in ignorance of him; but when this came, it was successful to bring the world to an acknowledgement of him. And this is evidential, that the Bible is the proper means for teaching the world concerning God... Since we have this light in our hands, let us prize it, and make use of [it]. O! what *a precious treasure have we*, in that we have this very revelation {of God's will}. Let us therefore not neglect, and let it lie by, as if it were good for nothing, a thing of no use... Shall we have this revelation in our hands, and not read and search it, and diligently use it from day to day?[1]

For Jonathan Edwards, the Bible was a precious treasure. Throughout his ministry he placed priority on relaying the "inexhaustible"[2] value in God's Word and the value in the Gospel far beyond "gold and all earthly treasures."[3] For most of his ministry, he served a colonial congregation well versed and culturally enmeshed in the Scriptures. However, in 1751 Jonathan Edwards found himself with a different mission and congregation to instruct in this *precious treasure* of God's Word. A majority of his new congregation could not understand Scripture spoken in English, much less

[1]Jonathan Edwards, "Light in a Dark World, A Dark Heart," *Sermons and Discourses, 1734–1738,* ed. M.X. Lesser, vol. 19, *The Works of Jonathan Edwards* (New Haven: Yale University Press, 2001), 721–722.

[2]Edwards, "The Excellency of Christ," *Sermons and Discourses, 1734–1748*, 584.

[3]Edwards, "Heeding the Word, and Losing It," *Sermons and Discourses, 1734–1738*, 44.

read the Bible. Setting out to serve his new Mohican[4] congregants in Stockbridge, Edwards evaluated the situation through correspondence with Timothy Woodbridge (appointed the schoolmaster of one of two schools for Mohican children at Stockbridge), noting even the children who could recognize the letters and vowels that made up English words, and correctly pronounce said words, could not understand the meaning of the words they were saying. As seen in a letter of Edwards to William Pepperell dated November 28, 1751, Edwards hoped to help the children understand not only the pronunciation but also the meaning of the English language. To do this, he would trust in the normative educational process he and his children used to speak, read, and write in English of reading a lesson to understand the meaning of words and sentences through reading the Psalter, the Bible, catechism, and then ask questions on biblical subjects. After finding answers from the catechisms, they would rephrase to show understanding.[5]

There was an inseparable tie between literacy and biblical literacy in colonial New England during the 18th century. Edwards would suggest the use of popular catechisms at the time.[6] What should be highlighted from the letter, though, is not only the Bible's mechanical use but also Edwards's emphasis on the children comprehending the material to increase biblical literacy. To Edwards, this was the starting point, the base level of instruction and growth in knowledge.

At first glance, attempting to choose a new topic to write about Jonathan Edwards may seem impossible, yet the vast written corpus left by Edwards provides many unexplored avenues. Specifically, his vast number of sermons still require a large amount of analysis.

Many books, articles, and dissertations on Edwards focus on the area of the theoretical. On the other hand, the area of practice is less analyzed. Specifically, though given great diligence, works on his preaching are only

[4]Throughout this work the terms "Mohican," "Mahican," "Indian," "Native," "Native American," "Mohawk," "Mohegan," and various other self-identifying terms will be used in reference, and with respect, to the various Native American groups of colonial New England.

[5]Jonathan Edwards, *Letters and Personal Writings,* ed. George S. Claghorn, vol. 16, *The Works of Jonathan Edwards* (New Haven: Yale University Press, 1998), 408

[6]Edwards, *Letters,* 408–410.

on his technique and topic. With few exceptions,[7] the *audiences* of Edwards's preaching are neglected.

Even so, with the exception of Roy Paul, Rachel Wheeler, and Michael Harder, whose research focuses on Edwards's mission to the Mohicans, no one has examined the sermons in light of their tie to the audience's biblical literacy, or the transition of pedagogy and methodology in Edwards's preaching due to his change in audience.

In teaching and preaching, the one giving a lecture/sermon needs to understand the level of knowledge their audience has of the topic they wish to present.[8] Without such knowledge, they may overwhelm their audience or, conversely, bore and lose their audience's interest, who may see the topic as elementary.[9] Alistair Begg writes that "preaching at its best maintains a balance between teaching and preaching. First, there will be careful exposition of God's truth, so that hearers clearly understand what God says, and then there will be an appeal to men and women's wills to respond with reasonable obedience." The more the pastor understands their congregation, the better they will be able to balance the teaching and preaching necessary in producing response.[10]

Thus, knowing the biblical literacy of a preacher's audience is vital to determine the preacher's reasons for employing his homiletical arrangement and delivery and to gauge his effectiveness.[11] How Edwards utilized, illustrated, and exposited the Bible to advance theology through sermons will be analyzed in light of Edwards's biblical literacy, his perception of his audience's biblical literacy, and how a shift in his audience (from Northampton

[7]A thorough list of works which analyze Edwards's hermeneutics and homiletics are listed in my dissertation which this volume is a revised adaptation of. See: John L. Inman, III, "A Treasure Taught: Jonathan Edwards's Preaching Methodology Based on Pedagogy and Biblical Literacy" (PhD diss., Midwestern Baptist Theological Seminary, 2024), fn. 4, pg. 3. For a full literature review again see: Inman, "A Treasure Taught," 8–25.

[8]"The speaker should have a general idea of the average level of comprehension of those addressed." Robert Thomas, "Exegesis and Expository Preaching," in *Preaching: How to Preach Biblically*, ed. John MacArthur (Nashville: Thomas Nelson, 2005), 117.

[9]"He (the preacher) should gear most of his remarks just below (the average level of comprehension), but periodically he should rise above that level a bit. This will challenge his people and keep them from getting bored with hearing so much that they already know." Ibid.

[10]Derek J. Prime and Alistair Begg, *On Being a Pastor: Understanding Our Calling and Work* (Chicago: Moody Publishers, 2004), 119–120.

[11]John MacArthur, "Moving from Exegesis to Exposition," in *Preaching: How to Preach Biblically,* ed. John MacArthur (Nashville: Thomas Nelson, 2005), 238.

to Stockbridge) changed the format and delivery of his sermons due to his perception of their biblical literacy.

The scope of Edwards's sermons selected for this project was chosen by examining Edwards's preaching at Stockbridge. Through examination of the *Chronological Sermons Index* from the *Jonathan Edwards Sermon Index* at the Jonathan Edwards Center at Yale, it was observed that several sermon "series" (two to three sermons building on the same passage or theme) were preached by Edwards at Stockbridge to his Native congregation. Harry Stout notes that second-generation ministers of the "plain-style" of preaching delivered two or more sermons on a particular text or prepared longer-running series that could extend months and even years (this is seen in Edwards's *Charity and Its Fruits* series preached at Northampton).[12] Because of this, his short couplet and tri-series of sermons provide the best opportunity to get a feel for his purpose in preaching at Stockbridge (with comparative series preached to colonial audiences examined in comparison).

Corresponding sermons on the same key texts, biblical themes, or books throughout Edwards's ministry among colonials were then chosen as parallel sermons to compare with those at Stockbridge. The sermons at Stockbridge show Edwards's methodology of instruction over several sermons at Stockbridge while also giving corresponding sermons that show Edwards's evolution of preaching over the breadth of his time in ministry among colonials. This comparison produced a useful method for analyzing how Edwards transitioned both as a pastor and, more specifically, as a pastoral and missional preacher in light of the Puritan teaching method.

Edwards is arguably the most influential thinker and preacher in American history (even notwithstanding his status as a colonial British citizen of the time). His influence on Evangelicalism and American religious history and practice make him a paramount figure for analysis.

His extensive corpus of sermons also affords itself to analyze how his method advanced over years and with various texts and biblical books. His personal views on Scripture, education, ministry, and preaching (and how they relate to the above time periods) are also well documented through his corpus of personal correspondence, journals, and notations on Scripture. Edwards is also beneficial to study due to his long tenure at Northampton. With his more than three decades of service as pastor at the church, his familiarity with his audience can be seen and shown through his sermons. Edwards's sudden departure and his unique change of ministry at Stockbridge (with

[12]Harry S. Stout, *The New England Soul: Preaching and Religious Culture in Colonial New England* (New York: Oxford University Press, 1986), 93.

Native Americans) also gives a dramatic contrast in the audience to analyze and prove his sensitivity in preaching based on his audience.

For all the reasons stated above, Edwards is a great example to analyze and apply to preaching even today. The purpose of this book is to show a preacher can be pastoral in guiding and encouraging their audience to seek, love, and utilize the Bible through preaching and application of sermons based on understanding the biblical literacy of their audience.

Outline

The first chapter will examine the enmeshment of the Bible and Puritan culture through looking at the confessions utilized by the Puritans (the *Westminster Confession* and the *Savoy Declaration*), catechisms and primers utilized by Congregational churches in New England will be examined to show the cultural context Edwards utilized. This will be done by first looking at the state of education and biblical literacy in the colonies in general. Then, the focus will be narrowed down to biblical literacy and education in Massachusetts, then Northampton. Edwards's view of a high biblical literacy for the congregation at Northampton was due to the emphasis on education in the area and colonial New England's educational tie to the Bible. This educational level will later contrast the lack thereof for those at Stockbridge and Edwards's admission of a lower biblical literacy at Stockbridge and his emphasis on education tied to biblical literacy for those he ministers to.

The second chapter will examine Edwards's Puritan training received from his Puritan roots handed down from his grandfather, Solomon Stoddard, and father, Timothy Edwards. This will be done by analyzing Edwards's writing on his pastoral upbringing and looking at the primary sources that shaped his homiletics. Edwards's role as a pastor and preacher in a colonial Congregational context will be seen through pastoral preaching biography that will examine Edwards's life in light of this role as pastor and preacher. The chapter will then conclude through looking at Edwards's view of the Biblical literacy of his colonial congregations.

With the educational and homiletical context of Edwards's role as pastor and preacher in a colonial Congregational context given in the second chapter, the third chapter will look at the short (2–4 sermons) series of sermons Edwards preached to colonial audiences before examining further sermons which align with sermons Edwards preached to Native American audiences at Stockbridge.

Chapter four will examine missions among Native Americans in colonial New England and the mission at Stockbridge (including Sergeant and Edwards's perception of their audience's biblical literacy and methods to address it). This will be done by looking at primary sources and accounts from Native American mission in colonial New England and from Edwards and those who ministered in Stockbridge. Jonathan Edwards's sermons (specifically sermon "series") during his ministry at Stockbridge will be analyzed. How he crafted his sermons in light of his new audience and his teaching method will be given. How the structure and content of those sermons differed from his previous sermons at Northampton will be explained. Sermons with the same key texts, though created anew when preached for a Native audience at Stockbridge, will be analyzed in view of how he modified them for his new audience to show his pastoral focus.

Finally, a conclusion and application will show how Edwards's pastoral commitment to preaching the Word faithfully for all of his congregations will be given as an example for today how one can encourage their audience (no matter their biblical understanding) to come fully into the presence of God's truth and change their lives to live and glorify God.

CHAPTER 1:
PURITAN TIES TO BIBLICAL LITERACY

Introduction

IN WRITING ON THE CULTURE of the 18th century, Mark Noll notes for those in colonial British America, "since a supreme deity actually existed and had communicated his will by revelation to humankind, all human life should be organized in response to that revelation."[1] Noll's main point from his work *In the Beginning Was the Word* is how the Bible guided Protestants in the New World above all other authority. "Biblicism," as Noll explains, was an "effort to follow 'the Bible alone,' absent or strongly subordinating other authorities, as the path of life with and for God."[2]

Noll credits John Sterling with the phrase "Biblicism" in connection to the Puritans as a comparative to the "Squirism" of those who supported King Charles I as Royalists. Sterling identified the Puritans as Biblicists due to their "ardent profession to follow only the Scriptures" as they would push for reforms to the Church of England.[3] Noll advances this further in alignment with Marsden's identification of the Puritan's desire to "set aside all intervening tradition and return to the purity of the New Testament

[1]Mark A. Noll, *In the Beginning Was the Word: The Bible in American Public Life, 1492–1783,* (Oxford: Oxford University Press, 2016), 3. Noll's work examines how the Bible was used commonly by various demographics in the public square during this time.

[2]Ibid., 7–8.

[3]Ibid., 8. Noll credits a version of Carlyle's *Life of John Sterling*, the same passage was found in Thomas Carlyle, *Life of John Sterling*, vol. 20, *Thomas Carlyle's Collected Works* (London: Chapman and Hall, 1851), 311–312.

practice."[4] The priority and practice of the Bible alone as a guide and authority emerged out of the Reformation, as will be seen below by looking at the confessions of the period.

With the momentum and events of the Reformation, many attempted to make the Bible the authority in all areas of life, unsuccessfully at first in England, with more limited success in New England. This limited success was in part due to less competition from other factions with different views of how to center Scripture for all of life.[5]

This chapter will look at how those in colonial Massachusetts (specifically Edwards's congregation through his writings) revolved their lives around and understood God's Word through formation and foundation. This examination continues the theme of this work of how Edwards's pastoral ministry of preaching centered on his audience's biblical literacy.

This chapter begins with the importance placed on the Bible as a definitive authority to the Puritans through their confessions, catechisms, and primers. The advancement of biblical literacy in colonial America will be seen in the Puritan primary sources of the period.

Biblicist Confessions Adopted by the Puritans

The fight for religious liberty to practice one's faith based on biblical convictions (and not on the authority of a state-endorsed church) began in the Reformation and continued through the lifetime and ministry of Edwards, the Revolutionary War, and beyond into the 19th Century. Edwards's ministry was spent among the Congregational and Presbyterian denominations. While other newer denominations faced continuing struggles for individual congregation practice, the churches Edwards served would be free in that regard.[6]

Confessions were a method for those emerging from the Reformation to show their alignment with the Bible and biblical doctrine. The first major confession adopted by the Puritans was the *Westminster Confession of Faith*. The *Westminster Confession of Faith* became the "dominant" confession for Reformed Protestants. Later confessions (such as the *Second London Confession* along with later confessions and catechisms created by Congregational and Methodist churches) used the *Westminster Confession of Faith* as a tem-

[4] Noll, *In the Beginning*, 8.

[5] Ibid., 72–73.

[6] Noll, *In the Beginning*, 12–14.

plate document upon which to build. The *Westminster Confession of Faith* was written during the English Civil War by the Westminster Assembly (who met from 1643–53) as a way to further the Protestant reform of the English Church. Scottish theologians helped shape the document. The Scottish Church more readily adopted the confession than the more traditionally Anglican southern Church.[7]

All ten points of the first article of the confession relate to the authority and importance of Scripture.[8] The tenth article gives a particular resonance to the confession's submission and exaltation of the Bible's authority and reliability for all matters as follows:

> The supreme judge by which all controversies of religion are to be determined, and all the decrees of councils, opinions of ancient writers, doctrines of men, and private spirits, are to be examined, and in whose sentence we are to rest, can be no other but the Holy Spirit speaking in the Scripture.[9]

Multiple scriptural allusions are saturated throughout the confession as the basis for each doctrine. One example is relates to Christ's role as Mediator.[10] Later, a synod of Congregational theologian leaders, including John Owen and Thomas Goodwin, met at Savoy Palace in London in October 1658 to revise the *Westminster Confession of Faith* (1647).[11] The revisions were to refute some "misrepresentations of Congregationalism" and to add some clearer explanations of where Congregationalists have diverged from Presbyterians and the *Westminster Confession* though "fully" assenting to its "substance."[12]

[7]Ibid., 189–192.

[8]"The Westminster Confession," *Creeds, Confessions, and Catechisms: A Reader's Edition* Chad Van Dixhoorn, Ed., (Wheaton, IL: Crossway, 2022), 192–198.

[9]*Creeds, Confessions, and Catechisms*, 192–198.

[10]Ibid., 212.

[11]James M. Renihan, "God Freely Justifieth...By Imputing Christ's Active...And Passive Obedience," *The Master's Journal* 32 no. 1 (Spring 2021): 64.

[12]Daniel W. Burrus. "The Confessional Journey of John Owen," *The Westminster Theological Journal* 84, no. 1 (Spring 2022): 82–101., 20–21. Of note for these changes is 1) in XXI "Christian Liberty and Liberty of Conscience where the *Savoy Declaration* edits out where the civil magistrate is given power to punish heresy; and 2) in XXVI "Of the Church" where the *Savoy Declaration* rejects the *Westminster*'s declaration of baptismal entry into the visible church, the inclusion of children as members of the visible church, and the statement of Sacrament's purpose in delineating between those in the visible church from those not in it. Albert Peel, ed., *The Savoy Declaration of Faith and Order, 1658* (London: Independent Press, 1939), 20–21.

Copying the language of the *Westminster Confession*, the first chapter of the *Savoy Declaration* is on the "Holy Scriptures" with the standard Protestant canon and a dismissal of the Apocrypha sandwiching the statement on the canon as all "which are given by the inspiration of God to be the Rule of Faith and Life."[13] The Scriptures are shown in the sixth point as the "whole Counsel of God" for God's glory, man's salvation, faith, and life (living). The authors argue whether it concerns worship of God or even the "Government of the Church," all things "common to humane actions and Societies" should be ordered "according to the general rules of the Word, which are always to be observed." This argument again provides insight into how life and thought were to be centered on the Scriptures, specifically for Congregationalists.[14]

Reformation Catechisms and Primers

Catechisms (and later Primers) were intended to make the doctrines accessible and teachable for children. The method of bonding education and uniformity in doctrine goes back to the ushering of publishing with the Gutenberg Press and early guides printed by the Catholic Church. The name primer denoted from the "authorized" primers were so named as they were not "school books being primary – manuals of church service."[15]

The Westminster Shorter and Longer Catechisms

The *Westminster Shorter Catechism* was a revised version of the larger *Westminster Larger Catechism*. Both catechisms were written in 1647 as companion texts to the *Westminster Confession of Faith* (1646). The *Shorter Catechism* was written as an outgrowth of the larger version but with a more personal, direct voice. The *Larger Catechism* was designed for formal use for groups such as churches and family groups. The *Shorter Catechism* was a tighter abridgment "capable of being memorized even by a child."[16]

Like the *Westminster Confession of Faith*, the *Larger Catechism* shows the esteem placed on the Word of God by asking and answering how the Scriptures are the Word of God in how they "give all glory to God," "convince

[13] *The Savoy Declaration*, 2.

[14] *The Savoy Declaration*, 2.

[15] Paul Leicester Ford, ed., *The New-England Primer: A History of Its Origin and Development with a Reprint of the Unique Copy of the Earliest Known Edition and Many Fac-Simile Illustrations and Reproductions* (New York: Dodd, Mead, and Company, 1897), 4–8.

[16] *Creeds, Confessions, and Catechisms*, 369–461.

and convert sinners," "comfort and build up believers unto salvation," but most importantly through the Holy Spirit "bearing witness by and with" God's Word to proof it being "the very Word of God."[17]

This question is echoed in the Shorter Catechism's third question about what the Bible teaches, "principally, ... what man is to believe concerning God, and what duty God requires of man."[18] The *Larger Catechism* also includes a call to read the Bible (with restrictions on who should read it in the congregation), though all should "read it apart by themselves, and with their families" noting it should be translated "out the original into vulgar languages.[19] The *Larger Catechism* also prescribes the Bible be read with a "high and reverent esteem of them, and with a firm persuasion that they are the very Word of God." And the Bible be read with prayer, obedience, and meditation.[20]

This is paralleled in the answer to the *Shorter Catechism*'s question ninety for how the Word is to be "read and heard," stating the Word be attended with "diligence, preparation, and prayer" and received with "faith and love" and practiced in their catechized lives.[21] The Westminster catechisms formed the basis for the primers that were essential in the ministry of Jonathan Edwards at Northampton and Stockbridge.

Puritan Confessions, Catechisms, and Primers

An aim and product of the Reformation, with an emphasis on the access to and priority of the Bible, was the renewal of personal experience and spiritual formation. Puritanism, though part of the broader spiritual awakening, was a "devotional movement dedicated to the spiritual regeneration of individuals and society."[22] The Puritans were a transatlantic movement who held influence both in England and the colonies. As they "first settled

[17]"The Westminster Larger Catechism," *Creeds, Confessions, and Catechisms*, 371.

[18]*Creeds, Confessions, and Catechisms*, 461. Like the *Larger Catechism*, the *Shorter Catechism* too is tied explicitly to Scriptural references.

[19]"The Westminster Larger Catechism," *Creeds, Confessions, and Catechisms*, 439.

[20]*Creeds, Confessions, and Catechisms*, 439. Questions 158–160 again esteem the Bible in qualifying who should preach the Word and what the listeners of the Word preached should do.

[21]"The Westminster Shorter Catechism," *Creeds, Confessions, and Catechisms*, 485.

[22]Charles E Hambrick-Stowe, *The Practice of Piety: Puritan Devotional Disciplines in Seventeenth-Century New England* (Chapel Hill: University of North Carolina Press, 1982), 51.

Massachusetts Bay," their "influence spread throughout New England and dominated those colonies until the Great Awakening of 1740s."[23]

The "fundamental Puritan concern – to which we shall return – was to shift the authority base of Christian faith from that which rested principally on either the Church and its hierarchy or the Crown and its law, to that which rested principally on the Bible."[24] At the center of Puritan godliness was the Bible. In his account of martyrs, John Foxe quotes the famous line of William Tyndale that "if God spare my life ere many years, I will cause the boy that driveth the plough shall know more of the scripture than thou doest."[25] The religious culture Jonathan Edwards lived was a culture that saw this pronouncement made a reality through an emphasis on scriptural guidance and devotion at church, in personal study, and as a guiding force in education.

The Puritans initially sought reform within the Church of England through encouragement for the state church to be conformed to God's Word. When those within the Puritan movement saw this would not be a reality according to their desires, many ultimately sought the New World as a place to plant a new community built on a biblically-centered culture.

In his sermon "God's Promise to His Plantation" (1630), the Puritan pastor John Cotton encourages his congregation as they prepare to embark on their journey to the New World. His encouragement for settling across the Atlantic in New England was tied to greater spiritual devotion and practices dedicated to God.[26]

Cotton's sermon, taken from 2 Samuel 7:10, uses the text as the biblical warrant to go and seek a place of spiritual dedication and growth. Cotton goes further, speaking about how the Word of God abide in them as they settle in the New World that they "have a care to be implanted into the Ordinances, that the word may be ingrafted into you, and you into it."[27]

The Puritan emphasis on biblical literacy was a result of the Protestant "insistence that individuals must be able to read their own Bibles." It was the availability and priority of the Bible that lessened the exclusive authority

[23]Robert S. Paul, "The Accidence and the Essence of Puritan Piety," *Austin Seminary Bulletin*, XCIII, no. 8 (May 1978): 8.

[24]Ibid., 10.

[25]Transposed from the online 1563 version of John Foxe's *The Acts and Monuments*. John Foxe, *The Unabridged Acts and Monuments Online (TAMO)* (Sheffield: The Digital Humanities Institute, 2011), 570.

[26]Hambrick-Stowe, *The Practice of Piety*, 53.

[27]Referencing Isa 27:2–3. Cotton, "Gods Promise to His Plantation," 18.

reserved for priests before. The new emphasis for Puritans was on personal experience and spiritual expression through literacy, meditation, and prayer.[28] Reading and writing for the Puritans was founded on the understanding of what "useful" or "good" literature was. The "purpose" of all speech and writing was to relay Biblical truth, which points the reader or listener to their woeful state without Christ and their blessedness because of Him.[29]

Just as Cotton's charge for those settling in the New World was to be Word-centered, the emphasis on the Bible in all manner of life was carried on by the Puritans who settled and lived in colonial America as reflected in their documents and preaching. Knowing precisely how many households individually owned and used the historical manuals (such as the *New England Primer*) that defined the Puritan movement is unattainable. However, the manuals themselves can be relied on to give insight into the popular experience within Puritan New England in two respects. The first is they correspond to surviving correspondence of the experience; and second, their wide distribution, multiple editions, and popular style point to their heavy usage by those in the Puritan tradition in New England, including by Edwards's family in their instruction and by Edwards throughout his ministry.[30]

In the *Lawes for Massachusetts*, enacted in 1648, the priority of literacy and its intrinsic connection to the Bible and religion is stated directly, as Edmund S. Morgan explains, due to Puritans insisting on education "in order to insure the religious welfare of their children."[31] This was preceded by a statute in 1642 enacting "selectmen" to see to the educating of children in the household. The legal focus of education, pious and common, was accustomed to in England. Similar laws would follow in Connecticut in 1650 and New York in 1665.[32] In the 1648 *Book of General Lawes and Libertyes Concerning the Inhabitants of the Massachusets*, regarding children and servants, it states there be "selectmen" to ensure those in the household

[28]Hambrick-Stowe, *The Practice of Piety*, 84–86.

[29]David D. Hall, "Readers and Writers in Early New England," *A History of the Book in America* (Chapel Hill, NC: University of North Carolina Press, 2007), 118.

[30]Charles E. Hambrick-Stowe, *The Practice of Piety: Puritan Devotional Disciplines in Seventeenth-Century New England* (Chapel Hill: University of North Carolina Press, 1982), 8.

[31]Edmund S. Morgan, *The Puritan Family: Religion & Domestic Relations in Seventeenth-Century New England*, rev. ed. (New York: Harper & Row Publishers, 1966), 88.

[32]Lawrence Cremin, *American Education: The Colonial Experience: 1607–1783* (New York, Harper and Row, 1970), 124–25.

teach "by themselves or others" their children and apprentices to "perfectly read the English tongue" and have knowledge of the "capital laws" and masters of the house catechize their children and servants at least once a week or be brought to trial.[33]

It was important for Puritan children in Massachusetts to be catechized on the Ten Commandments as the capital laws were based on those commandments, and "the capital laws alone had the distinction of being supported by biblical citation."[34] The Puritan's bibliocentric formation of law and order sometimes resulted in more lenient punishment (in the case of theft, which was not a death penalty offense in America, but was in England) or harsher punishment (in the case of adultery which had a punishment of death in America contrasted with England).[35]

A shift happened when the responsibility of catechizing children moved from solely within the household to the addition of clerical catechization from ministers before and after sermons. In the 1640s-1680s, many churches employed two ministers for each congregation, one of whom was appointed as a "teacher" who oversaw the "catechizing of youngsters."[36]

On November 11, 1647, a "school act" was passed, which influenced not only Massachusetts but New England as a whole. The act stated, "Every township in this jurisdiction, after the Lord hath increased them to the number of fifty householders, shall then forthwith appoint one within their town to teach all such children as shall resort to him to write and read."[37] Connecticut passed an identical statute in 1650, and Massachusetts would establish approximately twenty-three schools by 1689.[38]

Northampton did not have a school established until 1664. In 1662, it was recorded there were sixty-two male residents of the town who owned meadowland and thus were "householders." Northampton complied with

[33]Thomas G. Barnes, ed., *The Book of the General Lawes and Libertyes Concerning the Inhabitants of the Massachusets* (1648: repr., Pasadena, CA: Castle Press, 1975), 11. Note the expansion from a general rule of educating children in the 1642 ordinance to a more direct application of weekly education of children. Ibid.

[34]Morgan, *The Puritan Family*, 88.

[35]Abram Van Engen, "A City on a Hill: The Bible and 'Christian America,'" *Christian History Magazine, America's Book: How the Bible Helped Shape a Nation*, 2021.

[36]Cremin, *American Education*, 154–57. This was perhaps Jonathan Edwards duties while at Northampton under his grandfather Solomon Stoddard.

[37]Nathaniel B. Shurtleff, M.D., ed., *Records of the Governor and Company of the Massachusetts Bay in New England*, vol. 2 (Boston: William White, 1853), 203.

[38]Cremin, *American Education*, 182–83.

the "school act" of 1647, and on January 28, 1664, the town voted to give six pounds to James Cornish, hired as the town's first schoolmaster. The town also provided a schoolhouse and land voted on in 1670–1671.[39] The legal emphasis on civically sponsored biblical instruction is something that will be at the heart of Edwards's emphasis in Stockbridge (and the conflict between Edwards, John Woodbridge, and Gideon Hawley against the Williamses).

Richard Mather, in a 1657 farewell address to his congregation at Dorchester, Massachusetts, charges parents to instruct their children in the "Word and will of God, and to pray for them and with them, for Gods blessing to be upon their soules."[40] Mather goes on to state it is an "express Commandment and charge" to train their children in the Bible and commands of God. But this charge is not only for one's family but includes the entire household, including servants, or they would "not be able to give any good answer for it before the Lord, having lived in the neglect of so express and plain, so serious and solemn a Commandment."[41]

Mather states that parents who are not diligent in instructing their children in the Word must do no "more for the soules of your children then Pagans and Infidels would do for the soules of theirs?"[42] These commands given by Mather inform the reader of the heart of Puritan piety and the importance of biblical literacy for those under the Puritan minister. Further in his exhortation, Mather instructs on the means for this first through "the principles of *Catechism*, and afterwards higher points, and pray that and your endeavours with them and for them may be blessed. Tell them, so many of them as have been Baptized, and tell it them as soon as they shall be able to learn, what a solemn Covenant there is between the God of heaven and them."[43] Cotton Mather, in a later 18th-century sermon, "The Young Man Spoken to Another Essay, to Recommend and Inculcate the Maxims of Early Religion, Unto Young Persons; and Especially the Religion of the

[39] James Russell Trumbull. *History of Northampton Massachusetts: From Its Settlement in 1654* (Northampton: Press of Gazette Printing, 1898), 141–42, 218.

[40] Richard Mather, "*A Farewell Exhortation to the Church and People of Dorchester in New-England*" (1657; repr., Ann Arbor: Evans Early American Imprint Collection Text Creation Partnership, 2005), 9.

[41] Mather, 9.

[42] Mather, 10.

[43] Ibid., 12.

Closet" printed by Samuel Gerrish in 1712, likewise calls upon parents to train their children in the Scriptures.[44]

Thomas Foxcroft (1697–1769) also connects the reading of the Word and preaching when he insists upon the necessity of the Bible for "youths" for their salvation and sanctification in his sermon on Psalm 119. He states the "ordinary medium of conversion and sanctification" is through the Bible preached and written, but states it is "their necessary duty" for parents, "masters, mistresses and the like" who have children in their care to start early in teaching, catechizing, and reciting the Bible and other works of piety and doctrine.[45]

Richard Baxter, in his *Reliquiæ Baxterianæ* writes of preaching at Kidderminster twice each Lord's Day before the Seven Years War, but only once each Sunday after (and once on Thursday). Baxter shows his pastoral emphasis on the Word and preaching by meeting every Thursday night at his house to allow his "neighbours" to examine and question the sermon after one of them read it aloud.[46]

Baxter also charged the youth to meet every Saturday night and read aloud the sermon from the previous week and "to pray and prepare themselves" for the following day's sermon. He goes on to show his emphasis on biblically educating his congregation:

> Two Days every week my assistant and I myself, took 14 Families between us for private Catechising and Conference (he going through the Parish and the Town coming to me): I first heard them recite the Words of the Catechism, and then examined them about the Sense, and lastly urged them with all possible engaging Reason and Vehemency to answerable Affection and Practice... I spent about an Hour with a Family, and admitted no others to be present, lest Bashfulness should make it burthensom,

[44]Cotton Mather, "*The Young Man Spoken to: Another Essay, to Recommend and Inculcate the Maxims of Early Religion, Unto Young Persons; and Especially the Religion of the Closet*" (1712; repr., Ann Arbor: *Evans Early American Imprint Collection, Online Texts Creation Partnership*, 2009).

[45]Thomas Foxcroft, "*Cleansing Our Way in Youth Press'd, as of the Highest Importance: and Observing the Word of God Recommended, as the Only Sufficient Means* (1719; repr., Ann Arbor: *Evans Early American Imprint Collection, Online Texts Creation Partnership*, 2009), 176–177.

[46]Richard Baxter, "*Reliquiæ Baxterianæ*" (1696; repr., Ann Arbor: *Early English Books Online Texts Creation Partnership*, 2003), 83.

> or any should talk of the Weakness of others: So that all the afternoons on Mondays and Tuesdays, I spent in this.[47]

Baxter's works were among the many ministerial guides for Edwards, and Edwards used this methodology of individualized instruction as he assisted Stoddard at Northampton and after he took over following Stoddard's death. Many Bibles were family books, utilized under the spiritual leading of fathers in daily worship. These family devotions created "little churches" of the homestead. More religious families read and meditated on the Bible at various points in the day (either morning and evening or during mealtimes).[48] Though the "first experiments in religious education" in themselves had importance, it was the personal context of the homes that was even more important.[49]

Whereas in the modern context, one who is "uneducated" refers to material or scholastic knowledge, biblical/religious knowledge (specifically Christian knowledge) was the means and goal of education for Puritans. To bar a child from attaining literacy and knowledge barred them off from salvation. As Morgan writes, "The Puritans sought knowledge therefore, not simply as a polite accomplishment, nor as a means of advancing material welfare, but because salvation was impossible without it."[50]

The next section will analyze some of those written guides for caregivers to instruct and "educate" children in the salvific Word. The most prominent of these was the *New England Primer*, which Ford notes, "With it millions were taught to read, that they might read the Bible; and with these millions were catechized unceasingly."[51] These were the direct tools Edwards and Congregationalists would use to instruct and build a culture of biblical literacy among their congregations.

Puritan Catechisms

Upon departing for the New World, it is unknown which catechism the Puritans were primarily focused on (though Ford points to William Perkins' instructions as a possibility). Soon after their arrival, "a tendency towards

[47] Baxter, "*Reliquiæ Baxterianæ*," 83.

[48] Antracoli, "Mighty in the Scriptures," 72–74.

[49] Paul, 30.

[50] Morgan, *The Puritan Family*, 89

[51] Ford, *The New-England Primer*, 4.

the individualism implied by all dissent and especially by Congregationalism" lead to a lapse of catechizing among the early Puritan churches in the New World.[52] Seeing the situation as dire, many early Puritan "teachers," including John Cotton and Richard Mather,each produced one or more personal catechisms. Producing these catechisms also helped pastors formulate their own faith and to have catechisms readily available to their congregations.[53]

The difficulty in each minister publishing and training their congregations in their specific doctrines was when another minister took over the church, and their doctrinal positions did not align singularly with their predecessor. This caused quarrels and schism within the congregations. The later formulation and use of the *Westminster Catechisms* (though a Presbyterian catechism based on the *Westminster Confession*) unified the early colonial Puritans (to a certain degree).[54]

English philosopher John Locke wrote several works on education. One such work, "Some Thoughts Concerning Education (1705 edition)," presented the curriculum for children to learn and read brought over from England to New England and commonly had the "Ordinary road," which included the "Horn-book, Primer, Psalter, Testament, and Bible."[55] Locke continues stating that the "Lord's Prayer, the Creeds, and Ten Commandments" were memorized by children in their education and their instruction in literacy. Further, Locke notes, "as for the Bible, which children are usually imploy'd in, to exercise and improve their talent in reading,"[56] as another norm for the education of children and as a tie between literacy, Biblical literacy, and doctrinal literacy for children at the time.

The Protestant Tutor

The immediate predecessor to the *New England Primer* was the *Protestant Tutor*, whose initial publication is unknown (though a correspondence from John Dunton dates a publication of the *Protestant Tutor* by Benjamin Harris

[52]Ford, 10.

[53]Ibid., 10.

[54]Ibid., 11–12.

[55]John Locke, "Some Thoughts Concerning Education," in *The Educational Writings of John Locke: A Critical Edition with Introduction and Notes*, ed. James L. Axtell (New York: Cambridge University Press, 1968), 260. Also picked up by E. Jennifer Monaghan in "Literacy Instruction and Gender in Colonial New England," in "Reading in America," ed. Cathy M. Davidson, special issue, *American Quarterly* 40, no. 1 (March 1988): 19.

[56]Locke, *Educational Writings*, 261. Locke's thought on this matter may have originally been expressed in a letter to Edward Clarke sent on September 1, 1683. Ibid., 346–351.

to 1686). Like the *New England Primer*, the *Protestant Tutor* contained an alphabet, syllabarium, the "Alphabet of Lessons," Lord's Prayer, Creed, Ten Commandments, a poem of John Rogers accompanied with a picture of his martyrdom, "figures and numeral Letters," and the "Names of the Books of the Bible."[57]

The New England Primer

Like the *Tutor*, the exact date of publishing the first edition of the *New England Primer* is unknown. Again, Dutton's correspondence gives a relative date between 1687 and 1690 for the first printing of the *New England Primer*.[58] The *New England Primer* became the major text used for the next hundred years and was a "frequently reprinted choice for an additional hundred years."[59] It is worth noting the Congregationalist *New England Primer* was largely taken up with the Westminster Assembly's *Shorter Catechism*.[60] The addition of the *Catechism* helped spur the popularity of the *Primer*. The *Primer* was one of the first items in the instruction of children, followed by the "Psalter (the Book of Psalms)."[61]

As a note on its popularity, between 1749 and 1766, Franklin and Hall printed over thirty-seven thousand copies of the *Primer*. The reason for the *Primer*'s rarity is that it is a children's workbook and is more inclined to be corroded through use.[62] The copy reproduced by Ford is a facsimile from the original 1727 copy that was housed at the Lenox Library.[63] Of note was Bibles were not able to be printed in America (and were instead imported in from England) until after the Revolutionary War (save for John Eliot's Indian Bible).[64]

One of the various textual changes to the *Primer* was the "evangelization" of the "rhymed alphabet" by printers sometime between 1740 and 1760. Some examples include 1) "The moon gives Light, in time of night," which was changed to "Moses was he who Israel's host led thro' the Sea;" 2)

[57] Ford, *The New-England Primer*, 14–16.

[58] Ibid., 16–17.

[59] Ibid., 19.

[60] Paul, 44n86.

[61] Monaghan, "Literacy Instruction," 21.

[62] Ford, *The New-England Primer*, 20–21.

[63] Ibid., 56.

[64] Monaghan, "Literacy Instruction," 21.

Nightingales sing, in time of Spring," which was changed to "Noah did view the old world & new;" and others that were changed though the original had Scriptural references such as "Samuel anoints whom God appoints," which was changed to "Young Sam'l dear the Lord did fear."[65] A popular addition during the period of 1740–1760 was the addition of Isaac Watts's *Divine Song for Children, Cradle Hymn,* and his *Morning and Evening Prayers*.[66]

Most of the printed versions of the *Primer* contained either the *Westminster Shorter Catechism* or John Cotton's *Spiritual Milk for Babes* (or both).[67] Children were drilled in the *Shorter Catechism* daily at church and school.[68] Further, Cotton Mather instructed mothers also to catechize their children "every day . . . you may be continually dropping something of the *Catechism* upon them, some honey out of the Rock!"[69]

"The "rhymed alphabet" of the 1727 version of the *Primer* includes (or highlights) the importance of children cherishing the Bible." Under "B" is the phrase: "Thy life to mend, this book attend," with an illustration of the Bible. Under "H" is: "My book and heart shall never part." Having a care for the brevity of one's life is seen under "T" ("Time cuts down all both great and small" with an accompanying illustration of the figure of Death with its scythe), "X" ("Xerxes the great did die, and so must you and I" with an accompanying illustration of the Persian king in his tomb), and "Y" ("Youth forward slips, Death sooneth nips" with another illustration of the figure of Death this time wielding a spear to slay down the aforementioned youth).[70] The colonial culture's focus on the perilousness of life and the imminent possibility of death (and its emphasis in the period's preaching) was an important factor in the responsive actions during the Great Awakening among Edwards's congregation at Northampton.

Following the "rhymed alphabet" section was an alphabetical section with proverbs for children also to memorize. The final letteral proverb "Z" again was tied back to the importance of the Word (quoting directly from Ps

[65]Ford, *The New-England Primer*, 30.

[66]Ford, *The New England Primer*, 46.

[67]Ford writes of the improvement of Cotton's *Spiritual Milk on the Shorter Catechism*: "In place of one hundred and seven questions, there were but sixty-four and instead of replies ranging in length from eight to one hundred words, one answer was a single word, and the longest only contained eighty-four." Ford, *The New-England Primer*, 43–44.

[68]Ibid., 39.

[69]Cotton Mather, "Mather on Catechising (1708)," *The New-England Primer*, 267–68.

[70]"The New England Primer (1727)," *The New-England Primer*, 65–68.

119:139): "Zeal hath consumed me, because they enemies have forgotten the words of God." The letteral proverbs are then followed by the Lord's Prayer, the Apostle's Creed, and the Ten Commandments. Next was the duties of children towards their parents.[71]

Some verses which followed the "duties" section include another emphasis on the brevity of life:

> I in the burying place may see, graves shorter there than I; From Death's arrest no age is free, young children too may die; My God, may such an awful sight, awakening be to me! Oh! That by early Grace I might for Death prepared be.[72]

After the verses section were the accepted books of the Bible according to the *Primer*, followed by a table of Roman and English numbers. The disputed account of John Rogers's martyrdom was then given with an illustration of Rogers's burning at the stake with his wife and children watching (the presence of his wife and children is among the disputations of the account).[73] The *Shorter Catechism* (remarked on above) is given at the end of this edition of the *Primer*.

As noted earlier, the *Primer* was the first step in instructing children in reading and writing. Next would be the *Psalter*. Monaghan notes the importance of the *Psalter* as an instructive text in literacy with an instance where a schoolmaster (John Proctor) came before a group of Boston selectmen for his denial of children into the school due to their inability to "read in the *Psalter*."[74]

After the *Psalter*, children learned to "master" the New Testament and then the whole Bible (both Old and New Testament). This was a widespread and well-known practice of the period. An instance of the expectations of this is found in the New Haven town records, which state the newly hired schoolmaster's work "should be to perfect male children in English, after they can read in their testament or Bible."[75]

[71] *The New-England Primer*, 68–80. Another verse a page over states: "Awake, arise, behold thou hast they life a leaf, they breath a blast; At night lye down prepar'd to have thy sleep, thy death, thy bed, thy grave." Ibid., 81.

[72] *New England Primer*, 80.

[73] *New England Primer*, 81–95.

[74] Monaghan, "Literacy Instruction," 21.

[75] Franklin B Dexter, ed., *New Haven Town Records, 1649–1662* (New Haven: New Haven Historical Society, 1917), 97.

Jonathan Edwards was educated in a family and religious structure for the purpose of salvation and ministry. The household he grew up in was replete with Bible study and catechesis. From the generations before to his own household, theology was at the forefront of devotion and discussion. Education of children, in the ways of religion, for the Puritans, was the duty of parents in fulfilling their part in covenant with God.[76] As noted by Sweeney, "Puritan New England may have been the most biblically orientated and literate society in the world before the time of Edwards's ministry."[77]

Take note of this comparison between a "youth" used as a character in a fictional conversation between said youth, the Devil, Christ, and Death. The opening statement from the "youth" shows a stark difference from Jonathan Edwards's resolutions:

> Those days which God to me does send in pleasure I resolve to spend like as the birds I'th' lovely spring, sit' chirping on the boughs and sing, who straining forth their warbling notes do make sweet musick in their throat: So I resolve, in this my prime, in sports and plays to spend my time. Sorrow and grief I'll put away, such things agree not with my day. From clouds my morning shall be free, and nought on earth shall trouble me, I will embrace each sweet delight the earth affords me day and night. Thought parents grieve and me correct, yet I their counsel will reject.[78]

In the fictional narrative, the "Devil" is seen as pleased with the youth's carelessness, while Christ calls the "youth" to come to repentance. At first, the "youth" is seen to repent, but the "Devil," while at first disappointed, ensnares the "youth" by appealing to his laziness and false hope of a long life (again speaking to the idea of death stalking and striking at any time).[79]

The above narrative statement of the "youth" and his wasting of time unto death stands in contrast to Edwards's famous *Resolutions* to "never to

[76]Morgan, *The Puritan Family*, 91.

[77]Douglas A. Sweeney, *Jonathan Edwards and the Ministry of the Word: A Model of Faith and Thought* (Downers Grove, IL: IVP Academic, 2009), 27.

[78]"The New English Tutor (1702–1717)," *The New-England Primer*, 226. The *New English Tutor* was a variant of the *Protestant Tutor*, the aforementioned predecessor to the *New England Primer*. Ibid., 137.

[79]"The New English Tutor," *The New-England Primer*, 226–237.

do any manner of thing, whether in soul or body, less or more, but what tends to the glory of God; nor be, nor suffer it, if I can avoid it," or "never to do anything, which I should be afraid to do, if it were the last hour of my life."[80]

The Puritan poet Anne Bradstreet (maiden name Dudley 1612–1672), in a poem dedicated to her mother, Dorothy Dudley, writes of her mother's dedication to instructing her and her siblings writing "a true instructor of her family, the which she ordered with dexterity . . . And in her closet constant hours she spent; Religious in all her words and ways, preparing for death, till end of days: of all her children, children, lived to see, then dying left a blessed memory."[81]

Puritan "Confessions"

Nathaniel Eaton (1609–1674), the first head of Harvard College, writes of his upbringing in the Scriptures in his "confession" recorded by Thomas Shepard in "The Confessions of Diverse Propounded to be Received & Were Entertayned as Members" transcribed by George Selement as part of his doctoral dissertation. Eaton writes that "from a cradle that I was trained up to read scripture, and, frequenting means, in the appearance of some made a progress."[82]

Testimonies like those recorded by Shepherd were done so to show a confirmation of their faith as prospective church members. This became a standard protocol in New England congregations. The important element of the confessions for this study is, as Noll puts it, "unlettered servants" who were giving their confessions as "this selected slice of lay spirituality revealed a remarkably comprehensive spiritual biblicism."[83]

Solomon Stoddard, Edwards's grandfather, later criticized this practice of the earlier Puritan leadership in New England.[84]

[80]Jonathan Edwards, "Resolutions," *Letters and Personal Writings,* 753.

[81]Anne Bradstreet, "An Epitaph on My Dear and Ever Honoured Mother Mrs. Dorothy Dudley," *The Works of Anne Bradstreet: In Prose and Verse* (Charlestown: Abram E. Cutter, 1867), 369.

[82]George Selement, "The Means to Grace: A Study of Conversion in Early New England" (PhD diss., Calvin College, 1970), 132. Eaton goes on to write of his lostness and need for salvation, though having scriptural knowledge. Ibid.

[83]Noll, *In the Beginning*, 102.

[84]Solomon Stoddard, *The Doctrine of Instituted Churches Explained and Proved from the Word of God* (1700; repr., Ann Arbor, *Early English Books Online Texts Creation Partnership*, 2012), 6–8.

In one of the "confessions" by John Stedman (recorded by Shephard), Stedman shows his biblical literacy through Scriptural references from moments throughout his life. He recollects the passage preached during an uncle's funeral (2 Thess 1), another sermon on drunkenness (1 Thess 5), another on humility (1 Pet 5), and assurance of forgiveness (Gal 2:19).[85]

Barbary Cutter likewise shows her biblical literacy in her "confession" by citing Ezekiel 16, 2 Corinthians 5:19, 1 John, Psalm 3, John 13, John 21, Matthew 25, and Isaiah 35. Edward Collins remarks in his "confession" about being catechized as a child by his father and learning about the "fundamentals" of the faith.[86]

Katherine, a maid of John and Elizabeth Russell, in her confession, testifies to the usage and devotion to the Word for years, which clarified and confirmed her salvation for her "and so I had (an) abundance of comfort from the word."[87]

Of interest is a note from the "confession" of William Andrew, a mariner who, upon falling sick in Spain, testifies to his fellow sailors reading Psalm 16 to calm and comfort him in his distress. Another confessor, Martha Collins, writes of her father catechizing her as a child. In their "confessions," like Stedman and Cutter, many others write of hearing several verses as a progression of conviction and saving faith.[88]

Hambrick-Stowe notes that these "Confessions" reveal how the laity in New England Puritan culture exhibited an "awareness of the stages of redemption" while they did not have "a sense that the work of redemption was complete."[89] Antracoli notes that for the purposes of his research, it was hard to interpret some of the conversion narratives in relation to biblical literacy as many describe the hearing of the Word and, with the language, denote an interchange of reading and hearing the Word.[90]

Conclusion

Whether by oral recognition or through remembered readings, those who gave their "confessions" did so with a familiarity with the Scriptures. To note

[85] Selement, 154–156.

[86] Ibid., 154–156.

[87] Selement, 185–87.

[88] Selement, 185–187, 198–241.

[89] Hambrick-Stowe, 149–150.

[90] Antracoli, "Mighty in the Scriptures," 76.

and remember the impact placed upon them was to recognize not only the words of a particular passage but the doctrinal truths that they then applied to themselves and their state of salvation. "Confessions," like those collected by Shepherd, are a focal point for Edwards in his *Religious Affections*. As seen through the New England Puritan culture, most aspects of life and religion were connected to biblical literacy.

Through looking at the confessions, catechisms, and primers which served as a foundation of Puritan religious authority and culture, it is clear the Bible was the focal point of education, literacy, religion, and culture. This was the education and culture Edwards was formed in. He learned how to read using a primer such as the *New England Primer*. At church he developed his faith as a child through using the call and response of catechisms such as the *Westminster Shorter Catechisms* and would add to it through reading the Psalter and the Bible. We can see the results of this education in writings of Edwards such as his *Resolutions*, his "Miscellanies," and his notes on Scripture in the "Blank Bible."

Added to this foundation, in the next chapter we will see some specific influences on Edwards's preaching philosophy before looking at Edwards through a brief biography focused on his preaching philosophy.

CHAPTER 2: EDWARDS, BIBLICAL LITERACY AND PREACHING

THE FIRST CHAPTER DEMONSTRATED the Puritan ties to biblical authority and education. This was done by examining the two primary confessions utilized by the Puritans (and later Congregationalists): the Westminster Confession and its revision, the Savoy Declaration. Next, the Westminster Shorter Catechism was examined to show how biblical fidelity was ingrained in religious education. Finally, primers such as the Protestant Tutor and the New England Primer were examined to show how from the earliest beginnings of one's education, Congregationalists such as Jonathan Edwards learned how to speak, read, and write through rhyming alphabets and pictographic primers tied to the Bible and its characters. This was done in a manner leading to eventual study of the Psalms, the New Testament, and the whole Bible as part of one's education. This education was of highest priority to the legal system in colonial New England as the capital laws were linked with the commandments from the same Bible.

In this chapter, the aim will be to connect this personally with Edwards through his individual education in looking at the resources he utilized in his training to become a Congregationalist Pastor-Preacher. The primary sources seen below are a direct influence on Edwards's preaching and show Edwards's advancement of Puritan preaching philosophy and his role as pastor and preacher. This chapter will conclude with looking at Edwards's own view of his colonial congregations' biblical literacy and his purpose and method in preaching to this audience.

Introduction

George Marsden notes Edwards's dedication to his biblical studies in his biography. Edwards purposed to give his "best gifts" of biblical study and sermon preparation to his congregation. This was at the expense of making "pastoral calls on his parishioners as was usually expected of New England clergy."[1] Samuel Hopkins, in his biography of Edwards, writes of Edwards's focus on ministry and crafting sermons that he did not make a custom of visiting his parishioners in their homes unless they were sick or under "some special affliction." Instead, he preached frequently at private meetings in particular neighborhoods and called children and young adults to his own home. There, he would pray with them and engage in "treating with them" in a "manner suited to their years and circumstances."[2]

Edwards recited the *Westminster Catechism* with children every sabbath in the summer. According to Hopkins, Edwards thought visiting congregants "house to house" should not be a mandatory routine for a minister, instead, each individual minister should examine their respective ministerial talents and serve their congregations according to their gifts. While some ministers were known to be more relational, Edwards did not see this as a strength but a weakness of his. Perhaps because of his inclination to meditate and think over theological topics over a longer period of time, the idea of having to improvise answers and discuss doctrines without, as he would see it, care, was "unprofitable."[3]

Edwards's commitment of time to studying God's Word was for the purpose of preaching and leading in a pastoral context. Edwards's time in his study was used to craft sermons as his primary ministry for his congregation, in addition to meeting with those in his care, whether family, those he was mentoring, members of his congregation, or friends.

Puritan Education, Biblical Literacy, and Preaching in New England

Puritan William Ames, in his preaching guide *The Marrow of Sacred Divinity Drawne Out of the Holy Scriptures*, writes preaching should cause those

[1] Marsden, *Jonathan Edwards*, 3.

[2] Samuel Hopkins, *The Life of the Late Reverend, Learned and Pious Mr. Jonathan Edwards* (Boston: S. Kneeland, 1765), 49.

[3] Hopkins, 49–50.

who hear to be "pricked to the quick" by the Word, pulling imagery from Hebrews 4:12 of the Bible as a two-edged sword piercing to the very marrow of the heart.[4] Ames instructs preaching should not be dead but vibrant and "effectuall" for the purpose of affecting the hearer and them, in turn, worshiping God.[5]

Works such as *The Marrow of Sacred Divinity* were the guides Edwards read for instruction on how to develop a sermon and reach his audience as a pastoral preacher. As noted at the end of this chapter, Edwards observed congregants throughout his ministry leading to Northampton who regarded the Word and its preaching as tasteless, "insipid," or "dead," as Ames put it.[6]

In an early recounting of the Northampton revivals of the 1730s published in 1736 (*A Faithful Narrative*), Edwards writes of the state of Northampton when he both became the assistant pastor and later was made pastor at the death of Stoddard. Edwards attests there was an "extraordinary dullness" of religion, with most in the area concerned with "other cares and pursuits."[7] But, starting at Pascommuck, a village situated three miles away from the main town and tied to Northampton's congregation, a "remarkable religious concern" began with the deaths of some in the village, which opened a door for Edwards through the "solemnizing of the spirits" of many youths who became more concerned about religion. Edwards encouraged them to gather in groups to meet after they heard the sermons to and discuss and apply what was preached. This shows Edwards's thought to instruct and apply the Word after preaching the Word.[8]

Through the preaching of the Word, Edwards would see the fruit of the Spirit's working in response to his preaching. Some came gradually; others saw a "new manner" of their religious concerns awakened. But many were suddenly "seized" by convictions and have their consciences "smitten, as if their hearts were pierced through with a dart,"[9] relaying the imagery taken from Hebrews 4:12 of the piercing Word.

[4]William Ames, *The Marrow of Sacred Divinity Drawne Out of the Holy Scriptures* (1642; repr., Ann Arbor: *Early English Books Text Creation Partnership*, 2005), 179.

[5]Ibid.

[6]William Ames, *The Marrow of Sacred Divinity*, 179

[7]Jonathan Edwards, "A Faithful Narrative," *The Great Awakening*, ed. C.C. Goen, vol. 4, *The Works of Jonathan Edwards* (New Haven: Yale University Press, 1972), 146.

[8]Edwards, *The Great Awakening*, 146–148.

[9]Ibid., 160.

In a later work published in response to ongoing criticism of the Great Awakening revivalism published in 1743 (*Some Thoughts Concerning the Revival*), Edwards defended his practice of balancing both the explanation of the text aimed at understanding with the desire to raise affection for God and His Word. For Edwards, the objection to raised affections was built on the mistake of the objectors thinking those affections could not be raised without the "enlightening" of the "understanding" being lost.[10]

Edwards's view was those affections are raised either by "light" or "error/delusion" in the understanding of the doctrines. So, the true measure of the faithfulness of the revival was whether the affections were raised by true or false understanding. If the doctrines preached are true and faithful to the Word and deal with having a greater affection for God, then the manner by which they are preached should be in proportion to that doctrine of affection.[11]

The tension for the "faithful shepherd" was in their stylistic focus on prophetic and pastoral preaching. The mission of the faithful shepherd was (as seen in chapter three) to separate the pure "sheep" from the wicked "swine."[12] It was not plainness in "strict literary terms" which was evident in Puritan preaching, as many would include "art" and "conventions" (which Bernard would see as useful in bringing the thoughts of "men" back from wandering to the Bible), but was in utilizing "special exercises" to raise inner affection.[13]

As will be seen, Edwards sought to raise the affections of his hearers through a faithful exposition of Scripture and an earnest call to respond to the truth and power of the Word. This will be demonstrated first by examining the Puritan influences on Edwards's preaching. Next, Edwards's own thoughts, like those shown above, will be given, as well as observations by those closest to Edwards's preaching. In the following chapter, Edwards's sermons at Northampton will be examined in light of his desire to exposit God's Word in a faithful and earnest manner.

[10]Edwards, "Some Thoughts Concerning the Revival," *The Great Awakening*, 386.

[11]Edwards, *The Great Awakening*, 386–387. This is in line with John Edwards's (no relation) recommendation in *The Preacher* (1703) of preaching with "intense belief and feeling" with a focus on application. John Edwards, *The Preacher*, 2nd ed. (London: J. Robinson, J. Lawrence, and J. Wyat, 1705), 24.

[12]David D. Hall, *The Faithful Shepherd: A History of the New England Ministry in the Seventeenth Century* (Chapel Hill, NC: University of North Carolina Press, 1972), 48–49.

[13]Hall, *The Faithful Shepherd*, 49–53.

Puritan "Plain Style" Preaching

William Perkins originated "plain style" preaching in his foundational work, the *Arte of Prophesying*. The *Arte of Prophesying* introduced the tripartite sermon structure of exegesis, doctrinal extraction, and application. Both the Directory and Perkins's *Arte of Prophesying* were required reading both for ministers training under the Assembly and later for the Puritans and those who followed those traditions.[14]

The "plain style" of preaching involved a rejection of obfuscation of the text for the advancement of understanding for the hearer. The text would be analyzed, and the doctrine explained and illustrated to further advance knowledge and understanding of the passage as well as its implications. Perkins instructs in *The Art of Prophesying* that "human wisdom must be concealed" citing 1 Cor. 2.[15]

The idea of categorizing ideas and arguments to present them with the goal of better understanding came from the philosophy of Peter Ramus and was picked up in the "plain style" of preaching proposed by Perkins. McKim writes, "Ramus set forth a skeletal system (resembling a blueprint or branching tree) where all the elements of a subject were divided and then subdivided until each had its own location on the chart." Once a subject was charted, "the Ramist philosophy sought to simplify the prevailing scholastic logic with its elaborate descriptions of figures, models, and forms of syllogisms. For Ramus and his followers, the ultimate goal of all dialectic was discourse."[16]

A gift from Ramus's methodology for Perkins and Puritan preaching was its function as an "educational tool *par excellence*." It served as an important tool for memorizing and teaching doctrines from Scripture. It focused on the goal of pedagogy. Its method was moving from the "most general to the most particular elements. This made the teaching clear as concrete examples illuminated general truths."[17] This method was adapted in Perkins's "plain

[14]Chad Van Dixhoorn, *God's Ambassadors: The Westminster Assembly and the Reformation of the English Pulpit, 1643–1653* (Grand Rapids: Reformation Heritage Books, 2017), 178.

[15]William Perkins, "The Arte of Prophesying," *The Works of William Perkins,* vol. 10, ed. J. Stephen Yuille (Grand Rapids, Reformation Heritage Books, 2020), 7. John Edwards also notes a need for biblical exposition and knowledge matching that of the apostles in referencing Jesus's own preaching in Matt. 22:34 and Peter and Paul's preaching and scriptural knowledge in their preaching as recorded in Acts 17, 19, and 28. Edwards, *The Preacher*, 28.

[16]Donald K. McKim, "The Functions of Ramism in William Perkins' Theology," *The Sixteenth Century Journal* 16, no. 4 (Winter 1985): 504–6.

[17]McKim, "The Functions of Ramism in William Perkins' Theology," 510.

style" preaching as Puritan preachers emphasized the "need for changes in the lives and behavior of a congregation." Universal truths in Scripture could be applied specifically to the audience's experiences in their lives.[18]

The Ramist method for Puritans was "more suited to preaching the unadulterated Word."[19] The Ramist theory of rhetoric helped preserve a "forensic" ideal, though keeping it from becoming too "forensic." Logic was at the center before rhetoric had its place and before manufacturing arguments that were "pleasing before being true."[20] The outcome and application of biblical truths fit Edwards's desire to influence his congregation through pastoral preaching.

Both Increase Mather and Cotton Mather endorsed the "plain style" of preaching. Increase noted in his biography of his father, Richard Mather, that, "his way of preaching was plain, aiming to shoot his arrows not over his people's heads, but into their hearts and consciences."[21] Cotton Mather also commended John Eliot for his "very plain" style of preaching. Both William Williams (father of Edwards's cousin Elisha Williams) and Stoddard encouraged experiential ministry that "preached the Word 'not as if a man were telling a dull story' but with 'warmth and earnestness of spirit.'"[22]

Timothy Edwards's sermons contained the basic divisions of Text, Doctrine, and Application that Jonathan would adopt in his sermons.[23] Timothy would use multiple doctrines, many subheads or the simpler text, doctrine with several points, and a single application with "multiple admonishments."[24] Stoddard would use Text, Doctrine, and Application with only reduced subheads under the single doctrinal point. Stoddard was a "preparationist who believed God underwent a distinct process for preparing sinners for conversion." Stoddard would encourage Edwards to preach not only the "rhetoric of delight" but also to complement it with the "rhetoric

[18]Ibid., 511–512.

[19]Clint Heacock, "Rhetorical Influences Upon the Preaching of Jonathan Edwards," *The Journal of the Evangelical Homiletics Society* 12, no. 2 (September 2012): 17.

[20]Miller, *New England Mind*, 326.

[21]Increase Mather, "The Life of Richard Mather," reprinted from "The Life and Death of that Reverend Man in God, Mr. Richard Mather (1670)," *The Puritans*, Perry Miller, and Thomas H. Johnson (New York: Harper & Row Publishers, 1963), 2:494.

[22]William Williams's sermon "A Painful Ministry, the Peculiar Gift of the Lord," quoted in Philip F. Gura, *Jonathan Edwards: America's Evangelical* (New York: Hill and Wang, 2006), 53, Kindle.

[23]Heacock, "Rhetorical Influences," 13.

[24]Ibid., 14.

of terror."[25] Edwards's purpose was to "extract a theological axiom" from the passage and dispute the axiom in a "creedal order." The text was broken into its "constitutional elements" and then set out in propositions in the sermon. Edwards broke the sermon into a tripartite structure where the first section clarified the key text, the second elaborated on the doctrine, and the final section concluded with application of the text for the audience. This enabled notetaking and following along with the sermon.[26]

Turnbull writes, "Of William Perkins this can be said: No other exerted a greater influence upon Edwards as a literary model."[27] Other works that influenced Edwards included William Ames's 1638 work *The Marrow of Sacred Divinity*,[28] Richard Bernard's *The Faithfull Shepherd* (1627), John Wilkins' *Ecclesiastes* (1646), William Chappell's *The Preacher and the Art and Method of Preaching* (1656), John Edwards' *The Preacher* (1705), and Cotton Mather's *Manductio ad Ministerium*, which all subscribed to the "plain style" of preaching.[29] Edwards "fully exploited" the Puritan preaching form while never departing from its tradition. It was Edwards who advanced the style through an insistence on "a personal formulation of that heritage."[30]

William Perkins's *The Arte of Prophesying*

As mentioned, Perkins' work was the introduction and standard text for Puritan "plain style" preaching. In the work, Perkins rejected the fourfold sense of interpretation used by "the Church of Rome."[31] For Perkins, there was only the literal sense, with allegory seen as a way "of uttering the same sense" and analogical and tropology "ways whereby the sense may be applied" to the sermon. He advises the literal sense be the first rule (giving Acts 10:43 as an example) when it agrees with the "analogy of faith and with the holy Scriptures."[32]

[25] Heacock, "Rhetorical Influences," 14.

[26] Ibid., 15.

[27] Ralph G. Turnbull, *Jonathan Edwards the Preacher* (Grand Rapids: Baker Book House, 1958), 40, 57.

[28] Douglas A. Sweeney, *Edwards the Exegete: Biblical Interpretation and Anglo-Protestant Culture on the Edge of the Enlightenment* (New York: Oxford University Press, 2016), 21.

[29] Heacock, "Rhetorical Influences," 16.

[30] Heacock, "Rhetorical Influences," 11.

[31] Perkins, "The Arte of Prophesying," 561.

[32] Ibid., 561–575.

However, for "cryptical or hidden places" more difficult to align with the analogy of faith and Scripture, Perkins presents a second rule to seek "the other meaning," which aligned with the analogy of faith and Scriptures. Perkins gives the example of 1 Corinthians 11:24, where the literal sense is the Lord's Supper, continually being the literal body and blood of Christ taken by the saints. This is contradictory to "the article of faith (He ascended into heaven) and with the nature of a sacrament (as a memorial of the absent body of Christ)."[33]

The foundation for application for Perkins is whether the doctrine is about the Law (to show the sinner the "disease" of their sin without remedy) or Gospel (which points to belief and action in repentance). Perkins moves on to the seven "ways" or purposes of application "according to the divers conditions of men and people." The first condition is unbelievers who are "ignorant and unteachable." Perkins advises declaring the doctrine "generally" in "common terms or ordinary points."[34]

The second condition are those who are ignorant yet teachable, in which case they are catechized through the application of questioning. The third are those with some knowledge "but are not as yet humbled." They are to be humbled through applying the Law "which may beget contrition of heart or the horrors of conscience." After this, the Gospel is preached "whereof the Holy Spirit works effectually unto salvation."[35]

Those humbled (condition four) are given the Law and Gospel to "finish" the work of sorrow and humiliation, leading to hope and repentance. Those who do believe (condition five) are given the Law (without the dread of the curse of sin) to bring "forth fruits of new obedience," along with the Gospel of "justification, sanctification, and perseverance."[36]

The application for those who are fallen (condition six) is to preach the error at the root of their falling. Then they are pressed with the Gospel and "entreated to stir up in them . . . their faith . . . and that it would please them to struggle manfully in prayer either alone or with others."[37] Edwards will similarly, in *Miscellany 462,* write of how to deal with young congregants who have fallen:

[33]Ibid., 575.

[34]Perkins, "The Arte of Prophesying ," 614–617.

[35]Ibid., 621–623.

[36]Ibid., 623–625.

[37]Ibid.," 625–627. This is called "redargution" by Perkins. Ibid., 631–633.

> And when the children of the church are become adult, they should be put upon it to come and join with the church; but it should be understood as with those conditions, for 'tis presumed that they know how dreadful 'tis to come without them. If they don't come when they are become adult, it should be seen to what the cause is; and if they object their want of any of these conditions, as particularly of a believing the truth of the gospel, thorough care should be immediately taken to convince them: the elder should come and argue with them, books suitable for the purpose should be read, and he should never be left till he is convinced. If he objects that he is not willing to forsake all his sins and do all duties through all difficulties, then he will be condemned out of his own mouth; his own fault and inexcusableness will tare him in the face, and it will be easy to come at him with arguments, for he himself will open the way.[38]

The final condition is what Edwards and most preachers had: a mixed crowd. Perkins's advice is to mix the application of Law and Gospel to reach both groups as much as possible.[39] After expositing the purposes (or ways) of application, Perkins moves on to the four "kinds" of application. Two are mental (doctrine, redargution), and two are practical (instruction, correction). Doctrine instructs in correct doctrine, whereas redargution corrects erroneous thinking about God and the Gospel (as is seen above with both Perkins and Edwards). Instruction and correction (with respect to application "kinds") instruct practical action in living out one's faith.[40]

Perkins was against using visual memorization with mental images as he saw it as a threat of placing "absurd, insolent, and prodigious cogitations, and those which set an edge upon and kindle the most corrupt affections of the flesh."[41] In "uttering the sermon," Perkins laid two requirements for the preacher, including (as quoted above) "concealing human wisdom" and demonstrating the Spirit speaking through them. The preacher's speech must be gracious, with the sanctity of a good conscience, an inward feeling of the doctrine, fear of God, love of the congregation, venerable, and temperate.

[38]Jonathan Edwards, "Church Order," in *"Miscellanies," (Entry Nos. a-z, aa-zz, 1–500)*, ed. Harry S. Stout, vol. 13, *The Works of Jonathan Edwards* (New Haven: Yale University Press, 1998), 504–505.

[39]Perkins, "The Arte of Prophesying," 627–629.

[40]Ibid., 631–633.

[41]Ibid., 637.

It must also be spiritual speech, which is both "simple and perspicuous" with "neither the words of arts nor Greek and Latin phrases and quirks," which Perkins advises disturb the mind of hearers, hinder understanding, and "draw the mind away from the purpose to some other matter."[42]

Perkins concludes by advising the preacher speak clearly so "all may hear," with the volume more moderate during doctrine and in exhortation "more fervent and vehement." The legs remain "erect and quiet," and the eyes and hands lifted in confidence or cast down to signify sorrow and heaviness.[43]

William Ames's *The Marrow of Sacred Divinity*

William Ames (1576–1633), whose influential work *The Marrow of Sacred Divinity* included Ramist logic, was an early example of "theology from a Puritan perspective."[44] Ames was the leading proponent of Ramist theology, with *Marrow* not only a Puritan theology but also "a clear illustration of Ramist principles applied to theology."[45] In her dissertation on Ames, Jan van Vliet argues for the acknowledgment of Ames as the "architect" of federal theology as an improvement of Perkins's "largely medieval, Thomistic system."[46] Edwards would pick up on this federal theology and Ramist logic. *Marrow* was popular due to its "emphasis on method and practical divinity."[47]

In *Marrow*, Ames argues that because Scripture is so valuable for doctrine, reproof, correction, and instruction in piety (1 Tim 6:17), those who "invert and confound those parts, do not provide for the memory of their hearers," but actually hinder their ability to remember the Word and do the greatest disservice in their preaching.[48] Instead, Ames argues the preacher should make the text clear and memorable for their audience.[49]

[42]Perkins, "The Arte of Prophesying," 637–646. This is also why Perkins advises preachers to omit "the telling of tales and all profane and ridiculous speeches." Ibid.

[43]Ibid., 648.

[44]Keith L. Sprunger, "Ames, Ramus, and the Method of Puritan Theology," *The Harvard Theological Review* 59, no. 2 (April 1966): 133.

[45]Ibid., 140.

[46]Jan van Vliet, "William Ames: Marrow of the Theology and Piety of the Reformed Tradition" (PhD diss., Westminster Theological Seminary, 2002), iv.

[47]Sprunger, "Ames, Ramus, and the Method of Puritan Theology," 141.

[48]William Ames, *The Marrow of Sacred Divinity,* 176–178.

[49]Ibid., 182.

Richard Bernard's *The Faithful Shepherd* (or *The Shepherd's Faithfulness*)

Bernard, like Perkins and Ames, emphasizes the "plain style" style of bringing the text to the understanding of the hearer. Bernard saw the practice of expounding in Greek and Latin as an "unprofitable spending of time" as he advised that only "some few understand hardly the languages" while others would doubtless get lost in the exposition. For him, preachers rather be "faithful dispensers of God's secrets to the conscience of every believer, in every thing to the utmost of our power."[50]

In writing on the format of the sermon, Bernard notes after the delivery of the doctrine should be the uses of said doctrine. Therefore, the audience will know what to do with the biblical truth they have just learned.[51] Bernard's format slightly differs from Perkins's in that he separates doctrine from the uses of doctrine. Bernard gives the four uses (familiar in Perkins's *Arte of Prophesying*, with an additional use) of redargution (to "confute and overthrow and error or heresy"), instruction ("when the doctrine is used to bring us to the exercise of Christian duties"), correction ("when the lesson is used against corruption in manners, vice, and wickedness, whether it be for omission or commission"), and consolation ("when the doctrine is used to raise up the spirit with comfort ... and to encourage such as to be obedient").[52]

After the uses of the doctrine, Bernard advises the preacher to move to the application of the doctrine. This is done by going from the second person in pronouncing uses to the first and second person (when the preacher includes himself with his congregation) as a "nearer brining of the use delivered, after a more general sort ... to the time, place, and persons then present."[53] Bernard then moves to something that would become a strength of Edwards's preaching: the identification of the preacher from the self-knowledge of their sinfulness as the "old man."

Bernard compares the preacher in identifying the sin and "corruption of nature" to a physician "skillful of his patient's disease, he may fitly administer a right potion; or like a wise counselor in his client's cause, he may give

[50]Richard Bernard, *The Faithfull Shepheard: Or The Shepheards Faithfulnesse,* (1648; repr., Ann Arbor: *Early English Texts Online Texts Creation Partnership*, 2014), 17.

[51]Bernard, *Faithfull Shepheard,* 60–61.

[52]Ibid., 59–69.

[53]Ibid., 70.

sound advice for safety and defense."[54] After the application, Bernard advises the presentation and reproval of objections. This is advised to take away all excuses (with private conference advised for those who cannot be "fully satisfied") and not to make the "pulpit the place for a continual and full handling of controversies in a common auditory." Finally, after this is handled, the conclusion of the sermon is given.[55]

Richard Baxter's *The Reformed Pastor*

The final work representing the works Edwards used as instruction in preaching is Richard Baxter's *The Reformed Pastor*. An inscription from 1875 at the base of a statue dedicated to Baxter at Kidderminster, England, states Baxter was "renowned equally for his Christian learning and his pastoral fidelity. In a stormy and divided age, he advocated unity and comprehension, pointing the way to everlasting rest."[56] He had written over 130 books, including the seminal Puritan works *The Saints' Everlasting Rest* and the pastoral ministry handbook *The Reformed Pastor*. *The Reformed Pastor* influenced Edwards, George Whitefield, the Wesleys, and later Charles H. Spurgeon.[57]

In *The Reformed Pastor*, Baxter notes the public preaching of the Bible was "the most excellent" part of the pastor's work. Though Preaching was a work that required "greater skill, and greater life and zeal, then any of us bring to it."[58] He adds the work of a preacher is not easy as they have to speak plainly (picking up the idea of the "plain style"), "that the ignorant may understand us," and yet in such a somber tone "that the deadest hearts may feel us," and with such conviction "that the contradicting cavaliers may be silenced."[59]

According to Baxter, the "greatest, most certain, and necessary" truths must be emphasized. This emphasis was to get those preached to "well to heaven" where they "have knowledge enough." This was to "destroy men's sins" and "raise the hearts" of the hearers to God. Baxter saw truths that did

[54]Bernard, *Faithfull Shepheard,* 71–72.

[55]Ibid., 77–81.

[56]Paul C.H. Lim, "A Pen in God's Hand," *Christian History,* Winter 2006, https://christianhistoryinstitute.org/magazine/article/pen-in-gods-hand.

[57]Ibid.

[58]Richard Baxter, *Gildas Salvianus, The Reformed Pastor shewing the nature of the pastoral work, especially in private instruction and catechizing* (1656; repr., Ann Arbor: *Early English Texts Online Texts Creation Partnership*, 2005), 78.

[59]Baxter, *The Reformed Pastor,* 78.

not serve the purpose of preaching the Gospel as "needless ornaments" and "unprofitable controversies."[60]

As for the affections of the preacher (something Edwards would advance in his own preaching), the preacher must be "sincerely affectionate, serious, and zealous" in every public and private exhortation. Baxter saw the weight of the eternality of the Gospel as what "condemneth coldness, and sleepy dullness." The preacher is awakened themselves. making them "fit to awaken others."[61] Baxter, like others in the Puritan tradition, advocated for the "plain style" of preaching.[62]

As with Edwards's intentions in preaching, Baxter supported the education of those hearing the Word preached. He saw the benefit it brought in understanding the sermon and having a regard for the truths expressed from the Bible. He writes, "When you have acquainted them with the principles, they will the better understand all that you say." Baxter saw catechesis and biblical education as opening the hearts and minds of the hearers to the Word preached, where without the private instruction of the congregation in biblical literacy, the preacher is at risk of losing most of their "labour" and the less good they can do.[63]

For the pastor-preacher intimately involved in the private instruction of his congregation, it would also afford the benefit of more accurately knowing the spiritual state of their congregation and how to watch over them as their pastor.[64] While Baxter acknowledged and emphasized the practical benefits of catechesis and biblical literacy, he charged the pastor to never lose sight of the spiritual aspect of their work.[65]

In the next section, Edwards's role as pastor and preacher is examined. Edwards's use and advancement of "plain style" preaching for comprehension, and advancement of this "plain style" through affectionate, rhetorical, and illustrative preaching is shown as the purpose of Edwards in reaching an audience that was all too familiar with, and yet for many disinterested in, the Word they knew since childhood.

[60]Ibid., 120.

[61]Baxter, *The Reformed Pastor*, 127.

[62]Ibid., 123.

[63]Baxter, *The Reformed Pastor*, 316.

[64]Ibid., 317–318.

[65]Ibid., 128–129.

Edwards's Role as Pastor and Preacher

On October 5, 1703, in East Windsor, CT, Esther (Stoddard) Edwards gave birth to Jonathan. Jonathan Edwards was born into a pastoral family connected to such names as Mather, Hooker, and Stoddard.[66] His father, Timothy Edwards, was a Congregationalist pastor. His grandfather was a respected Congregationalist revivalist, Solomon Stoddard, who served as pastor of the congregation at Northampton, MA.[67] A religious life and education was all Edwards knew as the son and grandson of influential pastors in colonial New England. Western New England was on the "frontier" of British posts that saw frequent bouts of warfare. The French-Indian conflict with England previewed the sorrow and horrors for Edwards's extended family as Stoddard's daughter-in-law and step-grandchildren were massacred by Indians.[68]

Edwards progressed from the Reformed Puritan heritage of Stoddard and his father, Timothy.[69] Stoddard was imposing, tall, and known for preaching without notes. Stoddard's publications, which held advice for clergy, gave insight into his preaching methodology. Stoddard urged ministers not to use notes. Edwards, known for being meticulous, continued writing out manuscripts for the sake of advancing his expositional logic. Later in his career, his sermons were adapted to fit what, in his mind, was an audience that needed a more direct, relatable exposition. Stoddard was described as an animated conversationalist, and Edwards as a driven logician.[70] Timothy Edwards was like Stoddard in preaching extemporaneously.[71]

A break between Stoddard and the Edwardses in theological polity was over Stoddard's inclusion of an open communion at Northampton. Timothy disagreed with the practice and precluded it at his own congregation. It

[66]George M. Marsden, *Jonathan Edwards: A Life* (New Haven: Yale University Press, 2003), 32–33, 140.

[67]Sang Hyun Lee, ed., *The Princeton Companion to Jonathan Edwards* (Princeton: Princeton University Press, 2005), 1.

[68]Marsden, 3.

[69]Kimnach, *Sermons and Discourses 1720–1723,* 10–17.

[70]Marsden, 11, 119.

[71]Sereno Edwards Dwight, *The Life of President Edwards* (New York: G & C & H Carvill, 1830), 17.

later caused major issues for Jonathan, eventually causing his dismissal after Edwards attempted to restrict communion.[72]

Early on, Edwards was fascinated with nature, especially spiders, as seen both in an early scientific essay and in *Sinners in the Hands of an Angry God* (in his illustration of a spider dangling by a thread). This fascination with nature and science did not lead him away from orthodox theology but was founded on the idea of God ruling over creation.

Samuel Hopkins writes that, later in life, nature was Edwards's most common "diversion" when leaving the study where he commonly spent 13 hours. "His most usual diversion in the Summer was riding on horseback and walking. He would commonly, unless diverted by company, ride two or three miles after dinner to some lonely grove, where he would dismount and walk a while." He would carry his pen and ink with him, to note any thought or illustration that came to mind. Hopkins adds in the winter he took an ax and would chop wood "moderately for the space of half an hour or more."[73]

In 1722, at the age of 18, Edwards went to New York City (which at this time boasted a population of 7–10,000 inhabitants) to begin his pastoral career as a "supply" pastor of a small Presbyterian congregation that broke from a larger body. During this eight-month tenure, Edwards began writing his *Miscellanies*, a collection of theological meditations written in personal notebooks. He helped his congregation grow spiritually while his own faith grew in this "family-like atmosphere" the congregation provided.[74]

Even at a young age, when he was at the small Presbyterian congregation in New York City, Jonathan Edwards was known for a relentless logic personified in his sermons. The logic proposed from the beginning of the "doctrine" section of his sermons left no loopholes. Truths, proven through repetitive exposition, were applied as necessities to his congregants. This logical exposition was due to Edwards's extensive study of the Scriptures.[75]

When Edwards was at Bolton in 1723, his preaching took on a consistently cheerful note. The sermon (*A Spiritual Understanding of Divine Things Denied to the Unregenerate*) showcases another theme of Edwards, Spirit-led regeneration giving "holy joy" and a special form of spiritual insight and

[72]Marsden, 122–123.

[73]Hopkins, 40.

[74]Lee, *Princeton Companion*, 4.

[75]Marsden, 54–55; 474. John Carrick notes that Edwards's sermons were both known to be Theocentric and Christocentric when necessitated by the biblical text. Carrick, 25–27; 103–111.

appreciation of God denied to the "natural man."[76] He also wanted to pare down complex ideas into exposition his hearers understood. Edwards did this through analogy and imagery. Marsden illustrates this in *Nothing Upon Earth Can Represent the Glories of Heaven,* wherein Edwards used Revelation 21:18 to illustrate the varied "glories of the heavenly city." This was done by recounting similes used in Scripture to describe heaven, such as a crown, kingdom, treasure, and city.[77]

Noteworthy when examining the 17th century period and the homiletics used is the appreciation of the audience for the expositor and their craft. Sermons and the preachers who delivered them were considered integral to life and culture. While the perspective of sermon delivery and reception today values brevity, sermons were given ample space to be delivered at that time.[78]

In April of 1723, Edwards moved to East Windsor, where he composed and delivered his Master's *Quaestio* (a thesis to complete his degree). After finishing his studies, Edwards (through his father's desire to have him close to home) signed on to become the pastor in Bolton, a town recently settled with persons from Windsor and East Windsor.[79]

Edwards returned to Yale in the spring of 1724 when he was hired as a tutor. During Edwards's time at Yale, he was smitten with his future bride Sarah Pierpont, proposing to in 1725. In 1726, he was elected assistant pastor to his grandfather at Northampton. Ordained on February. 15, 1727 by the same church. Just two years later he was the pastor after the passing of his grandfather.[80] His sister Jerusha also died to diphtheria in the same year. Jerusha was the same age as Sarah and was close with Jonathan. Edwards named one of his daughters after Jerusha.[81]

Stirrings of revival occurred once again at Northampton in the early 1730s as Edwards saw the Spirit move in his congregation through the preaching of the Word. In an unpublished letter to Dr. Benjamin Colman,

[76] Marsden, 96–97.

[77] Marsden, 97–98.

[78] Arthur S. Hoyt, *The Pulpit and American Life* (New York: The Macmillan Company, 1921), 11–12.

[79] Ibid., 4–5.

[80] Marsden, 93–127.

[81] Marsden notes that both were examples of intelligence, grace, and piety. Marsden, 128.

the pastor of Brattle Street Church in Boston, Edwards reported on these movements.[82]

Edwards's account, however, was not the first account of the revival sent to Colman as William Williams (a pastor at Hatfield, MA, and Edwards's uncle) wrote Colman about the revival. Edwards's account was then reported in the May 1735 *New England Weekly Journal.* Colman abridged both revival accounts for publication; however, when Colman sent this abridged version of Edwards's account to John Guyse (a minister) and Isaac Watts (the renowned hymn writer), they asked for the unabridged version to publish in London under the title *A Faithful Narrative of the Surprising Work of God.*[83]

At first Watts read the account and worried it was hyperbole since he received an overwhelming number of inquiries concerning the authenticity of the narrative by Edwards.[84] However, Watts also read the account and saw potential for revival in England and beyond, and, as noted by Kidd, even portends of the eschaton. Edwards's *Narrative* influenced future revivals during the following century and revivalists journaling their own accounts.[85]

Whereas Stoddard's preaching was known for its bluntness, Edwards's was relentless in logically getting his points across through exposition.[86] Marsden credits Edwards's relentless and pointed preaching to the Awakening at Northampton in 1734–5. Several factors played a role in the moving of hearts, including the deaths of a number of youths in town, Edwards's preaching, and a community being moved by the Spirit.[87]

In his preface to "Discourses on various Important Subjects," Edwards defends the complex doctrine preached in the sermon "Justification by Faith Alone" on two occasions. In this defense, Edwards gives insight into his

[82]Jonathan Edwards, *The Great Awakening*, ed. C.C. Goen, vol. 4, *The Works of Jonathan Edwards* (New Haven: Yale University Press, 1972), 99.

[83]Thomas S. Kidd, *The Great Awakening: The Roots of Evangelical Christianity in Colonial America* (New Haven, Yale University Press, 2007), 21; Marsden, 172.

[84]Marsden, 172. Also noted in Philip F. Gura, *Jonathan Edwards: America's Evangelical* (New York: Hill and Wang, 2006), 75–94. Edwards had noted no fewer than thirty-two separate communities aside from Northampton that were awakened during this time of "awakening." Ibid.

[85]Kidd, 21–23. *Faithful Narrative* will be examined more thoroughly when looking at the biblical literacy of the congregation of Northampton in chapter three.

[86]Marsden, 128–29.

[87]Kimnach notes that Jonathan Edwards, like Stoddard, would preach in a style similar to those in the Connecticut Valley, which emphasized the importance of experience of conversion. Edwards, *Sermons and Discourses 1720–1723*, 12–14.

methodology for preaching to a biblically (and theologically) literate audience:

> The following discourse of justification, that was preached, (though not so fully as it is here printed), at two public lectures, seemed to be remarkably blessed, not only to establish the judgments of many in this truth, but to engage their hearts in a more earnest pursuit of justification, in that way that had been explained and defended; and at that time, while I was greatly reproached for defending this doctrine in the pulpit, and just upon my suffering a very open abuse for it, God's work wonderfully brake forth amongst us, and souls began to flock to Christ, as the Savior in whose righteousness alone they hoped to be justified: So that this was the doctrine on which this work in its beginning was founded, as it evidently was in the whole progress of it.[88]

By elevating the conversation to a discourse on justification, Edwards had ministered to his (and another) congregation's need to analyze what the doctrine of justification meant generally.[89] Edwards shows humility in addressing his own ability yet values what he believes is the "foolishness of preaching," which he sees as salvific for those who hear the Word prepared and pastorally delivered.

Edwards's sermon series on God's redemption in history (*Historical Narrative*) and on God's redemptive love (*Charity and Its Fruits*)[90] show how Edwards would work through a topical series with the same logical doggedness that served him well in theological debates.

In Northampton, Edwards and famed itinerant preacher George Whitefield met on October 17, 1740. When Edwards heard of Whitefield coming to New England, he "excitedly" wrote and invited him to Northampton. Edwards heard of Whitefield's success through published articles in the Boston newspapers. Whitefield also had heard of Edwards through reading

[88] Jonathan Edwards, "Preface to Discourses on Various Important Subjects," *Sermons and Discourses, 1734–1738*, ed. M.X. Lesser, vol. 4, *The Works of Jonathan Edwards* (New Haven: Yale University Press, 1972), 795.

[89] *Sermons and Discourses, 1734–1738*, 796.

[90] *Charity and Its Fruits* was a follow up series to a series based on Matthew 25:1–12 which became a nineteen-part series on the wise and foolish virgins preached in the winter of 1737–38. *Charity and Its Fruits* would become one of his most recognized sermon series which culminated in *Heaven Is a World of Love*. Edwards would depart from topical preaching with a wider text choice to preaching from 1 Corinthians. Marsden, 190–91.

Edwards's *Faithful Narrative* and about Stoddard through his works *A Guide to Christ* and *Safety of Appearing in Christ's Righteousness.*[91] Edwards would note the success of Whitefield's visit in a letter sent to Whitefield dated December 14, 1740:

> I have joyful tidings to send you concerning the state of religion in this place. It has been gradually reviving and prevailing more and more, ever since you was here. Religion is become abundantly more the subject of conversation; other things that seemed to impede it, are for the present laid aside. I have reason to think that a considerable number of our young people, some of them children, have already been savingly brought home to Christ. I hope salvation has come to this house since you was in it, with respect to one, if not more, of my children. The Spirit of God seems to be at work with others of the family. That blessed work seems now to be going on in this place, especially amongst those that are young.[92].

The most famous sermon preached by Edwards on July 8, 1741, at Enfield (a town just south of Northampton), was *Sinners in the Hands of an Angry God.* Eleazar Wheelock (a faithful companion in revival with Edwards) relayed to Benjamin Trumbull what he described as a crowd not conducting themselves in a "decent manner" for the proceedings. By the end, their hearts were awakened (credited through prayer and Edwards's preaching):

> There was an extraordinary instance of this at Enfield. While the people in the neighbouring towns were in great distress for their souls, the inhabitants of that town were very secure, loose, and vain. A lecture had been appointed at Enfield, and the neighbouring people the night before, were so affected at the thoughtlessness of the inhabitants, and in such fear that God would, in His righteous judgment, pass them by, while the divine showers were falling all around them, as to be prostrate before him a considerable part of it, supplicating mercy for their souls. When the time appointed for the lecture came, a number of

[91]Marsden writes of their contrast of styles: "In public, Whitefield was a born actor. He preached without notes, had a splendid voice that Benjamin Franklin calculated could readily be heard by 25,000, and was a master of painting vivid pictures that would draw an audience emotionally into the theme of the text." Marsden, 202–207.

[92]Jonathan Edwards, *Letters and Personal Writings*, 87

> the neighbouring ministers attended, and some from a distance. When they went into the meeting-house, the appearance of the assembly was thoughtless and vain. The people hardly conducted themselves with common decency. The Rev. Mr. Edwards, of Northampton, preach, and before the sermon was ended, the assembly appeared deeply impressed and bowed down, with an awful conviction of their sin and danger. There was such a breathing of distress, and weeping, that the preacher was obliged to speak to the people and desire silence, that he might be heard. This was the beginning of the same great and prevailing concern in that place, with which the colony in general was visited.[93]

Recently, Douglas L. Winiarski has disputed this claim of Edwards as a stoic disaffected by the enthusiasm of those who had become frenzied due to his preaching. He writes of those who most likely would have traveled to Enfield from the surrounding areas to hear Edwards preach. Winiarski theorizes Edwards came "uncomfortably close" to those later characterized as "enthusiasts" who would later form the New Light movement of revivalism in New England. Winiarski (by way of Ola Winslow's biography of Edwards) also refutes the idea of Edwards's centrality to the Enfield revival due to his last-minute replacement of Wheelock, scheduled to preach at Enfield instead. Winiarski's downplay of Edwards's importance to the revival at Enfield is correlated by his assertion that Edwards had deliberately chosen to "preach terror" after seeing the enthusiasm of those at Suffield.[94]

Whether as normative or deliberately at Enfield, Edwards's style of going after the affections of the heart was complimented by his explanation of doctrine, which in *Sinners* focused on an illustrative bombardment of the gravity in which sins pulled the unregenerate into hell. The spider's web, so poetically described in his observatory letter, was now used as an example of frailty in illustrating the sinner's precarious state. Edwards notes the need to preach to the affections of believers:

> I think an exceeding affectionate way of preaching about the great things of religion, has in itself no tendency to beget false

[93]Trumbull adds about how he obtained the information, "Mr. Wheelock went from Connecticut, who gave me information of the whole affair." Edwards, *Ethical Writings,* 145.

[94]Douglas L. Winiarski, "Jonathan Edwards, Enthusiast? Radical Revivalism and the Great Awakening in the Connecticut Valley, *Church History*, 74, no. 4 (December 2005): 683–728. See also, Ola Elizabeth Winslow, *Jonathan Edwards, 1703–1750: A Biography* (New York: Macmillan, 1940), 190.

> apprehensions of them; but on the contrary a much greater tendency to beget true apprehensions of them, than a moderate, dull, indifferent way of speaking of 'em. An appearance of affection and earnestness in the manner of delivery, if it be very great indeed, yet if it be agreeable to the nature of the subject, and ben't beyond a proportion to its importance and worthiness of affection, and there be no appearance of its being feigned or forced, has so much the greater tendency to beget true ideas or apprehensions in the minds of the hearers, of the subject spoken of, and so to enlighten the understanding: and that for this reason, that such a way or manner of speaking of these things does in fact more truly represent them, than a more cold and indifferent way of speaking of them.[95]

Edwards continues by advising it is his duty as the preacher to raise the affections of his hearers as high as possible, "provided that they are affected with nothing but truth, and with affections that are not disagreeable to the nature of what they are affected with."[96] Edwards argues reason and earnestness should not be in opposition for the preacher, though he sees this as a fashion of the time. The preaching and sermon should be more practical and less speculative in favor of clarity. Edwards continues:

> Was there ever an age wherein strength and penetration of reason, extent of learning, exactness of distinction, correctness of style, and clearness of expression, did so abound? And yet was there ever an age wherein there has been so little sense of the evil of sin, so little love to God, heavenly-mindedness, and holiness of life, among the professors of the true religion? Our people don't so much need to have their heads stored, as to have their hearts touched; and they stand in the greatest need of that sort of preaching that has the greatest tendency to do this.[97]

With the revival fervor sweeping across New England, Edwards's own household were affected as a spiritual enrapturement took place for Sarah

[95]Edwards, *The Great Awakening*, 386–387.

[96]Ibid., 387.

[97]Ibid., 387–388. With respect to Sinners and "hellfire preaching" Edwards notes in *The Distinguishing Marks of a Work of the Spirit of God*: "Some talk of it as an unreasonable thing to think to fright person to heaven; but I think it is a reasonable thing to endeavor to fright persons away from hell, that stand upon the brink of it, and are just ready to fall into it, and are senseless of their danger." Ibid. 248.

Edwards. She felt the Spirit encompass her being, which she described as leading to a state of joy beyond comparison.[98] Sarah was admired as a deeply religious person by the age of 13. Jonathan, himself, a minister in training, held an admiration for her to the point that he had written an apostrophe to her in a book's flyleaf, possibly with the intention of presenting to her in 1723.[99] Sarah's "experiences" (recorded by her and kept through the work of Jonathan and later Sereno) were transcribed from the original material and presented in a journal article co-written by Kenneth Minkema, Catherine A. Brekus, and Harry S. Stout. In the article, they write of how her bodily responses to the revival were noted (both positively and negatively) as encouraging revival.[100]

Nearly a decade later, Edwards's conflict with Northampton over open communion reached its culmination when Edwards (following his principles) would argue against it and seek to implement measures to assure church members were Christians (such as parents needing to make a profession of faith before baptizing their children).[101] Philip F. Gura writes that Edwards did not foresee "the degree to which the town continued to revere Stoddard and view his principles as little less than canon law."[102] The church revolted against this. They were led by Joseph Hawley III (a cousin of Edwards's), who later repented for his role both to Edwards and in print. Eventually, the congregation dismissed Edwards from the congregation, and he preached his last sermon as their pastor on July 1, 1750.[103]

After Edwards was ousted from the church, he left Northampton and settled in Stockbridge. He would lead the multi-ethnic (English and Mohican) congregation, school, and community. He took great care in preaching messages that related to the dual congregations and primarily used John Wauwaumpequunnaunt as an interpreter.[104] Edwards writes of his purpose at Stockbridge:

[98] Marsden (taken partly from Sereno Edwards), 240–249.

[99] Kenneth P. Minkema, Catherine A Brekus, and Harry S. Stout, "Agitations, Convulsions, Leaping, and Loud Talking: The "Experiences of Sarah Pierpont Edwards," *The William and Mary Quarterly* 78, no. 3 (July 2021): 494–95.

[100] Sarah Pierpont Edwards, "Mrs. Edwards's Experiences in Jan. 19 & 1742," Shepard Family Collection, Department of Special Collections, Yale Divinity School Library, New Haven, CT, as published in "Agitations, Convulsions, Leaping, and Loud Talking," 527.

[101] Marsden, 341–363.

[102] Gura, *Jonathan Edwards: America's Evangelical*, 61.

[103] Marsden, 341–363.

[104] Ibid., 392–93.

> If any shall offer this excuse for themselves, that they have the Bible and we can search that: I answer, A people ben't only obliged to read the word of God, but also to hear it preached. Ministers are set on purpose to explain the word of God, and therefore their people ought to hear them when they offer to explain it to them, when they don't know what light they may hold forth t 'em to enable 'em to understand the Scripture.[105]

This quote from Jonathan Edwards is a great example of his dual emphasis on preaching for instruction *and* understanding which will be fleshed out in the coming chapters. Of the thousand-plus sermons (over 1229 in the *Sermon Index* at Yale), this sermon on Isaiah 30:26 tragically stands out for another reason. *Our Great End in God's Appointing the Gospel Ministry* (dated March 1750) was written in pieces on the back of a receipt for the purchase of a slave named Venus. As John Lowe points out, "Edwards viewed slaves as property. Even though Edwards would eventually see spiritual equality with Africans and Native Americans, he did not transfer that perspective to a temporal view between himself and his slaves. Titus's worth was measured in money and his person was counted as property." So, too, was Venus.[106]

It is hard for the historian to look back over someone's life and pronounce judgment over the intention of their thoughts. The role of the historian, though, is to give the fullest context to an individual's life based on the context of their life, writings, and personal interactions. Where does Edwards draw the line internally over slaves and their humanity? In the end, Edwards signed a document that said a seller would deliver to Edwards "a negro girl named Venus aged fourteen years or thereabout to have & to hold the said negro girl named Venus unto the said Jonathan Edwards his heirs exercs. & assigns and to his & their proper use & behoof for ever."[107]

As will be seen, Edwards during his time at Stockbridge showed growth and unity with Native Americans he ministered to while there. But tragically, his advocacy of Native Americans, and the care he took in ministering to his varied congregations must be seen in light of his ownership and support of slavery in line with the majority of colonial America, and not with the

[105]Edwards, "Our Great End in God's Appointing the Gospel Ministry," *Sermons and Discourses, 1743–1758*, 454.

[106]John Thomas Lowe, "The Practice that Prevails': Jonathan Edwards, Slavery, and Race" (PhD diss., Vrije Universiteit Amsterdam, 2022)," 113–115.

[107]Edwards, "Receipt for Slave Named Venus," *A Jonathan Edwards Reader*, ed. John E. Smith, Harry S. Stout, and Kenneth P. Minkema, (New Haven: Yale University Press, 1995), 296.

rising abolitionism which both his mentee (Samuel Hopkins) and his own son Jonathan Edwards, Jr. would become flag-bearers of.

Many literature and religious history classes have used *Sinners in the Hands of an Angry God* to illustrate the fiery preaching and rhetoric of the colonial American preacher. However, Edwards's ability to illustrate topics elucidates such frightening imagery. Edwards's purpose in relentlessly pursuing the logical application of doctrine and his use of illustrative imagery for his congregations before Stockbridge was Edwards's way of reaching both the mind and the affections of his audience. Thus, he met their need to not only understand and accept biblical doctrine but also see the doctrine expressed in a way that illuminates it to their senses and imagination.

The next section examines Edwards's role in the advancement of the Protestant Tradition and Edwards's view of his audience's biblical literacy and his purpose in reaching them with the Bible in his preaching.

Edwards, the Bible, and the Protestant Tradition

The Protestant Reformation and the Puritan tradition, which sprung from the Reformation, came with a view of the primacy of Scripture for doctrine. Edwards embodied this primacy in key characteristics that he either followed or advanced further. The first was the Bible as the authority in life, as shown through the confessions and in the catechisms that arose from the Reformation doctrine of *Sola Scriptura*. It was the foundation for the laws in the New England colonies (specifically seen in the Massachusetts' 1648 *Book of General Laws*). Edwards saw the Bible as the authority for life and would judge a person's salvation not only for their fondness of the Bible but that fondness as found through the right reverence for the Word in context:

> What deceives many of the less understanding and considerate sort of people, in this matter, seems to be this; that the Scripture is the Word of God, and has nothing in it which is wrong, but is pure and perfect: and therefore, those experiences which come from the Scripture must be right. But then it should be considered, affections may arise on occasion of the Scripture, and not properly come from the Scripture, as the genuine fruit of the Scripture, and by a right use of it; but from an abuse of it. All that can be argued from the purity and perfection of the Word of God, with respect to experiences, is this, that those experiences which are agreeable to the Word of God, are right, and can't be

> otherwise; and not that those affections must be right, which arise on occasion of the Word of God, coming to the mind.[108]

The second characteristic carried to Edwards's time from the Reformation was the Bible as the compass to develop doctrine. Through varied confessions of faith arising from the Reformation, doctrine was developed and defended from Scripture. While certain doctrines had varied interpretations by different factions, most doctrinal statements in their confessions were tied to Bible passages and their interpretation and application therein.

For Edwards, he saw a harmony within Scripture, which carried the twin pillars developed from the *Westminster Confession of Faith*. The first was the "analogy of Scripture," wherein texts were read in the context of other biblical texts, and the second was the "analogy of faith," wherein more challenging passages to derive doctrine from were read "in view of the kerygmatic core and doctrinal drift of the Bible."[109]

Edwards stated a doctrine, argued its consequences, defended his view from criticism, and then brought "it to the touchstone of a number of key biblical texts, chosen and used as propositional criteria of different aspects of truth he has been expounding." The result for Edwards was to show how his doctrinal exposition aligned with each of those texts and the consequences of that doctrine.[110]

Edwards saw revelation as progressive in history, not only within the period of the Bible but beyond, as God revealed Himself more fully through history. Edwards viewed this as the continuing story of His redemption throughout history. However, as mentioned above, Edwards tethered helps such as post-biblical orthodox tradition to Scripture as the ultimate benchmark of its validity and a corrective against error.[111]

The third characteristic that concerned the Reformers and was emphasized by the Puritans and those following in their tradition was the cause of biblical literacy. If the Bible was the authority for all things in life and thought, and the Bible is what drove doctrinal beliefs and even civil law, the

[108]Jonathan Edwards, *Religious Affections*, ed. Paul Ramsey, vol. 2, *The Works of Jonathan Edwards* (New Haven: Yale University Press, 1993), 142–144.

[109]Douglas A. Sweeney, *Edwards the Exegete: Biblical Interpretation and Anglo-Protestant Culture on the Edge of the Enlightenment* (New York: Oxford University Press, 2016), 55, Kindle.

[110]William Sparkes Morris, *The Young Jonathan Edwards: A Reconstruction* (Brooklyn, NY: Carlson, 1991), 500.

[111]Michael J. McClymond and Gerald R. McDermott, *The Theology of Jonathan Edwards* (New York: Oxford University Press, 2012), 140–148.

necessity of biblical literacy for the household was a priority that Edwards wholly embraced.

The fourth major characteristic, related to the third, is the need for "plain style" preaching. The Puritan William Perkins would introduce the idea of "plain style" preaching through his work *The Arte of Prophesying*. This work would then influence the Westminster Assembly's *Directory for the Public Worship of God* and become a standard for training Puritan preachers (and those who followed the Puritan tradition, such as Edwards).[112]

Edwards knew and preached in this manner of preaching. However, he would strive to reach the "affections" of his hearers who had rejected the "sweetness" of those Scriptures. To do this, he preached "affectionately" or with a renewed sense of targeting the spiritual affections of the audience. This targeting of affections is most well-known through his use of illustrative language in *Sinners in the Hands of an Angry God*, but was also seen through his use of the same imagery in a number of sermons (including *Heaven is a World of Love*). Edwards notes there is not a dilemma for him in doing this:

> I think an exceeding affectionate way of preaching about the great things of religion, has in itself no tendency to beget false apprehensions of them; but on the contrary a much greater tendency to beget true apprehensions of them, than a moderate, dull, indifferent way of speaking of 'em.[113]

As will be seen in the final section of this chapter, Edwards had a high estimation of the biblical literacy of his congregation. Yet, he strove for his congregation to not only have a working knowledge of scripture but to embrace it as a "sweet fruit" or as sweet manna from heaven. Edwards's view of the need for greater holy affection for God's Word in light of an "insipid" familiarity will also be seen in his writings.

Edwards's View of the Biblical Literacy of His Congregation at Northampton

> Much of the Scripture is apt to seem insipid to us now, and as though there were no great matter of instruction in it, because

[112]Chad Van Dixhoorn, *God's Ambassadors: The Westminster Assembly and the Reformation of the English Pulpit, 1643–1653* (Grand Rapids, MI: Reformation Heritage Books, 2017), 178.

[113]Jonathan Edwards, "Some Thoughts Concerning the Revival," in *The Great Awakening*, ed. C.C. Goen, vol. 4, *The Works of Jonathan Edwards* (New Haven: Yale University Press, 1972), 386.

> those points of instruction that are most plainly contained in it, is old to us. 'Tis what we and everybody has been taught from our infancy, and has been most plainly taught this many hundred years in the world, so that the doctrines seem self-evident; so plain to us now, that there seems to have been no need of a particular revelation of such things, especially of insisting upon 'em so much. But it seems exceeding different to us now from what it would have done, if we had lived in those times when the revelation was given, when the things were in great measure new, at least as to that distinctness and expressness of their revelation. 'Tis so now with some of those that seem to us very plain points of what is now called natural religion. If we had an idea of the state the world was in then, when God gave the revelation, they would appear glorious instructions, bringing great light into the world, and most worthy of God. We are ready to despise that that we are so used to, and that is so common and old to us and to the world, as the children of Israel despised manna.[114]

In the above quote, Edwards reveals this permeation of the Bible, instead of leading to an attentive culture with abiding "affection" for the Word, was neglected as "flavorless." He likened the culture around him to the Israelites in the wilderness, who rejected the very "manna" of God. He writes above, in *Miscellany 598,* that this rejection is not from lack of instruction in the Scriptures but instead from apathy to it.

In August 1726, Edwards was asked to assist his aging grandfather, Solomon Stoddard, at Northampton. Stoddard was almost eighty-three years old at that time and served as Northampton's pastor twice as long as Edwards was alive. Every memory of his grandfather was tied to the congregation and church at Northampton. Whenever he visited his grandfather, he visited the church so he knew the families well, many of whom were his own cousins. After taking on the role of assistant pastor, the twenty-three-year-old Edwards served the congregation for twenty-three years.[115]

What view did Edwards have of his congregation? As shown above, the culture at the time was bent towards biblical primacy and education. The people were raised in the Word. They learned Bible lessons while

[114]Jonathan Edwards, *Miscellanies," (Entry Nos. 501–832)*, ed. Ava Chamberlain, vol. 18, *The Works of Jonathan Edwards* (New Haven: Yale University Press, 1998), 141.

[115]Sweeney, *Jonathan Edwards and the Ministry of the Word*, 52.

rehearsing their ABCs. The laws of the land required children brought up as biblicists. Every Sunday during the primary service (as there was also a second service on Sunday), there was a biblical text as a call to worship, an Old Testament reading with explanation by the pastor, a New Testament reading with explanation by the pastor, a sermon which expounded the text for 60–90 minutes, the singing of a psalm "metrically," and another reading of a different psalm.[116] No family honored this as much as Edwards's own family. His father, Timothy, was known to use his own parsonage parlor as a place for schoolboys to learn their lessons in the biblical and theological languages (Hebrew, Koine Greek, and Latin).[117]

Edwards began to learn Latin, Greek, and Hebrew by the age of twelve.[118] He had also led a group of boys in building a booth in the swamp of East Windsor to join together in prayer. Not satisfied to share only a secret swamp hut of prayer, Edwards built another forest dwelling to pray in further seclusion.[119]

Jonathan was not the only one who was raised in devotion to God. Sereno Edwards Dwight, writing on Edwards's sister Jerusha in his biography of Edwards, collected familial testimonials from Timothy, four of her sisters, and a family friend, which included this picture of her devotion:

> Habitually serene and cheerful, she was contented and happy; not envious of others, not desirous of admiration, not ambitious nor aspiring: and while she valued highly the esteem of her friends and of the wise and good, she was firmly convinced that her happiness depended, chiefly and ultimately, on the state of her own mind . . . Her religious life began in childhood; and from that time, meditation, prayer, and reading the sacred Scriptures, were not a prescribed task, but a coveted enjoyment. [120]

Of note from this portion of the extract is Jerusha's enjoyment of reading the Bible, praying, and meditation, which "began in childhood." The compliment of her pious pleasure is used as a contrast for the "prescribed task"

[116]McClymond and McDermott, *The Theology of Jonathan Edwards*, 495.

[117]Sweeney, *Jonathan Edwards and the Ministry of the Word*, 34.

[118]Ibid., 34.

[119]Jonathan Edwards, "Personal Narrative," *Letters and Personal Writings*, 790–91.

[120]Sereno Edwards Dwight, *The Life of President Edwards* (New York: G & C & H Carvill, 1830), 116–17. This accounting of Jerusha showcases the piety and dedication to Scripture and theology which was a feature of the church culture in which Edwards preached.

which for so many others was their duty, which also began "in childhood" (as seen above). Jonathan Edwards saw the earnest desire of his sister's piety and was driven by it to see hearts revived as he did during the Great Awakening revival at Northampton in 1735.

In writing to Benjamin Colman on the revival, he explains how those who had seen the Scriptures as "insipid" "manna" now saw God's Word afresh with a spirit of affection as he recounts many saw the Bible as "a new book to them, as though they never read it before."[121] He continues by illustrating their affection for the Bible as "a lover by the sight of his sweetheart," and the Sabbath as greatly prized among them and "longed for before it comes" and even moved by hearing the bell ring to announce the beginning of the Sabbath.[122]

Returning to the testimony of Jerusha, the testimonial further notes her joy at spending time alone with God or in reading with "deepest interest" theology "as a science," pursuing the "systematic study of the Scriptures" through examination with the help of "the best commentaries." Day by day, the testimony reads of Jerusha immersed in private daily prayer, meditation, and Bible reading in preparation for communal worship.[123]

Edwards was raised around a biblically-immersed society, but further than that, he had personally seen those in his own family who went beyond rote memory of the Bible and knowledge of doctrine to those who cherished and passionately lived it out, such as his sister. His desire was for the entire church to be those who went beyond mere rote knowledge and pursued God with an affectionate passion. His greatest concern for the church was those who had a "counterfeit religion" based on knowledge, not affection. In *Religious Affections,* he writes of the enemy's "greatest advantage," which is the damage "counterfeit religion" can cause the Church:

> By this means, he many ways, damps and wounds religion in the hearts of the saints, obscures and deforms it by corrupt mixtures, causes their religious affections woefully to degenerate, and sometimes for a considerable time, to be like the manna, that bred worms and stank; and dreadfully ensnares and confounds the minds of others of the saints, and brings 'em into great

[121] Edwards, *Letters and Personal Writings*, 54.

[122] Edwards, *Letters and Personal Writings*, 54.

[123] Dwight, *The Life of President Edwards*, 116–17.

> difficulties and temptation, and entangles 'em in a wilderness, out of which they can by no means extricate themselves.[124]

As apathetic religion was the fear for Edwards, Gura writes it was the joy and excitement of Scripture, or a higher "esteem of Jesus" operating against "the interests of Satan," that would confirm the Holy Spirit's presence in the revivals. Instead of an arrogance that caused a loathing of God and His Word, true revival for Edwards generated "Christian humility," signaling the presence of the Holy Spirit for Edwards.[125]

Edwards argues that true affection for God's Word is a true signal of earnest conversion and regeneration by the Spirit as it "establishes them more in their truth and divinity, it is certainly by the Spirit of God."[126] Humble searching and affection for God's Word is something Edwards argues is not what Satan desires people to do as "that divine Word, is that which God hath given to be the great and standing rule for the direction of his church in all religious matters and concerns of their souls, in all ages."[127]

The Word must be discerned rightly, as Edwards warns in *Religious Affections* that Satan can and will twist Scripture to delude those not regenerated of a false security. He illustrates Satan even used and twisted Scripture to tempt Jesus, and if the enemy was so brazen to do that, what would hinder him from doing it to those in his congregation.[128]

How, then, can one discern between natural and divine affection for Scripture? Edwards writes it is in the Scripture being rightly applied according to the Word's own standard. This harkens to the *Rule of Faith* as the test of whether affections or interpretations of Scripture are authentic or twisted to produce false confidence. He writes those experiences confirmed with Scripture are "agreeable to the Word of God, are right, and can't be otherwise: and not that those affections must be right, which arise on occasion of the Word of God, coming to the mind."[129]

Edwards responds in a similar manner to critics of the Awakening in *Some Thoughts Concerning the Revival*. It is Scripture Edwards cites as the

[124] Jonathan Edwards, *Religious Affections*, 86–88.

[125] Philip F. Gura, *Jonathan Edwards: America's Evangelical* (New York: Hill and Wang, 2006), 121.

[126] Jonathan Edwards, "Distinguishing Marks," in *The Great Awakening*, ed. C.C. Goen, vol. 4, *The Works of Jonathan Edwards* (New Haven: Yale University Press, 1972), 253.

[127] Edwards, "Distinguishing Marks," 253.

[128] Edwards, *Religious Affections*, 144.

[129] Edwards, *Religious Affections*, 143–144.

criterion for judging the revival. He charges the critics of the revival of mixing select verses with "philosophical notions they entertain of the nature of the soul." Critics would dismiss all religious passions as compounded with "affections that are very flashy," which Edwards even writes as "little to be depended on." However, Edwards states true religious affections, which pertain not only to the will but to the soul, are the "very life and soul of all true religion."[130]

Edwards saw the effects of this firsthand with his wife after the visit of itinerant Samuel Buell to Northampton in 1742. Buell was becoming known as a "stirring itinerant" and was ordained by the New Haven Association. During Buell's visit, Edwards was out of town in Worcester County on an itinerant preaching tour of his own.[131]

In a letter to Thomas Prince, Edwards writes that Buell had spent most of his time in "religious exercises" with those at Northampton, either in public or private. Edwards compares the work of God attending Buell's visit with the revival that had taken place under George Whitefield's itinerant preaching in the Spring of 1740, though Edwards writes of this revival attending greater results with "religious affections being raised far beyond what they ever had been before."[132]

Edwards took the opportunity to encourage his congregation in their devotion by leading them "into a solemn public renewal of their covenant with God." Edwards drafted a covenant and distributed it for the people to join in. His final remarks to Prince show his great concern (seen above) with distinguishing true affections from false and how, in the revival of 1735–36, there was a great "visible" show of "high" affections, but many had now shown subtle, yet more mature signs of affections. Edwards was more encouraged by this revival. However, Edwards blamed an infection "from abroad" of that "greater visible commotion," which caused doubt among his people and "a deep and unhappy tincture" Edwards struggled to counsel his people through.[133]

His wife Sarah also wrote of Buell's visit and her experiences. Her testimony from the event demonstrates those true affections, which Edwards mentions in his analysis of the revivals that had taken place (notable in *Religious Affections*). Sarah writes repeatedly of a new sense of God's pres-

[130]Edwards, "Some Thoughts Concerning the Revival," 296–297.

[131]Gura, *Jonathan Edwards*, 105.

[132]Edwards, *Letters and Personal Writings*, 122–126.

[133]Ibid., 122–126.

ence that she felt was heightened during the revival under Buell.[134] These descriptions can be compared to Jonathan Edwards's language in *Religious Affections* of the regenerate's new perception:

> From hence it follows, that in those gracious exercises and affections which are wrought in the minds of the saints, through the saving influences of the Spirit of God, there is a new inward perception or sensation of their minds, entirely different in its nature and kind, from anything that ever their minds were the subjects of before they were sanctified.[135]

Edwards goes on to illustrate the affectionate sense given by God to which the unregenerate is blind, comparing it to the sense of taste for fruit or the sweetness of honey to one born without it. Edwards notes one could visually perceive a piece of fruit as having beauty or the visual smoothness of honey, but to one who has no sense of taste, it is rendered useless in truly experiencing the sweetness of honey or the refreshing and sweet taste of fruit. He relates this blindness of sense to a natural affection one may have for the Bible, or church, or church members, or even the thought of God, but those natural and true spiritual loves are "entirely and exceedingly diverse" due to that lack of sense of the goodness of God and holiness.[136]

Sarah relates in her experience she was filled with "an inexpressibly sweet and pure love to God, and to the children of God." She goes on to write that she was "entirely swallowed up in God" as her "only portion," stating again a greater "love to the children of God" with a love as to her "own soul."[137]

Sarah conveys that this experience was one of not only the loss of the sense of self but also the profit of a new sense of oneness with God and His Church. She writes she had "never felt such an emptiness of self-love, or any regard to any private, selfish interest of my own." She describes this pure love and connection with God and those in His Church as "exceedingly

[134] Sarah Pierpont Edwards, "The Narrative of Sarah Pierpont Edwards," *Family Writings and Related Documents*, vol. 41, *Works of Jonathan Edwards Online*, ed. Jonathan Edwards Center. Also seen in Sereno Edwards Dwight, *The Life of President Edwards*, 178.

[135] Edwards, *Religious Affections*, 205.

[136] Ibid., 205–209.

[137] Sarah Pierpont Edwards, *Family Writings and Related Documents*.

sweet and ravishing," connecting her experience to Edwards's illustration of honey or fruit.[138]

Sarah writes of the connection between her experience of oneness and unity with God and His Church with the high priestly prayer of Christ in John 17:21 (citing the *King James Bible*):

> I felt at the same time an exceedingly strong and tender affection for the children of God, and realized, in a manner exceedingly sweet and ravishing, the meaning of Christ's prayer, in John xvii. 21, "That they all may be one, as thou Father art in me, and I in thee, that they also may be one in us." This union appeared to me an inconceivable, excellent and sweet oneness; and at the same time I felt that oneness in my soul, with the children of God who were present.[139]

It is not a surprise this is similar to the view of heavenly love expressed by Edwards in his *Charity and Its Fruits* series sermon *Heaven is a World of Love*, that there "is undoubtedly an inconceivably pure, sweet and fervent love between the saints in glory; and their love is in proportion to the perfection and amiableness of the objects beloved."[140] Edwards preached on heavenly love, and Sarah, in her testimony, describes a heavenly sense of joy at the bliss of oneness of herself with God and those in His Church:

> At the same time, my heart and soul all flowed out in love to Christ; so that there seemed to be a constant flowing and reflowing of heavenly and divine love, from Christ's heart to mine; and I appeared to myself to float or swim, in these bright, sweet beams of the love of Christ, like the motes swimming in the beams of the sun, or the streams of his light which come in at the window. My soul remained in a kind of heavenly elysium. So far as I am capable of making a comparison, I think that what I felt each minute, during the continuance of the whole time, was worth more than all the outward comfort and pleasure, which I had enjoyed in my whole life put together. It was a pure delight, which fed and satisfied the soul.[141]

[138]Sarah Pierpont Edwards, *Family Writings and Related Documents.*

[139]Ibid.

[140]Edwards, "Heaven is a World of Love," 375.

[141]Sarah Pierpont Edwards, *Family Writings and Related Documents.*

Sarah's experience recalls the first question from the *Westminster Shorter Catechism*: "What is the chief end of man? Man's chief end is to glorify God, and to enjoy him forever."[142] In writing of Edwards's beatific vision, Kyle Strobel shows Edwards's view of man's ultimate purpose through ultimate unity with God and His Church, relayed above by Sarah of her own experience. Strobel describes it as a "stream of love flowing fully to Christ," which is communicated through Christ to His Church. The Church participates as receptors of God's love as "secondary and derivative realities of God's inner-triune love."[143] Thus, through regeneration, man experiences ultimate fulfillment in union with this "inner-triune love," or, as Strobel writes, "the elect drink from this fountain of love as persons who partake in God's own personal beatific-delight."[144]

Conclusion

In this chapter, Edwards's motivation in spending countless hours in his study was for the purpose of ministering through what he saw as his greatest strength as a minister: his study, exposition, and illustration of Scripture and its themes. Edwards desired for his audience to know God, to know God's Word, and to have joyous affections towards God. As Edwards was educated both in his home, at school, and later at college and seminary, he does not squander any opportunity to delve into the rich pool of resources at his disposal to engage, refine, and formulate doctrines for himself and his congregation at Northampton.

Edwards wrote thousands of entries (miscellanies) on every topic that came to mind. Many of those entries formed the basis for doctrinal works he refined over the course of his life. However, as will be seen in the next chapter, in his sermons, Edwards wanted more than rote knowledge and biblical and doctrinal accuracy for his congregation. He wanted them to go beyond the biblicist and religious culture they grew up surrounded by but were abandoning in their affections. He wanted them to experience God's Word and God's church through a true, affectionate union with God and His people.

[142] "The Westminster Shorter Catechism," *Creeds, Confessions, and Catechisms*, 462.

[143] Kyle C. Strobel, *Jonathan Edwards's Theology: A Reinterpretation*, T&T Clark Studies in Systematic Theology 19 (London: Bloomsbury Publishing, 2014), 106.

[144] Ibid., 106.

As will be seen in the following chapter, Edwards will relentlessly pursue his congregation with God's truths and use the gifts given to him through study and resources to elicit affectionate hearts receptive to God's Word. He will strive that they go from seeing God's Word as "insipid manna" and truly care to see the beauty and privilege of living in the time they did where access to God's Word was never as attainable and usable in the history of the church. The next chapter will show the advancement Edwards made of his Puritan heritage in his colonial preaching ministry. His affectionate preaching went beyond the normative "plain style" through a controlled affectionate pleading of God's truth in application. This demonstration will be a starting point to compare how Edwards will then respond to a new audience at Stockbridge.

CHAPTER 3: EDWARDS'S HOMILETICS AT NORTHAMPTON

Edwards's Puritan Preaching During His Colonial Ministry

The Value of Salvation[1]

Date: Spring/Early Summer 1722
Key Text: Matthew 16:26 – "For what is a man profited, if he gain the whole world, and lose his own soul, or what shall a man give in exchange for his soul?"

The earliest Edwards sermon to observe is one of four "candidating sermons" Edwards composed for his trial appearances to minister at the New York pastorate. The text is from Matthew 16:26. Thirty years later, Edwards chose Matthew 16:24 to preach among the Stockbridge Indians. Wilson H. Kimnach notes this sermon is significant as it is more of a lecture than a sermon, with its doctrinal section stretching three times as long as the application. When Edwards re-preached this sermon at Northampton, he lengthened the application without shortening the doctrinal section. The original sermon filled two octavo booklets with eight leaves each. When it was modified, it had one added to the first and two to the second.[2]

[1] Jonathan Edwards, "The Value of Salvation," *Sermons and Discourses 1720–1723*, ed. Wilson H. Kimnach, vol. 10, *The Works of Jonathan Edwards* (New Haven: Yale University Press, 1992), 308–337.

[2] Wilson H. Kimnach, "The Value of Salvation," 308–310.

Edwards does not begin with an explanation of the context of the verse or characters but assumes knowledge therein of who Peter, Jesus, and the disciples are and instead moves to the prideful context of Peter's motivations. Edwards gives the narrative of what happens with Christ's rebuke of Peter and His expectation of self-denial for the disciples as context for the value of the soul by Christ in Edwards's chosen text from Matthew. This leads to the doctrine that "the salvation of the soul is of vastly more worth and value than the whole world."[3]

Under doctrine, Edwards gives eight particulars that prove his doctrine. The first is that "all worldly things shall have an end." He references 2 Peter 3:10, Matthew 24:35, and Revelation 20:11 to show the world and all of its works will pass away.

Not only will everything in general end as in Edwards's first particular, but every person's connection to the world will also end with their death. He again gives a rich illustration in comparing the vain trappings of the temporal world for those who are affluent with the worms and bugs that will be their trappings at their death. He then uses the biblical illustration from Luke 16:19 of the rich man who planned to expand his wealth, not knowing of his forthcoming death that night. This shows Edwards's emphasis on visual imagination illustrating biblical doctrine for his hearers.[4]

Edwards gives a practical point that earthly things are often unreliable even before death. He gives Job as an illustration of this and the fleeting assurance of earthly gain. Through this sermon, Edwards does not try to explain the passage itself (which he only briefly does at the beginning), but rather focuses on helping his audience understand the significance of the meaning of the passage. Why does the soul have more value than riches? Why does that matter for the person in his congregation? Edwards wants his audience to move past understanding the passage to understanding, more than anything, the personal application of the passage.[5] This is seen again in his fourth particular of the soul's immortality in comparison to the temporal state of the world he has explained.

The Bible is central as the authority in Edwards's homiletics. In the fifth particular, Edwards exposits the little value of the world, even if it were to last for eternity. He uses Solomon and the Book of Ecclesiastes as an example of the vanity of possessions. Solomon's example is compared to

[3]Edwards, "The Value of Salvation," 311–313.

[4]Ibid., 371, 313–314.

[5]Edwards, "The Value of Salvation," 314–316.

his sixth particular of the "life and salvation of the soul" as of "inestimable worth and value." This is given for two reasons: first, it shows salvation as the "deliverance" of the soul from "so great misery," and second, it shows the happiness to be enjoyed in that salvation.[6]

In speaking of the misery those saved are delivered from, Edwards again uses illustrative language to explain how the things to which those of this world cling will prove meaningless in everlasting condemnation.[7] Edwards uses rich imagery to show the terror of judgment in juxtaposition to the temporal comforts they desire on earth. This is Edwards's primary means of shocking and awakening his colonial audience. In the next paragraph, Edwards makes assumptions of his audience's biblical literacy as he references Abraham, Isaac, and Jacob; Matthew 8:11–12; the frightening judgment of Jesus declaring those He does not know will be cast out as "workers of iniquity"; and the wedding feast and those denied entry into it.[8] Next, Edwards moves on to the eternal happiness of believers. The first benefit is deliverance. The second benefit is the "enjoyment of all good."[9]

Edwards again assumes biblical knowledge as he references without explanation the Queen of Sheba, Job, David, Elijah, the thief on the cross who went with Jesus to heaven, "the Beatifical Vision of God," and Moses's viewing of the glory of God. In highlighting the eternal happiness, Edwards shows again his goal of moving beyond understanding to encouraging affection for God and His salvation:

> This happiness shall be eternal. This crowns [it]: however great the happiness of heaven were in itself, yet it would detract from it if it were not to be eternal. If the saints in heaven were sure they should enjoy heaven some thousands of years, and after that it should be at an end, it would cast a great damp upon their joys and delights; it would much grieve them to think that they should lose so great [a] happiness, and at last it would be a cloud in their light, a bitter in the midst of their sweet. But it

[6] Ibid., 316–320.

[7] Ibid., 320–321. This shows similar illustrative language Edwards uses in *Sinners in the Hands of an Angry God*.

[8] Edwards, "The Value of Salvation," 321–322.

[9] Ibid., 322–324.

is not so; they are sure that they shall enjoy it forever, and this redoubles the joy: Rev. "And they shall reign forever and ever."[10]

Just as Edwards uses visual imagery to picture the terror of judgment, he uses imagery to capture the eternal delights of salvation. Edwards's seventh particular is the worthlessness of the world for the soul that is lost. This is a re-application of the truth that the body cannot properly enjoy creation without the soul being in alignment with God. Finally, in his eighth particular, Edwards shows the soul's worth due to God's valuation of it. In moving to the use (application) portion of the sermon, Edwards makes two inferences. First, man's "miserable and lost estate by nature." Second, the foolishness of the worldly who neglect to do anything about the lostness of their soul.

His first exhortation is to not neglect their souls with a direct quote from the key text.[11] Under this first exhortation, he gives three points of application. The first two are that they should consider the danger and inexcusableness of neglecting the salvation of their souls, with the third application urging care of their souls.

Edwards's second exhortation (which was added to the Northampton sermon and not present in the New York sermon) is to do their utmost to "forward the salvation of other men." A third and final exhortation added to the Northampton version of the sermon called on the congregation to pray for others' salvation and for a movement of revival.[12] In *The Value of Salvation*, Edwards uses rich biblical imagery to capture the terror of judgment and the beauty and joy of eternal salvation to help a biblically literate audience grasp the value of their salvation

Poverty of Spirit[13]

Date: Summer 1722-Spring 1723
Key Text: Matthew 5:3a – "Blessed are the poor in spirit: for theirs is the kingdom of heaven."

Like *The Value of Salvation*, *Poverty of Spirit* is a lecture-driven sermon from New York. In this sermon derived from the Sermon on the Mount,

[10]Ibid., 325.

[11]Edwards, "The Value of Salvation," 326–329.

[12]Ibid., 329–336.

[13]Jonathan Edwards, "Poverty of Spirit," *Sermons and Discourses 1720–1723*, 493–505.

Edwards compares the liberation brought about by Moses and Christ. The sermon booklet, an octavo, was revised at least three further times it was preached at Bolton, Glastonbury, and Northampton. The only major revision was the addition of a half-page for Northampton.[14]

The introduction for *Poverty of Spirit* begins with a comparison of the "terrible" and "dreadful" voice of the Law brought to Moses to the "sweet voice of Jesus Christ" on "whose lips grace is poured." It is a biblical illustration of the sweetness of the Gospel and its liberation of the Christian into relationship with God, compared with the previous dreadfulness of the Law without grace. Edwards gives this illustration to an audience he knows would be aware both of the picture of Moses at Mount Sinai receiving the Law and of Christ's incarnation. With this illustration given to introduce his subject, Edwards gives the doctrine of the sermon: "Those persons that are poor in spirit are happy and blessed, because the kingdom of heaven is theirs."[15]

To prove his doctrine, Edwards gives four particulars describing a person poor in spirit, showing the kingdom of heaven as theirs, explaining why God bestows the kingdom of heaven on them, and why they are blessed on this account. In this sermon, Edwards is not interested in giving an exposition of what the text is, but instead, what the doctrine means, both in general and specifically for his audience. His first particular is to explain what it means to be "poor in spirit" as a way of showing this as commendable to his audience. He explains why they should be humble and "sensible of" their "filthiness by sin."[16]

What is the reward for embracing this humility? Edwards shows the reward in his second particular that they receive the kingdom of heaven because it belongs to them. The meeker and humble they are, and the more they embrace seeing themselves as "vile and filthy," the more Edwards argues God will replace those "filthy garments and clothe them with royal apparel, shining with glory." This glory, according to Edwards, is a transcendent beauty above anything that can be created or "bestowed" on the earth. This shows again Edwards's method of enticing and stirring the affections of his audience for godliness and the rewards of true affection for God.[17]

[14]Kimnach, "Poverty of Spirit," 493–494.

[15]Edwards, "Poverty of Spirit," 495–497.

[16]Edwards, "Poverty of Spirit," 497–500.

[17]Ibid., 500.

The reasons God will replace their garments and those poor in spirit deserve it are threefold for Edwards. First, those who are unfit are like the fallen angels who want all the glory and power for themselves. Not having a humble and contrite spirit leaves one unfit for heaven. Those who are fit are those who are humble. Secondly, those who are not humble in spirit do not want the heavenly gifts anyway, as they already see themselves as richer and more deserving of greater gifts. Finally, those who are not humble are obsessed with this world instead of Christ and His kingdom.[18] This section also shows Edwards's focus not on the explanation of information but on the encouragement of affection for humility and godliness (or discouragement for haughtiness and worldly affections).

For the final particular of his sermon's doctrine, Edwards uses a number of scripture references to show the contentment and reward of the humble. He cites James 4:6, Proverbs 16:19, 29:23, 2 Corinthians 6:10, and Mark 10:28–30 (closing on Jesus's promise that those who sacrifice all for Him will "receive an hundredfold" for what they give up on His account).[19] Edwards closes on this before moving on to the application of the sermon.

In the application, Edwards lists four improvements of the doctrine. The first is to "mortify" the things of pride and worldliness. The second is to lament the pride and worldliness around them. The third is for those who are poor in spirit to be comforted. And fourth, to exhort all with the doctrine of poverty of spirit because "it is the highest, most excellent inheritance, that most excellent kingdom in the universe," showing again Edwards's focus on convincing his audience of their need for God.[20]

Christ, the Light of the World[21]

Date: Summer 1722-Spring 1723
Key Text: John 8:12 – "I am the light of the world."

Kimnach notes *Christ, the Light of the World,* is Edwards's "earliest extant sermon to have a metaphor wholly adequate to the rhetorical foundation of its argument."[22] Like later sermons, less space is given for the doctrine,

[18] Ibid., 500–501.

[19] Edwards, "Poverty of Spirit," 501–502.

[20] Ibid., 502–504.

[21] Jonathan Edwards, "Christ, the Light of the World," *Sermons and Discourses 1720–1723*, 533–547.

[22] Kimnach, "Christ, the Light of the World," 533.

although there is more exegetical exposition. The sermon was most likely repreached at Bolton and, as indicated by different colored markings, several times at Northampton.[23]

At the beginning of his sermon, Edwards makes a notable proposition in communicating who Jesus is in relation to His identifications in the Bible. First, Edwards notes other terms of identification, such as His being a lion, a lamb, the bread of life, the true vine, the life of the soul, the bright and morning star, and the sun of righteousness. But it is the key text, in Christ being the light of the world, that Edwards makes this notable proposition, Christ as the "communication" of God the Father's "infinite fountain of light."[24]

This is notable because Edwards proposes Christ as who was the member of the Trinity present in the burning bush for Moses or appeared to the patriarchs, or who "went before the children of Israel in a pillar of cloud by day and a pillar of fire by night," or who appeared to Moses at Mount Sinai. Next, Edwards observes the universality of Christ's presence as the light, the exclusivity of His being the only light, the global nature of His enlightenment (as it is offered for all people), and His efficacy to come in being recognized as it. His observations include references to John 1:9, Isaiah 2:2, Malachi 1:11, and Jeremiah 31:34.[25]

As with the previous sermons, there is no thought for explaining the text; instead, his focus is on encouraging his audience to consider the meaning of Christ's identification as the light of the world. His doctrine is Christ is the light of the world. What Edwards proposes through his doctrine is to show how the world is in darkness without Christ, how it is enlightened by Him, and what are the means Christ uses to communicate "his light."[26]

First, Edwards shows how the world is in perpetual "midnight" consumed in "barbarous idolatry and superstition" introduced into the world by the devil. Using 2 Corinthians 4:4 as a prooftext, Edwards explains this is the power of Satan as the "god of this world." Like in his other sermons, Edwards, with an eye on his audience, moves from the more general darkness of the world to the personal darkness of the individual in his audience. Edwards preaches:

[23]Edwards, "Christ, the Light of the World," 533–535.

[24]Ibid., 535

[25]Ibid., 536.

[26]Edwards, "Christ, the Light of the World," 537.

> Dreadful is our blindness and ignorance by nature; our souls are naturally like a dark, hideous dungeon where the sun, moon, nor stars never found an entrance for their beams. How dull are men while in their natural state of ignorance and unbelief! Their eyes are closed that they cannot see, and their ears heavy like the deaf adder that cannot hear the voice of charmers charming never so wisely. How blind are they to spiritual things; how impossible is it for any but God to persuade them of their danger, and of the importance of things of eternity, although it be as plain as the sun that those things which will last forever are a thousand times more to be regarded than those that will presently have an end; yet how impossible is it to persuade men of it, so full are their minds of darkness. How blind are they when they look on God! They can see nothing excellent or lovely in him, although he is infinitely glorious and infinitely amiable, and his glories appear everywhere throughout the whole creation; there is nothing that we converse with, but what God may easily be seen in it by those whose minds are not full of darkness.[27]

Edwards contrasts this darkness of soul and blindness with light's property to "make manifest" things to be seen and then relates this to Christ, who "makes glorious things manifest to him that he never saw before."[28] Further, light's property is beauty and pleasantness. As such, Christ is the most "beautiful and glorious object in the world." The contrast is Satan, who blinds those who follow him into dark blindness, with Christ, who "manifests" light and sight of wondrous things to those who follow him. As before, Edwards's style in this sermon is to illustrate blindness and glorious sight (metaphysical) language for his listeners who may have heard and read about Christ as the light of the world or about spiritual blindness many times before. Edwards hopes that they get a feeling for these spiritual images. What does it truly mean to be spiritually dark and blind, and how does it feel then to be awakened into glorious light. This is what Edwards hopes will stir his audience not only for spiritual knowledge but also for spiritual affection.

Edwards's third way in which Christ is the light of the world is that He revives and warms the world through faith like the sun does the earth with its warmth. He compares spiritual darkness to winter, which ends through

[27] Ibid., 537–538.

[28] Ibid., 538–539.

the warmth of spring brought about by the sun or how the sun revives plants and trees, quoting Canticles 2:10–13. He also concludes his section on Christ as the light by showing how the sun's light helps fruit bloom and increase. To finish, Edwards explains that Christ communicates "his light to the souls of men" through the Bible (quoting Ps 19:7–9 and Heb 4:12) and the Holy Spirit.[29]

In his exhortation, Edwards asks his audience to come to Christ since He is the light of the world. Those who have come are to continue to walk in the light of Christ and to follow the command of Ephesians 5:8 to walk in holiness in all ways. This sermon is another illustration of how Edwards seeks to stir affection beyond knowledge into action. Edwards is unconcerned with explaining what the passage is; instead, he explains what it means for his audience and how they should feel, forsaking their spiritual blindness to walk in the light of the world, Christ.[30]

That We Ought to Make Religion Our Present and Immediate Business[31]

Date: Summer 1724
Key Text: Psalm 119:60 – "I made haste, and delayed not to keep thy commandments."

Edwards's introduction to the sermon guides the listeners to his theme for the sermon, the immediate obedience of God as stated in the key text. The doctrine is like the introduction: "We ought to make religion our present and immediate business."[32]

In illustrating his doctrine, Edwards gives several reasons not to delay making obedience "our present and immediate business." First, for Edwards, obedience is the reason all are created, especially mankind, who are over creation. He uses Luke 13:7 to admonish that those who are not obedient and "don't bring forth the fruits of righteousness" are "as barren trees and cumberers of the ground." This admonishment shows Edwards's focus on moving beyond knowledge to action. Second, religion is a business of greatest importance. Again, Edwards juxtaposes those who have "eternal

[29]Edwards, "Christ, the Light of the World," 539–542.

[30]Edwards, "Christ, the Light of the World," 542–547.

[31]Jonathan Edwards, "That We Ought to Make Religion Our Present and Immediate Business," *The Blessing of God*, 89–105.

[32]Edwards, "Our Present and Immediate Business," 90–91.

misery" and "eternal happiness" by how they respond to faithfully following God. His purpose is to cause the thought of the eternal consequences of where their hearts lie and to stir affection for godliness.[33]

The third argument Edwards makes is not to delay, as all time is God's, and there is no knowing when it runs out. Because all time is God's, those who procrastinate actually rob God, a point which Edwards illustrates with Hosea 2:8–9. Likewise, procrastination casts "great contempt" and "manifests a great slight" on God's authority, glory, and excellency (Edwards's fourth and fifth arguments). Edwards moves again beyond explanation to application for his listener:

> Every filthy lust and desire must be served before him, and every creature is exalted above the Creator, and the high and mighty God must come in the rear of all such contempt as this. Those who delay to keep God's commandments do most certainly cast upon God. They delay to hearken to God for the sake of their ease, their sensual and sinful pleasures. Placing God lowest in their affections and last as ten times. Giving sin and the world their youth, their strength, and the bloom of their life.[34]

This sets up Edwards's next argument that delaying obedience is the "greatest abuse of God's mercy and patience." He closes his doctrinal section by charging his listeners not to put off being obedient because of laziness or "for any other case or business."[35] In his application, Edwards encourages his audience to be obedient so they would not live in fear of God or judgment or regret waiting like those who have regretted being obedient on their deathbeds. He argues it is easier to be obedient before their hearts are hardened. Edwards also gives ways "immediately to set about the work of our souls." These include using known means for instruction and conversion (like primers and biblical instruction) and seeking God through prayer.[36]

[33]Edwards, "Our Present and Immediate Business," 92–93.

[34]Ibid., 94–95.

[35]Ibid., 95–97.

[36]Edwards, "Our Present and Immediate Business," 98–105.

All God's Methods are Most Reasonable[37]

Date: Fall 1727 (most likely September 24, 1727)
Key Text: Isaiah 1:18–20 – "Come now, let us reason together, saith the Lord: though your sins be as scarlet, they shall be as white as snow; though they be red like crimson, they shall be as wool. If ye be willing and obedient, ye shall eat the good of the land: but if you refuse and rebel, ye shall be devoured with the sword: for the mouth of the Lord hath spoken it?"

An ambitious three-unit series by Edwards during his time as an associate minister at Northampton, *All God's Methods* was his most extensive "sermonic treatment of a text" he had then attempted. The sermon is an attempt to balance God's sovereignty (predetermination and foreknowledge) and human liberty. The sermon is written on thirty-seven duodecimo leaves. There were a number of revisions to the sermon before it was repreached later.[38]

Edwards begins with an explanation of the context of the passage from Isaiah and the exposition of the text. He also gives Isaiah 43:27 and 41:21 as textual parallels. Edwards explains the theme of his message is God's reasonableness (as explained by Edwards) in God's "readiness to pardon their sins," the terms of God's favor and blessing seen in the text, and the justice in God's "anger and punishment." This leads to the doctrine that "All God's methods of dealing with men are most reasonable."[39]

Six heads represent the particulars of the doctrine Edwards gives in showing how God is most reasonable in "decreeing and permitting sin," choosing some for salvation and others to "perish in sin," His covenants, commands, punishments, and "providence in this world." Edwards's goal is to show there is nothing in those particulars "but what is agreeable to perfect justice and the highest wisdom, and nothing contrary to infinite goodness."[40]

In his first head, Edwards gives a note on God's determination as to sin's existence. Though God does not sin nor cause the action of sin, He also does not intervene so that no sin should happen. Edwards states in relation to God's non-interference that "yet he withholds that grace and influence that

[37] Jonathan Edwards, "All God's Methods are Most Reasonable," *Sermons and Discourses 1723–1729*, ed. Kenneth D. Minkema, vol. 14, *The Works of Jonathan Edwards* (New Haven: Yale University Press, 1997), 161–197.

[38] Minkema, "All God's Methods," 161–163.

[39] Edwards, "All God's Methods," 164–167.

[40] Ibid., 167.

would restrain the creature from sinning, which grace being withheld, sin doth certainly follow."[41]

Edwards explains that God is not obligated to intervene, making it impossible for any of His creatures to sin. Edwards uses Judas as an example for his second argument, explaining that while a sinful action may be determined to happen from eternity by God, the sinner who commits such an act is free in their personal choice to commit the sinful action (such as Judas's betrayal of Christ). This argument shows Edwards's rhetorical ability to argue a point through his preaching:

> Necessity is not opposed to liberty, but to contingency, to the accidentalness of a thing. And compulsion is opposed to liberty. Liberty don't consist in an exact indifference to an action, so that when it is done it shall be done merely accidentally; but it consists in acting according to one's own choice, to the counsel of our own will. And he that acts according to his own choice, acts freely, however God has determined that choice; and it was absolutely certain from all eternity that the man should make such a choice. That is all the notion that any man can, with any propriety, have of liberty: that a man acts as he himself chooses and as he pleases, without considering how he came to choose as he did. And a man may act just according to his own will and pleasure, and yet it be determined from all eternity absolutely that he should so act. And that he should act so out of choice, it is not at all inconsistent. So that God's making of it necessary that the thing should so fall out, don't in the least stand in the way of our liberty. Necessity may be distinguished into necessity of compulsion.[42]

Edwards does a masterful job above in arguing for the necessity of compulsion as guided by God's sovereignty. This shows his pursuit of his audience through logical rhetoric. Edwards's next two arguments for his first doctrinal head include the benefit of the existence of sin in the righteous fear of God and the thankfulness for God's grace. For this sermon, Edwards then moves to application for his first doctrinal head that his listeners should understand sinners are responsible for their sin (without excuse),

[41] Ibid.

[42] Edwards, "All God's Methods," 168–169.

and because of this, God's people should be "filled with His praises for saving them from sin."[43]

Edwards moves on to God's reasonableness in choosing some for "eternal life, and not others." He explains the decision was made from all eternity and without merit from anyone (citing Rom 9:11–13). He then argues against the idea of apathy of the means of salvation due to the preordination of it. Edwards takes the idea of apathy and instead offers an improvement portion for this doctrinal head, which includes meditating on the reasonableness that God may have "things in the works of a Being that's infinitely greater and wiser than they, that so little a creature as man can't understand," and secondly that no one is excused from the "diligent use of the means of your salvation," and finally to let God have the glory of His sovereignty in so doing" in the choosing of anyone for salvation.[44]

For the third doctrinal head, Edwards notes the reasonableness of the covenants and how they do not differ because they were through Adam as a head, not offered in particular to each person to covenant and fall (as Edwards argues they would have). God's sovereignty in choosing Adam as the federal head of humanity is shown by Edwards as reasonable due in part to His right as Creator to order it in that manner. Because of this, Edwards argues his audience should "bewail and humble" themselves for their fall (under Adam). The audience is told they should look to the need for their Savior and thank God and "admire" Him for offering a second covenant and for Christ's federal headship as the Savior (citing Rom 5:12). The objection over man's inability to save themselves is argued against by Edwards in his return to his third doctrine by pointing again to man's sin and its causal effect for that inability.[45]

The fourth doctrinal head concerns God's reasonableness in His commands, both in His right to give them and their reasonableness as coming from Him. Edwards cites Leviticus 18 and Numbers 3 to show God's "absolute right" and "sovereignty over us."[46] The commands are shown then by Edwards as "most just and equitable" because of God's station, as noted here by Edwards:

[43]Ibid., 169–171.

[44]Edwards, "All God's Methods," 171–175.

[45]Ibid., 175–182.

[46]Ibid., 183.

> What can be more reasonable than that we should with all our hearts love and fear and adore him who is an infinitely perfect and glorious Being, and who is our creator and Father and our constant preserver?... What can be more reasonable than that we should love our neighbors as ourselves, and do by them as we would have them in like circumstances do by us, and live in the exercise of justice and equity, charity and faithfulness towards our fellow creatures, that have the same nature as we ourselves?... What can be more equal and just than those laws and rules of the Most High? Surely God's commands are purer than gold tried in the fire. Psalms 19:7–9, "The law of the Lord is perfect, the testimony of the Lord is sure. The statutes of the Lord are right: the commandment of the Lord is pure. The fear of the Lord is clean: the judgments of the Lord are true and righteous altogether." And Psalms 119:128, "I esteem all thy precepts concerning all things to be right."[47]

Edwards reminds his audience of God's infinite personhood and authority and then argues for the reasonableness of His creation to follow His commands. Edwards also shows those commands are for man's benefit and only difficult due to mankind's sinful hearts, with God argued as also reasonable in His punishment of sin. Furthermore, Edwards explains sin itself is a cause of "everlasting misery" (citing Prov 8:36 and Duet 29:18). It is also an "affront and an injury to an infinite majesty." Edwards goes on to explain the infinitude of God (highlighting the weight of sin against such a one as God).[48]

Likewise, since sin is against an "infinite authority" in God, it deserves eternal punishment, according to Edwards. This is in line with Edwards's next point that an infinitely majestic and authoritative God should also have an " infinitely dreadful anger." Edwards then tells those in his audience afraid of hell to see how just it is that they should be condemned to it and that no one would be to blame but themselves.[49]

The final doctrine then is resumed with Edwards arguing for God's providential actions as "most reasonable." Edwards advises his audience to "yield and resign" themselves to God's providence. For his general application,

[47] Edwards, "All God's Methods," 183–184.

[48] Ibid., 184–188.

[49] Ibid., 189–191.

Edwards cites Ezekiel 33:17, Isaiah 43:26, Micah 6:2–3, and Jeremiah 2:5, showing that those who rebel are unreasonable. He shows their unreasonableness by citing their use of the gifts of God against Him (Hosea 2:8), returning evil for good (Isaiah 1:2; 5:4), and refusing to be commanded or drawn to God by any method.[50]

Edwards concludes by showing how the faithful should depend on God's faithfulness as the only peace for their minds and give God "the glory that belongs to Him" on account of His reasonableness in dealing with them, according to "perfect wisdom" and not being inconsistent with His "perfect goodness." Edwards then charges his audience to praise God and cites Revelation 19:1–2.[51] This sermon showed Edwards's ability to rhetorically argue to a biblically literate audience doctrines of God's sovereignty and His authority.

The Spiritual Blessings of the Gospel Represented by a Feast[52]

Date: August 1728-February 1729
Key Text: Luke 14:16 – "Then said he unto him, A certain man made a great supper and bade many."

Kenneth P. Minkema notes this is the earliest Edwards sacramental sermon manuscript. It was likely delivered between August 1728 and February 1729. Edwards used the opportunity to combine the ideas of "personal and communal piety" with his unique sense of the saint's and the church's union with God. Through Christ's purchase of redemption are blessings to be enjoyed, including points Edwards has emphasized in his preaching at Northampton leading up to this sermon, including sanctification and spiritual knowledge.[53]

In his introduction, Edwards gives a short introduction to the text and its context. He begins with Christ's rebuke of pride in Luke 14:11, then explains Jesus's words of instruction in Luke 14:12–14 before finishing with explaining the final verse before his key text of Luke 14:16. He closes the

[50]Edwards, "All God's Methods," 192–196.

[51]Ibid., 196–197.

[52]Jonathan Edwards, "The Spiritual Blessings of the Gospel Represented by a Feast," *Sermons and Discourses 1723–1729*, 161–197.

[53]Minkema, "The Spiritual Blessings of the Gospel Represented by a Feast," 278–279.

introduction with an explanation of the parable as an invitation into the kingdom of God by way of the Lord's Supper (a feast).[54]

This sets up the doctrine of the sermon: "the spiritual blessings of the gospel are fitly represented by a feast." For his doctrinal section, Edwards has eight particulars of "how gospel provision is well represented by a feast," which include the expensiveness of gospel blessings; as free as guests are invited to a feast, so are sinners freely invited "to partake of gospel blessings;" because the Gospel "nourishes the soul as food does the body;" because of the excellency of the Gospel; because of the abundance and variety of gospel provision; the friendship and love measured of Jesus Christ and Christians; the communal (communion) aspect of it; and finally the joy of Christianity.[55]

The first particular of the expense is naturally related to Christ's sacrifice and is juxtaposed with the second particular of how freely it is offered for sinners. Edwards supports this second particular with references to Isaiah 55:1, John 7:37, Revelation 3:20, 22:17, and Proverbs 9:2–5. Edwards enhances the nourishment of the soul given in the third particular by explaining the quality of the nourishment given in his fourth particular (that it excels normal nourishment). Edwards notes of its excellency:

> Doubtless, that food which cost the Son of God his blood and life is pure dainties, when it is procured. And it is everywhere represented as the richest and most noble and excellent food. It is called the "bread of heaven" and "angels' food" (Psalms 105:40). So we are invited in Isaiah 55:2 not to "spend money for that which is not bread, and labor for that which satisfieth not," but to come to Christ, to eat "that which is good," that our souls may delight themselves in fatness. So this feast in Isaiah 25:6 is called "a feast of fat things, of wines on the lees, of fat things full of marrow, of wines on the lees well refined." This feast is a royal feast, the feast of a king.[56]

Like with his other sermons examined, Edwards is dogged in inviting his audience not only to apprehend what he is preaching but also to experience it through affection for God and His Word (in this case as a "royal feast"). Edwards does this by communicating Christ's invitation to take in this spiritual food with "no such virtue as temperance" in their feasting upon the

[54]Edwards, "The Spiritual Blessings of the Gospel Represented by a Feast," 280–281.

[55]Ibid., 282–288.

[56]Edwards, "The Spiritual Blessings of the Gospel Represented by a Feast," 282–285.

spiritual feast. The unity and community of Christ's people are explored in his sixth and seventh particulars, which then culminate in his final point of showing the joy of the church blessed richly by Christ's feast.[57]

Under application, Edwards explains what his audience has seen, including the appropriate wisdom of the Lord's Supper and the appropriateness of admiring God's grace towards those He saves. He then gives an invitation for "the poor, the maimed, the halt, and the blind [to come] unto this feast." He charges them to consider how long the invitation to "the feast" will last and the eternality of the feast, demonstrating Edwards's mastery of sermonic visualization and application. He applies further in giving directions to those considering the invitation a command to "choose the kingdom of God," to work at getting their "soul clothed with Christ's righteousness" and "Christ's mark" set upon them, and finally to "be contented while here to bear the cross" of Christ.[58]

Receiving the Blessed Fruits of Religion by Practicing it With Our Whole Hearts[59]

Date: Late 1729-Early 1730
Key Text: Psalm 119:2 – "Blessed are they that keep his testimonies, and that seek him with the whole heart."

Justin Hawkins observes Edwards in this sermon examines what it is to follow Christ, which should be done with the "whole heart" or affections. The sermon was preached either in late 1729 or early 1730 (at the beginning of Edwards's sole pastorate at Northampton after the death of Stoddard) and was preached a second time with brackets placed for what passages he wanted to emphasize.[60]

As with *Spiritual Blessings,* Edwards begins by giving textual context to the passage he will preach. He gives the theme of the Psalm (the excellency of the Word and Law of God) and the immediate verse before the key text. Edwards also gives the point of the key text of "keeping his testimonies"

[57]Ibid., 285–288.

[58]Edwards, "The Spiritual Blessings of the Gospel Represented by a Feast," 285–293. Edwards's parting words are that the "Christian life is a warfare, and the crown is promised only to those that overcome." Ibid.

[59]Jonathan Edwards, "Receiving the Blessed Fruits of Religion by Practicing It With Our Whole Hearts," ed. Justin Hawkins, Jonathan Edwards Sermon Index (Sermon 146), (New Haven: Jonathan Edwards Center, Yale University), 1–18.

[60]Hawkins, "Receiving the Blessed Fruits," 1–2.

and "seeking of him" as an observation and conformity to God's Law with one's "whole heart" to receive the blessing of God. Edwards concludes his introduction by giving the context of the following verses in Psalm 119 of what blessedness looks like in obedience to God and life in Him.[61]

The introduction sets up the doctrinal theme of the sermon, "the way to receive the blessed fruits of religion, is to practice it with our whole hearts." For this sermon, Edwards has two doctrinal particulars which he expounds upon. The first is an examination of practicing "religion with the whole heart." The second is that Edwards and his audience must do this to "obtain the blessed fruits of religion."[62]

The examination of what it means to practice religion "with the whole heart" includes all the faculties, with full resolution, with "free inclination" and not forced, not superficially or with "transient affections," without competition in the heart against "God and religion," and embracing religion "without reserve." Edwards's rejection of transient affections parallels his thoughts in his later sermon series in 1742–43 that would form the basis of his *Treatise Concerning Religious Affections*.[63] In this sermon, he uses oil for a lamp as an illustration:

> But he [who] practices religion with his whole heart, he has not only religious affections, but he feels a new nature, a living principle of holiness inwardly breathing, influencing and governing his heart. His lamp not only flames for a few minutes, but he has oil in his vessel that keeps it alive. His seed abideth in him; it takes deep root in his heart, and will grow till it comes to perfection.[64]

Under his second particular point of doctrine, Edwards gives four reasons for the necessity of practicing religion with the whole heart, including the inability to serve God with less than one's whole heart, there not being a form of obedience without whole-hearted obedience, that if the blessings of religion could be obtained without whole obedience there "would not be sufficient provision made for the securing of holiness of life and conversa-

[61]Edwards, "Receiving the Blessed Fruits," 3–4.

[62]Ibid., 4–5.

[63]Ibid., 5–8.

[64]Edwards, "Receiving the Blessed Fruits," 8.

tion," and if God is not served with a whole heart, God is not served "with any true and real respect at all."[65]

For application, Edwards invites his audience to examine if they truly are serving and obeying God with a whole heart and gives two evidences of a heart not truly "engaged in the practice of religion." The first evidence is seeming to have a religious life but seeing a known, observable sin "that is harbored and indulged." Second is when someone who seemed to be a believer does not hold on to the end, signifying they never truly were. These evidences are another example of Edwards's concern for an audience that may know about the Bible and religious thinking but contains many that have no true "affection" for God or His Word and do not practice their faith.[66]

Edwards finishes with three exhortations to search out what is the reality of religion, to see the vanity of creation and "God's all-sufficiency," and to count the cost[67] of following God and facing "difficulties" or "enduring God's wrath to all eternity" for not following God in line with giving blunt argumentation of wrath and reward.[68]

The Pure in Heart Blessed[69]

Date: Early 1730
Key Text: Matthew 5:8 – "Blessed are the pure in heart: for they shall see God."

Because one final leaf of the sermon was lost and two others were seriously damaged, the editor, Mark Valeri, utilized the published version in Dwight. He notes in the manuscript how the sermon was repreached twice, once in a neighboring parish to Northampton and once to the Stockbridge Indians. The sermon's focus, similar to *Receiving the Blessed Fruits,* is on the blessings of God, in this case, the blessing for the believer in seeing God.[70]

Edwards begins by giving the context of how believers are shown in the Bible to have "seen" God. Using Exodus 19:16–21, 24:9–11, Hebrews 1:1–2, John 1:17, 38, and Matthew 23:23–27 he shows the context of those who

[65] Ibid., 8–13.

[66] Ibid., 14–17.

[67] Edwards, "Receiving the Blessed Fruits," 14–17.

[68] Ibid., 17.

[69] Jonathan Edwards, "The Pure in Heart Blessed," *Sermons and Discourses 1730–1733*, 57–86.

[70] Ibid., 57–58.

are pure in heart tied to the Beatitudes and the great privilege for the Jewish people to see God.[71]

For this sermon, Edwards utilizes a dual doctrine: to see God is truly "happifying to the soul of men," and to know that having a pure heart is the only certain way to come to this happifying "blessedness of seeing God."[72] In explaining what it means to see God, Edwards explains it is not something one does with their "bodily eyes" but is a spiritual sight of God. Even in the Old Testament, Edwards explains God showed Himself by way of external signs, though not revealing Himself personally (only His works and His glory). This is further juxtaposed with the beauty of Christ's body "that will be beheld with bodily eyes will be ravishing and delighting chiefly as it will express his spiritual glories," a body that was only seen (as Edwards explains) by the three disciples at the "transfiguration upon the mount."[73]

Edwards explains God can be seen intellectually by the soul, not merely by hearsay or speculative reasoning, but by having "an immediate and certain understanding of God's glorious excellency and love." In expounding this point, Edwards details what it means to apprehend the sense of God's presence and glory through using biblical references to Hebrews 11:27, 2 Corinthians 3:18, and John 14:7. The spiritual sight of God's glory (the spiritual body of Christ) is seen as equal to what the "saints in heaven's" visible sight of Christ's corporeal body will be:

> The saints in heaven, they will see the glory of the body of Christ after the resurrection with bodily [eyes], but they will have no more immediate or perfect way of seeing that visible glory than they will of beholding Christ's divine and spiritual glory. They won't want eyes to see that which is spiritual as well as we can see anything that is corporeal. They will behold God in an ineffable, and to us now inconceivable, manner.[74]

Next, the reasons this spiritual sight of God's glorious presence will make the beholder truly happy are because it is most suitable to the "nature of an intelligent creature," it is the soul's "highest perfection and excellency," it is a "pure sweet without any mixture," it is satisfying as from "the fountain that

[71] Ibid., 59–61.

[72] Edwards, "The Pure in Heart Blessed," 61–66.

[73] Ibid., 61–62.

[74] Ibid., 62–75.

supplies it being equal to man's desires and capacity," and it has an unfailing foundation. Seeing God as a "pure sweet without any mixture" is where Edwards spends the most time, giving several subpoints of explanation.[75]

Edwards explains the privilege the believer has in seeing God through the revelation of Himself revealed in His Word. This leads the believer to a sense of the "heavenly state" and a desire and longing after it. This connects Edwards's desire to encourage his congregation to long after and desire God and His Word with their whole heart. As he closes on the first particular of doctrine, he states, "A life of holiness is the pleasantest life in this world, because in such a life men have the imperfect beginnings of a blessed-making sight of God."[76]

After explaining the need to be "pure in heart" to truly have the "blessedness of seeing God," Edwards has a significantly shorter application for this sermon. He gives a use of instruction on how great it is to be an "upright and sincere Christian." He then charges them to reflect on whether they are pure in heart. Finally, Edwards exhorts them to make themselves pure in heart if they are not so. Even though he states it is God's work of regeneration, the individual is responsible for "cleansing their hands," quoting from James 4:8. Edwards closes the sermon with a quote from Isaiah 4:4 of the cleansing of the Lord done through a baptism of fire.[77]

Honey from the Rock[78]

Date: Fall 1730
Key Text: Deuteronomy 32:13 – "And he made him to suck honey out of the rock, and oil out of the flinty rock."

Like *The Pure in Heart Blessed*, Edwards deviates from the singular doctrinal formula, giving three doctrines in a two-preaching-unit sermon. Instead of giving three applications for the three doctrines, Edwards only gives applications for his first and third doctrinal statements. There is no indication the sermon was repreached or edited further from its original version.[79]

[75]Edwards, "The Pure in Heart Blessed," 65–72.

[76]Ibid., 72–76. For his second particular Edwards gives a thorough explanation of the need to be "pure in heart" to have the "blessedness of seeing God" without the taint of sin and spiritual blindness. Ibid., 76–83.

[77]Edwards, "The Pure in Heart Blessed, 76–83.

[78]Jonathan Edwards, "Honey from the Rock," *Sermons and Discourses 1730–1733*, 121–138.

[79]Valeri, "Honey from the Rock," 121–122.

In the introduction (explication) portion of his sermon, Edwards explains the doctrinal themes (made explicit in the doctrinal portion of the sermon) of "honey from the rock" (how God causes good to "arise" from His people even when they are very far removed from Him), even though it would seem impossible for this to occur. He further states God's desire to bring good out of unlikely places. Edwards closes the explication by showing how Christ is the Rock, out of which living water (which he later shows refers to honey) flows (referencing 1 Cor 10:4).[80]

In giving the first doctrine that "God causes good to arise to his elect people when they are in a state as that they are most remote from it," Edwards explains first the elect to whom God causes this good to arise are very remote from any good. Edwards references Deuteronomy 8:15–16, 32:10, and Jeremiah 2:6 in giving the biblical narrative of the Israelite journey through the wilderness. Like Israel, the lost are in a state of great barrenness and misery since they are in a state of guilt and cast away from the "fountain of living waters." This is quoting Jeremiah 2:13, which he supports with references also to Hebrews 12:9 and James 1:17. Further, quoting Romans 7:14, he shows how sinners are under the dominion of sin and "mortal disease," leaving them "blind, deaf, halt, and maimed."[81]

However, in the second part of the first doctrine, good does come from God even when the elect are very far off. This good consists of giving them grace in their hearts, pardoning all their sins, and comfort and peace. Edwards then breaks the usual sermonic formula and gives his first section of application for the first doctrine. First, those in his audience who are regenerated should reflect on their current position compared to their lost one. Second, to praise God and remember and not become discouraged when things become dark. For those in his audience who are "awakened sinners," he encourages them to see their state and not become discouraged but to see they are in a helpless, miserable desert, which is just the place "you will be in the likeliest way to be delivered."[82]

Edwards next goes back to the doctrinal portion of his sermon, moving on to the second doctrine: "God is wont to bring good to his people out of those things that seem most unlikely to yield it." For this doctrine, Edwards uses the biblical story of Samson eating honey out of a lion's carcass in

[80]Edwards, "Honey from the Rock," 123–124.

[81]Edwards, "Honey from the Rock," 124–125. Edwards further states they are incapable of helping themselves, others are of no use, as are everything else in creation. Ibid., 125–127.

[82]Ibid., 125–130.

Judges 14:9 and also uses Hebrews 12:11, 2 Corinthians 7:11, and John 21:15–17 to illustrate and challenge his audience. It is clear that though Edwards is not preaching in a verse-by-verse expository manner, he does give credence to Samuel Hopkins's description of Edwards's biblical literacy in preaching.[83]

In his biography of Edwards, Hopkins notes his preaching ability resulted from three essential qualities that made Edwards an eminent preacher. These included the wealth of time spent in the Word, his biblical literacy, and his self-awareness of his own sinfulness. Hopkins writes of his biblical literacy in preaching seen above in *Honey from the Rock*:

> His great acquaintance with divinity, his study and knowledge of the Bible. His extensive and universal knowledge, and great clearness of thought, enabled him to handle every subject with great judgment and propriety, and to bring out of his treasury things new and old. Every subject he handled was instructive, plain, entertaining and profitable; which was much owing to his being master of the subject, and his great skill to treat it in a most natural, easy, and profitable manner. None of his composures were dry speculations, or unmeaning harangues, or words without ideas. When he dwelt on those truths which are must controverted and opposed by many, which was often the case, he would set them in such a natural and easy light, and every sentiment from step to step, would drop from his lips, attended with such clear and striking evidence, both from scripture and reason, as even to force the assent of every attentive hearer.[84]

Edwards further uses the illustration of honey in his third doctrine: "By causing his people to receive such great blessings from Jesus Christ, he does, as it were, cause them to suck honey out of the rock." Here, Edwards references 1 Corinthians 10:4 and Deuteronomy 32:4–31 to set up his first particular, "Christ is fitly compared to a rock." Edwards first notes his appearance and references Isaiah 53:2, Matthew 13:55, John 1:46, and Genesis 12:3. Next, Edwards compares Christ's perfection with a rock's sturdiness. He again makes several biblical references to Proverbs 16:2,

[83]Edwards, "Honey from the Rock," 130–131.

[84]Samuel Hopkins, *The Life of the Late Reverend, Learned and Pious Mr. Jonathan Edwards* (Boston: S. Kneeland, 1765), 46–47.

Daniel 5:27, Jeremiah 23:28, Hosea 13:3, Deuteronomy 32:4, and 1 Peter 2:22.[85]

Edwards shows Christ as a rock for believers in two ways: a firm foundation (Matt 7:24) and a rock of defense (Isa 33:15–16). For the final part of his doctrinal section, Edwards shows that "the blessings that the saints receive by Jesus Christ are exceeding sweet and precious" (like honey and oil). They are thus because they are first peaceful in their purity from evil, and second, they (the blessings received by believers) are "most nourishing and perfective of their nature." They are also refreshing, delightful, and satisfying by their nature.[86]

After the doctrinal section resumes, Edwards gives his final application, first to understand the "glorious work of God" as an argument for praise. Second, for his audience to trust in Jesus Christ "both from the things signified in his being called a rock and from the rich and sweet blessings that flow therefrom." He ends the sermon reiterating Christ's strength, immutability, faithfulness, and that Christ is a sure foundation to build their hope upon:

> They that build their hope of heaven upon Christ Jesus, they build them upon the rock of ages; and whence they never will, nor can, fall. And the great and precious benefits which he yields to those that come to him should draw our hearts to him. We are in a needy state; we are often called to Jesus Christ. There we have honey out of the rock. And in him, whoever is weary and heavy laden may find sweet rest; [whoever is] sick [may be] healed.[87]

So, this sermon shows Edwards's ability to use illustrative language again to affect the hearts of his listeners in apprehending biblical themes of the sweetness of the Gospel and the firm foundation built on Christ.

Serving God in Heaven[88]

Date: March 14, 1731

[85] Edwards, "Honey from the Rock," 130–134. Edwards utilizes several other biblical passages to illustrate Christ (in comparison to a rock) as durable/everlasting and immovable/faithful. Ibid., 133–134.

[86] Edwards, "Honey from the Rock," 134–136.

[87] Edwards, "Honey from the Rock," 136–138.

[88] Jonathan Edwards, "Serving God in Heaven," *Sermons and Discourses 1730–1733*, 251–261.

Key Text: Revelation 22:3 – "And there shall be no more curse: but the throne of God and of the Lamb shall be in it; and his servants shall serve him."

Edwards combined this text (Rev 22:3) with Psalm 115:17–18 for a second repreaching of the sermon. Valeri notes this sermon has themes that were further explored in the previously examined sermon series *Charity and Its Fruits,* preached in 1738, and his theological treatise *The End for Which God Created the World* (published posthumously in 1765).[89]

The introduction to this sermon is brief, with references to Revelation 3–5, 21:14, 24, and 22:2 to describe the glorious state of heaven and blessedness for those who reside therein, noting their description of service as part of that blessing. The introduction then leads into the doctrine stated as "the happiness of the saints in heaven consists partly in that they there serve God." The particulars show how the "happiness" of mankind consists of serving God, and particularly how this is manifest for the saints' happiness in heaven.[90]

First, Edwards ties happiness for a created being not to idleness but to action. Second, he notes mankind, in particular, was created for the service of God above other created beings. This service ties to the "rational service" noted by Edwards in Romans 12:1. Finally, the act of service is for the "most excellent king" man is created for and is an especially important part of saints' happiness in heaven.[91]

The saints' regenerated delight is seen as taking the greatest pleasure in serving God in justice and equity. Edwards explains through their regenerated perspective, believers in heaven see God as truly right and "sensible" as their ruler and redeemer, and because of this, see it only fitting that they serve Him. Second, the believer in heaven is seen as taking delight in their service of God, seeing God's plans and directions as best.[92]

Third, Edwards explains delight for the believer in heaven comes from being conformed to the holiness of God, especially Christ. He uses Psalm 40:8 to show this obedience as natural and then uses 1 Corinthians 15:28 to state, "Christ will be subject to the Father." Fourth, believers will delight in seeing their service as "pleasing and acceptable to God." God receiving glory is something in which saints will take great delight. The pleasure of

[89]Valeri, "Serving God in Heaven," 251–252.

[90]Edwards, "Serving God in Heaven," 254.

[91]Ibid., 254–256.

[92]Ibid., 256–257.

expressing love as the believer's delight in serving God in heaven concludes the doctrinal part of the sermon.[93]

To close out this sermon, Edwards applies it by reiterating how service to God has purpose and pleasure for the truly regenerated. He notes idleness should be reproved as antithetical to those wishing to spend their eternity in heaven. Also, those who grumble about their service to God should be reproved. He concludes by exhorting his audience to devote themselves to God's service. In comparing *Serving God in Heaven* to the later closing sermon of the *Charity* series, *Heaven is a World of Love,* the reader notices they are different in tone and purpose. Whereas *Heaven* has as its purpose to illustrate heavenly love through moving, illustrative prose, Edwards uses *Serving God* to argue for the rightness of service to God logically and to exhort his audience not to become idle or complacent. Both have Edwards's theme of wanting to exhort beyond idleness to affection and religious action in common.[94]

Self-Examination and the Lord's Supper[95]

Date: March 21, 1731
Key Text: 1 Corinthians 11:28–29 – "But let a man examine himself, and so let him eat of that bread, and drink of that cup. For he that eateth and drinketh unworthily, eateth and drinketh damnation to himself, not discerning the Lord's body."

This is one of Edwards's earliest sacramental sermons at Northampton. Valeri notes Edwards, at this point, does not wade into the communion controversy, which later sees him forced out over his view of a closed communion in opposition to Stoddard. Instead, Edwards gives a straightforward sermon about self-examination before partaking in the Lord's Supper. He also encourages those who are too self-critical not to forsake the Supper as it is a sacramental privilege for those who believe. Of note at this point is Edwards's own working through the doctrine and application of the sacrament in his "Miscellanies" entries during this period (462, 464, 466, and 485) and later entries 610 and 612. Edwards would repreach the sermon in October of 1756 (with three to four additions after the original composition).[96]

[93]Edwards, "Serving God in Heaven," 257–258.

[94]Ibid., 258–261.

[95]Jonathan Edwards, "Self-Examination and the Lord's Supper," *Sermons and Discourses 1730–1733*, 262–272.

[96]Valeri, "Self-Examination and the Lord's Supper," 262–263.

In the introduction, Edwards gives the context of the key text by examining Paul's rebuke of the Corinthians from 1 Corinthians 11:17–28 and tying it to the practice as described in Acts 2:46 and 20:7. He then finished the explication with the context of Paul's direction on how to avoid partaking of the Lord's Supper "unworthily" and the punishment of such action. This contextual introduction sets up his doctrine that "persons ought to examine themselves of their fitness before they presume to partake of the Lord's Supper, lest by their unworthy partaking, they eat and drink damnation to themselves."[97]

For the doctrine, Edwards lays out his argument of the "fitness or unfitness here spoken of," the particular things one should examine to determine their unfitness, and how they should examine themselves to avoid drinking judgment in their unfit partaking of the Lord's Supper.[98]

Edwards states first that fitness (or unfitness) is not contingent on what they deserve, as Edwards clarifies that all are unworthy of partaking. Second, he notes not all unfitness renders the believer "defective" in their attendance of the Supper, but only that which "renders the ordinance void." To examine oneself, Edwards gives a checklist to follow. First, one should check if they live in any known sin. Second, Edwards moves from the visible to the invisible conscience and how one should examine if they are resolute in avoiding sin and living in obedience. Third, they should seek if they have any envy or bitterness towards another. Finally, they should examine their motives for coming to the Lord's Supper.[99]

For the final portion of the doctrinal section, Edwards gives a list of reasons to avoid eating and drinking "damnation to themselves." The reasons include the "horrid contempt of the ordinance" and what it signifies. Edwards compares those who do so fitly as "eating and drinking for spiritual food and nourishment as worthy partakers" to others who do so "as a wild beast eats his prey" and further do so "out of a murderous bloodthirstiness." Next, he argues those who do so unfitly mock and make a "dissimulation" of the ordinance and the covenant it represents.[100] The focus of the sermon shows Edwards's intention on his audience and their context. He preaches

[97]Edwards, "Self-Examination and the Lord's Supper," 264–266.

[98]Edwards, "Self-Examination and the Lord's Supper," 266.

[99]Ibid., 266–269.

[100]Ibid., 269–272. The application of this sermon is the shortest of those examined thus far in this chapter containing only a simple charge to carefully examine oneself before partaking in the Lord's Supper. Ibid., 272.

to an audience familiar with the Lord's Supper and presses them to evaluate themselves and whether they have taken it for granted. This evaluation is in line with examining whether the Lord's Supper, God, and His Word have become something devalued in their hearts instead of having an earnest affection and reverence for them.

East of Eden[101]

Date: Summer 1731
Key Text: Genesis 3:24 – "So he drove out the man; and he placed at the east of the garden of Eden cherubims, and a flaming sword which turned every way, to keep the way of the tree of life."

Valeri notes *East of Eden* could be a lecture-sermon about the ramifications of the Fall. Yet, the sermon has illustrative language conveying the importance of what was lost from Eden.[102] Edwards begins by explaining the state of Adam and Eve before the fall and how they knew good, yet not evil. He gives context through Genesis 3:5, 19, and 22–24. He then previews the dual doctrines of the sermon of how man was driven away from their former blessedness and how man "procured the displeasure" of God to an extent they lost (without hope of re-attaining) the life and eternal blessing they should have attained.[103]

Edwards lists several propositions under the first doctrine of the sermon. These were when man fell he "lost all his former blessedness," when he fell, there was "a necessity of his parting" with his former blessings, and it was due to God's displeasure at man's provocations that he was driven from his former blessedness.[104] In a picture of what would be fleshed out in his *Charity* series, Edwards notes the harmony of relationship in the Garden before the Fall and the brokenness brought about by it:

> And as God was man's friend, so were the angels. And man, besides, enjoyed the pleasure of human society: our first parents mutually in each other in perfect love, without anything to interrupt or spoil their joy... All this happiness was lost when man sinned against God. He was no longer free from what was

[101] Jonathan Edwards, "East of Eden," *Sermons and Discourses 1730–1733*, 329–348.

[102] Valeri, "East of Eden," 329–330.

[103] Edwards, "East of Eden," 330–332.

[104] Ibid., 333–336.

> troublesome. He immediately began to know what sorrow and affliction were. The earth lost its beauty and pleasantness. There was a curse brought upon it; there was, as it were, a deathly darkness brought upon things here below... That bloom and beauty and joy that all nature seemed to [be] clothed with was gone.[105]

Edwards not only says what happened (the Fall) but illustrates the weight of the Fall and what it meant to be cast out of Eden, to be corrupted by a sin nature after the Fall, and to be at enmity with God. For the second doctrine, Edwards likewise gives three propositions that are direct expositions of his second doctrine for the sermon: the hopelessness of man retaining on their own an ability to be restored to Eden's blessedness and eternal life (assured to mankind before the Fall) due to God's "displeasure" with man. Under the third proposition of man's helplessness, he gives four arguments: God's displeasure with sin, the justness of God's anger at man, the implacability of this anger due to God's infinite holiness, and the resentment (before noted as just) of God towards man due to the sin as casting "contempt upon God's majesty."[106]

For the application, Edwards then pivots. He speaks first of the joy for the believer due to the Gospel and the horror of being cast out and at enmity with God for those under the Fall. Edwards relates Christ as the "tree of life" spoken of in Revelation 2:7 that believers are invited to partake of (to "eat of the fruit of this tree without any sort of terms"). Edwards also answers the rhetorical question of how it came to be there was a way to make the impossible a reality, namely to reconcile a righteous and wrathful God with man. This, Edwards notes, is because of the plan of divine wisdom, in the form of a divine person (Christ), who took guilt upon himself and "did the work which Adam should have done and performed, that perfect obedience which he failed of," as the second Adam (referencing 1 Cor 15:45).[107]

Edwards closes by giving a fourfold explanation for man's "vain and dangerous" attempt at attaining eternal life themselves. The reasons for this attempt include man's disagreement with perishing, the righteousness required for the favor of God, and man's ignorance of the need to be saved by another's righteousness, something men do not seek because of the "proud

[105] Edwards, "East of Eden," 334.

[106] Ibid., 334–342.

[107] Edwards, "East of Eden," 342–346.

conceit of their own goodness," which they see as sufficient. Continuing in this attempt, Edwards warns, leads to futility and being "slain by the flaming sword of God's vengeance."[108] Again, it is seen through this sermon Edwards's understanding and focus of reaching an audience casual about their salvation and the practice of their faith.

The Time of Youth the Best Time To Be Improved To Religious Purposes[109]

Date: August 1731-December 1732
Key Text: Ecclesiastes 12:1 – "Remember now thy Creator in the days of thy youth, while the evil days come not, nor the years draw nigh, when thou shalt say, I have no pleasure in them."

A sermon directed at youth, *The Time of Youth* is a sermon about the advantage of the "freest opportunity" at religion for those in their youth. Edwards gives recommendations in the application for the youth to seek out "private religious meetings" and to focus on sermons, secret prayer, and godly conversation. These are all activities Edwards benefitted from in his youth and encourages those in his congregation to attend. The preaching directed by Edwards to the youth would see what he termed a "flexibleness" among them, leading to the beginning of the awakening in the Connecticut Valley.[110]

In the introduction to this sermon (and possibly in line with the audience he is directing the sermon to), Edwards begins with an exposition of Ecclesiastes 11:9–10 and its contextual foundation for this sermon. He explains two main points from the context of the preceding verses and the key text for the sermon: first, to remember their Creator in the days of their youth, and second to remember without delay as there is an end point to this opportunity (the time of youth) when the "evil days will come."[111]

The reminder of evil days refocuses the sermon on its main doctrine that "the time of youth is the best time to be improved to religious purposes." Edwards gives six particulars revolving around youth having the "freest opportunity" to spend seeking God and salvation and the greater success in

[108] Ibid., 346–348.

[109] Edwards, "The Time of Youth the Best Time to be Improved to Religious Purposes," ed. Charles T. Thaluri, *Jonathan Edwards Sermon Index* (Sermon 214), (New Haven: Jonathan Edwards Center, Yale University), 1–16.

[110] Charles T. Thaluri, "The Time of Youth," 1–2.

[111] Edwards, "The Time of Youth," 3–5.

attainting it.[112] Edwards sticks with a straightforward, logical explanation of each particular, choosing to explain and rationalize rather than illustrate. One example is when he argues that the older one is, the harder it is to be pliable.[113]

Edwards's method of logical argumentation (seen above) continues in his application as he gives motives for why the youth hearing the sermon should respond to his invitation to take advantage of their youth in "improving" upon their religious purposes, including their mortality and the potential to provoke God's wrath (quoting from Prov 23:36 and 7:1 to emphasize this point).[114] In the end, Edwards gives two directions to the youth in his congregation: First, remove any distractions and think over the "deep concern about the affair" of their souls. The second is to use all methods which "have a tendency" to fix their focus on the state of their souls. Those that distract include going into great company and conversing with those who are living in vanity. That which helps improve one's religious thinking includes diligently attending preaching, secret prayer, conversing with those living religiously (or who are thinking through religion), and the aforementioned "private meetings." Again, this reinforces the goal of building a culture around the study and application of the Word preached for daily living.[115]

God is the People's Portion, and the People are God's Portion[116]

Date: August 1731-December 1732
Key Text: Jeremiah 10:16 – "The portion of Jacob is not like them: for he is the former of all things; and Israel is the rod of his inheritance: the Lord of hosts is his name."

A sermon manuscript written in two preaching units, *God is the People's Portion,* was first preached sometime between 1731 and 1732 and

[112]Edwards, "The Time of Youth," 6–10.

[113]Ibid., 8–9.

[114]Ibid., 9–13.

[115]Edwards, "The Time of Youth," 13–15. As seen in Edwards's sermons on *Charity and Its Fruits* and during his final season at Northampton, the frivolity and dispassion of the youth in his congregation were of utmost importance to Edwards, even until his termination at the congregation.

[116]Edwards, "God is the People's Portion, and the People are God's Portion," ed. Tom Koontz, *Jonathan Edwards Sermon Index* (Sermon 219), (New Haven: Jonathan Edwards Center, Yale University), 1–25.

repreached in November 1757 (with a reference to Ps 16:4 for the second delivery of the sermon). The sermon focuses on the inheritance of God for the believer and the believer as the inheritance of God.[117] The sermon's introduction begins with a contextual look at the preceding verses of Jeremiah 10 as Edwards explains the chapter's comparison of God and idols and their inheritance. This sets up the dual doctrine: "That God is his people's portion" and "That the people are God's portion."[118]

In explaining the first doctrine, Edwards seeks to show his audience that God is His "people's portion" and how God comes to be this for His people. Like with earlier sermons, Edwards explains his first doctrine and then gives an application for the first doctrine before doing likewise with the second doctrine's explanation and application. Like with other sermons to colonial audiences, Edwards is less concerned with using the sermon to explain the passage but instead uses the sermon to explain what it means for his audience to become inheritors of God. Edwards jumps from verse-to-verse to show how the believer inherits God through their adoption (Rom 8:17), with respect to possession in three manners: God being for them (Rom 8:31), in them (1 John 3:24; 4:12, 15, 16), and "seen and enjoyed by them" (Matt 5:8, 1 Cor 13:12, John 14:21; 17:24, 1 John 3:2 among other verses cited). Again, this sermon shows Edwards's biblical, though not verse-by-verse, exposition as he explains the concept of the believer's inheritance of God.[119]

After preaching of the believer's portion in God generally, Edwards then argues for the "peculiar" manner in which the believer inherits God as their portion.[120] Edwards explains this inheritance is free, yet through purchase in Christ's blood. This leads to the application of this first doctrine through Edwards's encouragement of his audience to self-examine whether they have chosen God for their portion and are sensible of their "poverty and emptiness" without God. This self-examination then leads to Edwards's exhortation not to excessively grieve over worldly loss but to rejoice and be content and willing to part with worldly things and their lives.[121]

Edwards's exhortation naturally sets up the second doctrine of "God's people" as "God's portion." God's people are illustrated as a treasure and jewel by Edwards. This second doctrine's explanation mirrors the first as

[117] Tom Koontz, "God is the People's Portion," 1–4.

[118] Edwards, "God is the People's Portion," 3–5.

[119] Edwards, "God is the People's Portion," 5–9.

[120] Ibid., 9–10.

[121] Ibid., 10–13.

Edwards seeks to explain that God's people are His portion and how this came to be. Edwards juxtaposes God's inherent worth with the worth placed upon man by God as His treasure. Edwards explains this is not intrinsic or merited but placed upon them by God through His separation of His people from those who "are given to other gods."[122]

Edwards explains this difference between the general creation (mankind) of God and those created anew to worship God as His "portion." Edwards further illustrates being created anew as God's portion by using marble and jewels as an image of something crafted specially to become a unique possession by the craftsman through his further shaping of the object. This is an image Edwards uses to then expound upon the work of redemption in creating a greater inheritance than a creature has in its initial creation. They are created anew in relationship with Him through this redemption by Him (using the picture given in John 17 of Jesus's high priestly prayer of unification between the Disciples, Jesus, the Father, and all believers).[123]

Edwards shows how God's people became His possession through "free election," through purchase by Christ's blood, and finally through "effectual calling." Edwards's argumentation is again peppered with scriptural references to tie the points to the biblical passages they are from. For this application, Edwards instructs his audience to understand their blessing and behave accordingly. This should be done by devoting themselves to God, not only in theory but through their behavior, laboring to be more like God purified "as vessels sanctified and made for your Master's use" so that they would see God's face in service for all eternity.[124]

Gracious Mourning the Way to True Comfort[125]

Date: August 1731–1732
Key Text: Matthew 5:4 – "Blessed are they that mourn, for they shall be comforted."

Gracious Mourning is a sermon preached by Edwards either in the latter half of 1731 or sometime in 1732. It was repreached at some point later with a notation of having used Isaiah 61:1–2 in the second delivery. The

[122]Edwards, "God is the People's Portion," 13–15.

[123]Ibid., 16–19.

[124]Ibid., 19–24.

[125]Edwards, "Gracious Mourning the Way to True Comfort," ed. Albert Ypma, *Jonathan Edwards Sermon Index* (Sermon 227), (New Haven: Jonathan Edwards Center, Yale University), 1–14.

manuscript was written on eight duodecimo leaves, and Albert Ypma notes the conclusions of both the doctrine and application become more "outlinish."[126] Edwards begins this sermon with a focus on explaining the "paradox" and the "reason" of how those who are blessed by mourning and the promise of comfort in mourning. This leads to the doctrine that "mourning is the way to true comfort."[127]

Edwards will explicate his doctrine with three points. The first is what mourning is being spoken of by Christ, how this mourning "is the way to comfort," and "what comfort it is the way to." Edwards then gives the reasons for those in the world to mourn, including God's (and Christ's) daily dishonor in the world (in comparison to His eternal worthiness, glory, love, and lordship), the "fountain of sin and corruption" seen by Christians who still dishonor God themselves. These things should be mourned for, Edwards explains, through seeing God's worthiness and through "gracious humiliation and self-abasement."[128]

Mourning is the way to "true comfort" through its mortification of sin, preparation of the heart for comfort, and its entitlement of the repentant believer to the "pardon and favor of God." As Ypma explains, this is where Edwards's manuscript becomes "outlinish" in Edwards's use of short sentences, possibly as a way of emphasizing the points he makes here. This is seen in his third inquiry of "How they shall be comforted":

'Tis the way to most comfortable discoveries of God and Christ.
[They see that God is] infinite, excellent and beautiful.
[They see that God is] infinitely gracious, of infinite love.
'Tis the way to a comfortable view of what is past, of what God and
Christ has done for them: [they are] elected; Christ died [for them]; [their]
sins [are] pardoned; [they are] adopted.
'Tis the way to comfortable hopes.
[It is the way to the] comfort of God's promises.
[It is the way to] comfort in all affliction.
[It is the way] to the joy and comfort of a full enjoyment of God.[129]

For his application, Edwards notes Christians should beware of "excessive mirth" because of the wickedness of the world and the lostness of it. He

[126] Albert Ypma, "Gracious Mourning," 1–2.

[127] Edwards, "Gracious Mourning," 3–4.

[128] Ibid., 4–9.

[129] Edwards, "Gracious Mourning," 10–11.

adds that "carnal mirth" by those in the world is not a sign of true happiness, portending the addictive nature of temporary frivolity.[130] Edwards likewise closes with a brief exhortation of four lines:

1. It argues a wise and right consideration of and judgment of things.
2. It argues a rectified disposition of holiness.
3. The mourning has a pleasure mixed with [it].
4. It is but short, but the comfort everlasting.[131]

This is a good example of Edwards's beginning of outlining his sermons to become more connected with his audience, which will be a consistent format for both his sermons to colonials and Native Americans later in his ministries.

'Tis Not Inconsistent with God's Attributes to Punish Ungodly Men With Eternal Misery[132]

Date: Summer 1731–1732
Key Text: Revelation 19:2–3 – "For true and righteous are his judgments: for he hath judged the great whore, which did corrupt the earth with her fornication, and hath avenged the blood of his servants at her hand. And again they said, Alleluia. And her smoke rose up forever and ever."

In a sermon certain to evoke the later characterization of Edwards as a "Fire and Brimstone" preacher, *Tis Not Inconsistent*'s theme is a defense from Edwards of God's eternal punishment of sinners. Revelation 19:2–3 is the passage Edwards chooses to evoke the right image of God as judge and executioner of judgment on sinful mankind, with angels celebrating and delighting in God's righteous pronouncement of eternal condemnation. It is a call to sober thought on the eternality of torment for those in his congregation who are not regenerated.[133]

[130]Edwards, "Gracious Mourning," 11–12. Edwards writes "Hence, carnal mirth is no sign of happiness. Many are ready to look upon them as the happiest men, that enjoy most carnal mirth and jollity. They call those happy that, careless of their souls, addict themselves to their pleasures and are under the best advantages to give themselves a swing at their carnal and sensual delights, and are ready to look upon the more sober and serious sort of people as being in an undesirable condition. And therefore the condition of the other is ordinarily much more sought after and envied." Ibid.

[131]Ibid., 12–13

[132]Edwards, "Tis Not Inconsistent with God's Attributes to Punish Ungodly Men with Eternal Misery," ed. Kenneth P. Minkema, *Jonathan Edwards Sermon Index* (Sermon 265), (New Haven: Jonathan Edwards Center, Yale University), 1–30.

[133]Minkema, "Tis Not Inconsistent," 1–4.

Edwards begins the sermon with a contextual exposition of the previous chapter of Revelation and ties it to the thematic observance in his sermon, the praises of those mentioned in the key text of God's punishment on the Antichrist, and how they are valid as are God's judgment and punishment of wickedness. He also ties the key text with 2 Corinthians 11:2. He finishes by noting the eternality of the punishment and the repetition of acclaim for this punishment (seen in the key text).[134]

Edwards gives the doctrine that God's attributes show it not inconsistent that He would punish the ungodly with an eternal "misery." Before Edwards begins to give his particulars, he gives a thorough exposition of what eternal damnation and suffering will be using scriptural references (Ezek 18:32; Lam 3:33) and illustrative narration:

> They must as it were wear out the visible world. When the sun is grown so old that he grows pale and has lost his light, their torments will be as extreme as ever; when the heavens wax old as a garment, and are as it were worn out, so severe is God upon them, that he won't abate at all of their misery. Their torments shall never grow old, but be always fresh and in full strength. When they have worn out a thousand such ages as the age of the sun, God won't at all acquit 'em then, nor in the least abate 'em of their torment. And if you multiply all that again by another thousand, or when they have suffered a thousand times so long as that--as that time will come, when it may be so said that they have suffered so long--yet then their torments will be but young; they will be fresh and strong as ever, without any abatement.[135]

Like with *The Value of Salvation*, the portion above shows Edwards's rich ability to illustrate the terror and eternality of judgment. After acknowledging the potential objector of this doctrine, Edwards gives the purpose of preaching "for the vindicating of the name of God in this his dispensation." He notes it is not against God's attributes to punish in this manner as it is deserved. Edwards then shows how the crimes are "infinitely heinous" due to being against God, whose "loveliness, honorableness, and authority are infinite." He goes on to illustrate God's infinite attributes:

> God is a being infinitely great and glorious, a being of majesty, infinitely exalted above the kings and potentates of the earth, or

[134]Edwards, "Tis Not Inconsistent," 5–7.

[135]Ibid., 7–8.

> archangels of heaven; and therefore, it is infinitely more faulty in men to cast contempt upon him, than them. It follows from the last particular. And the ground of his righteousness to us, and to our obedience, is infinitely strong: he, being infinitely worthy [to] be obeyed in himself, being infinitely high and glorious, wise and holy; and we, having an absolute and universal and infinite dependence upon him.[136]

After answering objections, Edwards moves to his second argument that God is not inconsistent with his merciful nature to punish ungodly "men" with eternal misery. Edwards argues the view of God being moved contrary to His nature of justice and righteousness to relent on punishing sin stems from a misguided view of God and His immutability (citing Jas 1:17 and Num 23:19). He then argues it is also an attribute of God to be infinitely just, and not limited in His justice or at odds with His infinite mercy. However, they are both infinite and immutable. The infiniteness of the offense against God's majesty and the deservedness of infinite justice as vindication is then expounded upon by Edwards in his rhetorical manner.[137]

Edwards finishes his doctrinal section by showing that the infinite punishment should be carried out for the purpose of consistency with the fact of its threat. If the threat is righteous and consistent with God's justice, then the punishment would be as well. Threatening but not carrying out punishment would be seen as inconsistent with God's righteousness. For application, Edwards advances that if what he has argued is right, then those who "contend" with God over His righteous justice are to be seen as "miserable" and "foolish."[138]

For "Use," Edwards notes those above should not "flatter themselves with hopes" of God's relenting on justice and punishment (citing Mark 9:44; Matt 25; Rev 14:10–11; 20:10). He then advises them to consider both eternity and the extremity of those eternal torments, the uncertainty of escape, how near death is (and the uncertainty of its nearness).[139] *Tis Not Inconsistent* showcases Edwards's ability both to visually illuminate points (the terror and eternality of judgment), and logically argue for God's authority, immutability, and sovereignty.

[136]Edwards, "Tis Not Inconsistent," 9–13.

[137]Edwards, "Tis Not Inconsistent," 17–24.

[138]Ibid., 24–27.

[139]Edwards, "Tis Not Inconsistent," 27–29.

The Sins of Youth Abide to the Grave[140]

Date: March 1733
Key Text: Job 20:11 – "His bones are full of the sins of his youth, which shall lie down with him in the dust."

The Sins of Youth is a sermon with a target audience of unmarried youth between the ages of sixteen and twenty-six, who were an issue in the Northampton congregation for Solomon Stoddard and Edwards. The sermon is a call to piety, not for salvation in itself, but at the least to not quench the Holy Spirit in bringing regeneration for those who were lost in their youth. The sermon was written on ten duodecimo leaves and was repreached in January 1756.[141] For his introduction, Edwards explains the key text (the words of Zophar in Job) are figurative (paralleling Ezek 32:27, where the bones of the dead would still carry the sins of the guilty who had perished). For the purpose of his sermon, Edwards argues those who sin are not separated from their sin by death but carry it (and their guilt) within their souls into eternity unless it is removed. For his doctrinal section, Edwards lists two propositions: many "spend their youth in sin," and many are never freed from the guilt of their sins and carry them into eternity.[142]

Edwards theorizes the causes for his first proposition (bad company, vanity, or Satan's schemes). He then gives seven arguments (reasons) for the validity of the eternal attachment of sins to the souls of those who commit them. These include God's denial of their excuse of youthful indulgence (citing Job 14:17 and Eccl 11:9), God's remembrance of their youthful sins even in their old age (citing Mal 3:16 and Matt 12:36), the best opportunity of conversion (youth) missed while living in sin (tied to quenching the Spirit in conversion, and God's provocation (reminiscent of *The Time of Youth*).[143]

For his application section, Edwards begins with a use of self-examination to those who are young to examine themselves for the youthful sin that may be "in sinful courses" and "spending away" their youth in sin. Like the previous sermons examined above (*All God's Methods* and *Tis Not Inconsistent*), Edwards shows the eternality of sin and its consequences:

[140] Edwards, "The Sins of Youth Abide to the Grave," ed. Carol King, *Jonathan Edwards Sermon Index* (Sermon 274), (New Haven: Jonathan Edwards Center, Yale University), 1–16.

[141] Carol King, "The Sins of Youth," 1–2.

[142] Edwards, "The Sins of Youth," 3–7.

[143] Edwards, "The Sins of Youth," 7–11.

> The sins that you are now daily committing, and that you make so light of, ben't such light matters as you are ready to think. They'll be no pleasant things to think [of] when you lie a-dying, and when they follow you into another world. They will be no pleasant companions, when you come to stand before God. And the guilt of 'em will never wear out in hell. After you have burnt in hell a million ages, the guilt of the sins of your youth will remain still, as full as ever, and you will have never the less to suffer for 'em for the future: for what is suffered already, there will be an eternity of suffering for 'em behind, and all to as great a height as ever.[144]

Edwards's final use is an exhortation for the youth not to spend their youth in sin but in "the practice of virtue and religion," arguing that while they think spending their youth in sin is something of comfort and pleasure, it is leading to a foundation of uneasiness and "bitter reflections all your life." In juxtaposition, Edwards argues living their youth in piety will lead them to an "abundantly pleasanter" life (citing Prov 3:17 and 24:13) through having "peace with God" who is to be their "father and friend" while they are "safe from hell" and have confidence that if they die, they shall go to heaven and "enjoy eternal glory and happiness." This fits too with Edwards's purpose in encouraging religious affection and pious living among the youth in his congregation. Edwards's preaching of terrible and pleasant eternal options, like *The Value of Salvation*, shows Edwards's care in presenting biblical argumentation for his audience familiar with the Bible.[145]

The Lord's Supper Ought to be Observed in Remembrance of Christ[146]

Date: June 1734
Key Text: Luke 22:19 – "This do in remembrance of me."

This is another sermon by Edwards in preparation for celebrating the Lord's Supper, and he chooses Luke 22:19 as his key text for this manuscript. It was a sermon first preached in June 1734 and then repreached later.

[144]Edwards, "The Sins of Youth," 11–13.

[145]Ibid., 14–16.

[146]Edwards, "The Lord's Supper Ought to be Observed in Remembrance of Christ," ed. R. Craig Woods, *Jonathan Edwards Sermon Index* (Sermon 328), (New Haven: Jonathan Edwards Center, Yale University), 1–17.

Woods notes it is a sermon about duty in performing the ordinance and an intimate responsibility in partaking of the ordinance.[147] The introduction is a summary of what will be preached by Edwards: who is commanded in the text (the followers of Christ compared with those in the wilderness given the Ten Commandments), the command "this do" from the key text of partaking in the Lord's Supper, and the manner in which to do it ("in remembrance of Christ"). This leads to the doctrinal charge that Edwards's audience should keep up the Lord's Supper and "attend" it "in remembrance of Christ."[148]

Edwards gives two propositions for his doctrine, first speaking to the duty of Christians to continue and attend the Lord's Supper and to do so in remembrance of Christ. The ordinance is to be done to remember Christ and what He has done and to stir "suitable affections towards Christ," not only in memory (head) but in "suitable exercises" (heart).[149] These propositions shows Edwards's focus on the heart and affection for God.

In his application, Edwards gives two reproofs to those who do not attend the sacrament or who attend it without remembering Christ. Why this ordinance is commanded is given, including how Christ is "infinitely worthy" to be remembered by his audience as their "infinitely" best friend. His exhortations to the audience include partaking in the Lord's Supper in remembrance of Him, engaging "to live to him," and finally uniting their hearts as those who are His.[150]

Light in a Dark World, A Dark Heart[151]

Date: August/November 1737
Key Text: 2 Peter 1:19 – "We have also a more sure word of prophecy; whereunto ye do well that ye take heed, as unto a light that shineth in a dark place."

Like *Christ, the Light of the World* (examined above) and *A Divine and Supernatural Light* (one of Edwards's most well-known sermons), in *Light in a Dark World, A Dark Heart,* Edwards illustrates the nature of God's light as it illuminates the darkness of the world. M.X. Lesser notes the theme of

[147] R. Craig Woods, "The Lord's Supper," 1–2.

[148] Edwards, "The Lord's Supper," 3–5.

[149] Ibid., 5–9.

[150] Edwards, "The Lord's Supper," 10–16.

[151] Edwards, "Light in a Dark World, A Dark Heart," *Sermons and Discourses 1734–1738*, 704–733.

light not only in the mentioned sermons but also in Edwards's treatises "Of the Rainbow" and "Of Light Rays," written at Yale, to his "Speech to the Mohawks" in January 1751, which opened with a call for those present to "rejoice" the hearts of "all good men" with their coming to faith as "coming into greater light and knowledge in the Christian religion." The sermon *Light in a Dark World* was preached as a two-fold lecture in August and November 1737.[152]

Edwards begins the sermon by noting the context of 2 Peter and its eschatological message. This is given as the judgment to come of those who are proponents of the "dark place" as those (at the time of both Peter and Edwards) who would charge the apostles with following "cunningly devised fables" (taken from 2 Peter 1:16–18, the preceding verses before the key text). Edwards argues that the light of revelation (prophecy) Peter refers to is personally witnessing Jesus and His transfiguration (noting Matt 16), and the testimonial authority given to the apostles to write what would be the New Testament.[153]

This introduction leads to the doctrine that "divine revelation is like a light that shines in a dark place." Edwards gives a two-fold explanation of where this light shines (and where the dark places are) in the world and the heart of man. Edwards uses biblical history as his vehicle for illustration of the dark world where divine revelation shines (noting the darkness of the times of Noah, Job, and Melchizedek) before showing the time of the Exodus and the breaking of the covenant by Israel in worshipping idols. Edwards notes these idols were thought to have done debauched things, which their worshippers interpreted as permission to imitate.[154] The darkness before Christ is compared to the light of revelation brought by Christ's coming in the flesh and what follows from the Incarnation:

> The Son of God, who is in the bosom of the Father, came to be "the light of the world" (John 8:12), "a light to lighten the Gentiles" (Luke 2:32). He came and preached the glorious gospel, and sent forth his disciples to teach all nations, and [to] that end, sent down the Holy Spirit from heaven; who first in a remarkable manner came on them, on the day of Pentecost, and thenceforward abode upon them, giving them such a revelation

[152] M.X. Lesser, "Light in a Dark World," 704–707.

[153] Edwards, "Light in a Dark World," 707–710.

[154] Ibid., 710–714.

> of God's mind and will, that the former revelation under the Old Testament had in comparison of it no glory, "by reason of the glory that excelleth" (2 Corinthians 3:10). And thus divine revelation was sent forth into other nations besides the Jews, and it was to them like the rising of the sun after a long night of darkness. Christ, who is the Sun of righteousness, then rose; and then the nations of the world, who time out of mind had remained in such gross darkness, as we have heard, and whose countries were regions of the shadow of death, saw a great light.[155]

The above portion is like Edwards's sermon series, *A History of the Work of Redemption,* showing his ability to trace the redemption arc (in this case, God's light of revelation). This is further illustrated by Edwards' explanation of the response of the darkness of the world to this revelatory light through persecution and the burning of the Word. Edwards pauses and examines the time of Constantine and sees it as a turning point for the darkness of the world to be once again enlightened by the Gospel. He then gives historical and contemporary examples of places that had, as of his time, not received the Gospel light or who had rejected it. Edwards gives three groups in particular as examples of those where "divine revelation has been rejected in places that have enjoyed it." These include Muslims, the "Papists," and the deists of his day.[156]

For Edwards's application of his first point, he gives four brief uses, including the unreasonableness of those who reject the Bible, the thankfulness they should give for having it, how they should prize and utilize the Bible, and how they should pray for the Word to reach the world with God's revelatory light. Edwards moves on to how the light shines in the dark place of man's heart. In reading the manuscript, one can see how this was broken up into two sermons with two applications. And in looking at Edwards's *Sermon Index,* the reader can also see how he continued with this light-themed sermon in a sermon preached again on 2 Peter 1:19b in November 1737.[157]

In his doctrinal point, Edwards notes the light's ability to discover the secrets of the heart, those discoveries (in light of the Gospel) as being sweet, and the direction pious acting gives to the heart. In making these

[155] Ibid., 714.

[156] Edwards, "Light in a Dark World," 715–720.

[157] Ibid., 720–724.

subpoints, Edwards again peppers his discourse with biblical references to Ephesians, Psalms, Proverbs, Ecclesiastes, Ephesians, 2 Corinthians, and Luke. Edwards shows how the heart of the believer, even when guided by the Gospel light, is still as dark as the world it inhabits due to the fallen nature of the heart before resurrection and renewal.[158] This dark heart is precisely why Edwards notes the believer should be encouraged and prize the divine light that continues to shine in this dark place.[159]

This leads then to the second application for Edwards's two-part sermon lecture. Edwards again relays to his audience the necessity of prizing the treasure of God's Gospel light. Edwards utilizes the fountain of light typology he gives to Christ as something to love for the believer and notes how they should "earnestly seek that this light may shine into our hearts . . . 'until the day dawn," as taken from the key text. A possible later additional exhortation is specifically to "take heed of this light of God's Word."[160] The mixture of light metaphor with God's Gospel, Word, and work in the world shows Edwards's ability to encourage his audience with the beauty of redemption.

The Foundation of a Good Hope of Heaven is Laid on a Rock[161]

Date: January 1739
Key Text: Luke 6:47–48 – "Whosoever cometh to me, and heareth my sayings, and doeth them, I will show you to whom he is like: he is like a man which built an house, and digged deep, and laid the foundation on a rock: and when the flood arose, the stream beat vehemently upon that house, and could not shake it: for it was founded upon a rock."

This sermon, *Foundation of a Good Hope,* was preached at "New Town" (possibly the part of Northampton eventually named Southampton) in January 1738/9. The sermon bears the markings of Edwards's interest in God's working in nature as he compares geological stone with the picture given of the foundation built on the spiritual "Rock of Ages."[162] To begin, Edwards gives the context of the key text taken from Jesus' Sermon on the Mount

[158]Edwards, "Light in a Dark World," 724–730.

[159]Ibid., 729–730.

[160]Edwards, "Light in a Dark World," 730–733.

[161]Edwards, "The Foundation of a Good Hope of Heaven is Laid on a Rock," ed. R. Craig Woods, *Jonathan Edwards Sermon Index* (Sermon 502), (New Haven: Jonathan Edwards Center, Yale University), 1–19.

[162]Woods, "Foundation of a Good Hope," 1–2.

and connects it with how it is recorded in Matthew 5–7. The believer's sure hope through a good foundation, that sure hope compared to an earthly foundation, and surety of either foundation is the context given for the key text before the doctrine is given by Edwards that "they that would build a hope of heaven well, should dig deep and lay their foundation on a rock."[163]

Edwards's two subpoints to explain his doctrine show what it is to dig deep for the foundational Rock and how the "good hope of heaven" is laid on this Rock. Digging deep, as explained by Edwards, includes "great labor." In explaining this, Edwards utilizes biblical illustrations, including the unfaithful steward of Luke 16 and the labor for treasure as seen in Job 3:21 and Proverbs 2:4. Next, Edwards explains the process of digging also involves sifting through what is between the man and the foundation (including their own righteousness—"a fair profession, or a mere form of godliness"). This digging also involves stooping low in humility.[164]

Edwards then moves on to the Rock, on which those who build their hope well lay their foundation. Jesus Christ is given as this Rock by Edwards, who makes biblical reference to Christ as the rock Moses smote given in 1 Corinthians 10:4, the rock used by Manoah in Judges 13:19, the Rock of His people's salvation in Deuteronomy 32:15, and the Rock and Redeemer of His people in Psalm 78:35. Edwards gives the visual of Christ's as a rock by way of two comparisons. The first is compared to a fortress, as seen in Psalm 18:2, 61:2, 94:22, and Isaiah 33:16. Secondly, Edwards shows how Christ as the Rock is compared with the foundational rock, seen in the key text. He uses not only the key text but also Isaiah 26:4, 28:16, and 1 Peter 2:6–8.[165]

Jesus is given by Edwards (through biblical references) as a sure Rock to build a hope of salvation because of His sufficient worthiness, His strength and because Jesus is an "immortal and everlasting Savior." Because Christ is a sure Rock upon which to build this foundation of hope in salvation, He will not be able to be removed like the "carnal confidences" that will pass away like land "swept away by a flood of waters." Edwards concludes his doctrinal section by quoting Psalm 125:1, Hebrews 7:25, 28, and Revelation 1:18.[166]

In his application, Edwards warns his audience about the dangers of not clearing away the earth (worldly attributes), which can falsely be used to

[163]Edwards, "Foundation of a Good Hope," 3–4.

[164]Edwards, "Foundation of a Good Hope," 5–7.

[165]Ibid., 7–10.

[166]Edwards, "Foundation of a Good Hope," 10–11.

build one's foundation. He warns them not to be like "the Pharisees," who were the "sort of men that looked upon themselves – and were looked upon by others – as the most likely of all to have eternal life ... and yet, [they were] dreadfully disappointed. [They] not only perished, but had their place in the bottom of hell."[167]

Edwards then guides his audience to examine if they have given themselves "to Christ without reserve" and are sincerely inclined to practice "those things Christ has said."[168] He finishes the sermon with a short third point to examine their fruit.[169]

Foundation of a Good Hope has a similar theme to *Honey From the Rock*: Christ as the foundation. It also features Edwards's passion for stirring affections from apathy.

Mercy and Not Sacrifice[170]

Date: January 1740
Key Text: Matthew 12:7 – "But if ye had known what this meaneth, I will have mercy, and not sacrifice, ye would not have condemned the guiltless."

Mercy and Not Sacrifice was a sermon Edwards preached against the religious rituals of groups such as Catholics and Muslims, comparing them to Pharisees who had empty religiosity. This, to Edwards, was a "formal hypocrisy" the text shows Christ criticizing. Edwards employs rhetorical reason in this sermon to convince his audience of his doctrine that duties towards fellow men are "more important and essential" parts of faith than the hypocrisy of meaningless ritual.[171]

Edwards begins by noting Christ's quote of Hosea 6:6 and connects the context to Hosea and Exodus 16:23–25. He sets up the doctrine of the sermon and forecasts his intention to exposit "some things needful" for their right understanding of the doctrine, his intention to prove its truth and give reasons why it is true. Edwards shows religion as the "creatures' exercise and the manifestation of respect to the Divine Being, with its duties in kind with respect either to God or man, are distinct acts of obedience or sacrifice, those duties with respect to God are either internal or external, and moral

167 Ibid., 11–14.

168 Ibid., 14–18.

169 Edwards, "Foundation of a Good Hope," 18.

170 Edwards, "Mercy and Not Sacrifice," *Sermons and Discourses 1739–1742*, 111–135.

171 Stout, Hatch, and Farley, "Mercy and Not Sacrifice," 111–114.

duties to man are no more essential than acts to God." Edwards then shows that moral duties to man are seen as essential both in the Old and New Testament, with an emphasis given by Edwards on the Old Testament.[172]

When the duties to God and man are spoken of together, the duties to man are "plainly preferred before the external act of worship." Edwards gives biblical references to reason with his audience from Isaiah, Amos, Micah, Zechariah, and Jeremiah before relating those passages back to the key text in Matthew. Edwards further explores in the Old and New Testament how hypocritical acts of external "worship" by the "self-righteous" abound, though acts of charity towards their fellow man are scarcely written of. Edwards advances further, showing it is the fruits of charity that are given as direction in Scripture (citing James and 1 John). Ultimately, he notes, man is judged more for those benevolent acts (or in their absence) than external acts of "worship."[173]

Edwards finishes by giving the reasons, including how external signs are only worthwhile as a reflection of internal affection and worship; earnest external worship is tied to external acts; how there is greater self-denial in acts of service that give God more honor in their performance than external acts of worship; and how there is more good to external acts of service making them more wholesome (citing Matt 5:16, Rom 14:17–18, and 1 Tim 4:8).[174]

For application, Edwards notes the doctrine of the key text confirms Scripture's sacredness in speaking to the heart of the believer, in a parallel to *Religious Affections* that illustrates how to discern someone's true "eminence in piety" and further to "judge the state of religion in a town." Edwards then moves to exhortation, charging his audience to not place their import on external worship but on duty towards each other:

> Let us therefore hearken to this exhortation. Let us apply ourselves to such duties as these. If you do truly love God, you won't be content not to express your love. Yea, you will want to express your love a great deal. You have now been told which is the most acceptable way of expressing love to God. Therefore seek to express your love much in this way, by being very much in such deeds of righteousness, faithfulness, mercy and love towards

[172]Edwards, "Mercy and Not Sacrifice," 115–119.

[173]Edwards, "Mercy and Not Sacrifice," 119–124. This is shown thorough Jesus' words recorded in Matthew and Luke. Ibid., 124–125.

[174]Edwards, "Mercy and Not Sacrifice," 124–130.

> your neighbor. Christ delights to have his spouse show her love to him in such things as these, and these are the pleasant fruits which she lays up for her beloved.[175]

Like *Foundation of a Good Hope,* the above portion shows Edwards's passion for his audience to have not only biblical knowledge but also pious action.

Zeal an Essential Virtue of a Christian[176]

Date: April 1740
Key Text: Titus 2:14 – "Who gave himself for us, that he might redeem us from all iniquity, and purify unto himself a peculiar people, zealous of good works."

Zeal an Essential Virtue is a sermon composed by Edwards to stir affections. Edwards had noted twelve years earlier his congregants had become "sermon proof" and that the Word had become "insipid" to them. It was five years since the last revival at Northampton, and Edwards desired to stir earnest "zeal" for the Lord and His Word. This is reminiscent of his writings on revival and affection (notably showing his thoughts worked out in *Religious Affections*), whereby the Spirit should stir affections for revival and awakening. This sermon also builds off of *Mercy and Not Sacrifice* in the key text of people zealous for good works. The sermon was a continuation of a previous sermon of the first part of Titus 2:14a, which was preached earlier in March 1740.[177]

Edwards begins with what he plans to observe in the key text: the virtue of being zealous for good works, those having this virtue's membership in the invisible church, and what Christ has done to endow His people with this virtue (zeal) stated in the doctrine as an essential virtue of a Christian. For his doctrinal section, Edwards shows what zeal for good works is a virtue and the reasons for its being an "essential qualification of a Christian." For his first part of doctrine, Edwards shows zeal as a virtue inasmuch as it relates to having a "holy fervor" for doing good works for God. This zeal desires that God be glorified and has an aversion to "what is contrary to God's command and glory." Those with proper zeal are also shown by

[175] Ibid., 130–135.

[176] Edwards, "Zeal an Essential Virtue of a Christian," *Sermons and Discourses 1739–1742,* 136–155.

[177] Stout, Hatch, and Farley, "Zeal an Essential Virtue," 136–138.

Edwards to have a "spirit of jealousy for God" and courage to serve God, "enervating the difficulties" in the way of doing His will and in the face of those that "oppose His glory."[178]

Edwards then moves to his second doctrinal point, noting those earnestly zealous for God stand apart from those who are lukewarm (referencing Rev 3:15–16). Edwards references Luke 24:32 ("Did not our hearts burn within us while he talked to us by the way, and while he opened to us the scriptures?") in showing true zeal for God distinguishes itself from hypocritical outward expressions (in alignment with his exhortation in *Mercy and Not Sacrifice*). Indifference (or having a lukewarm spirit), Edwards argues, is not what becomes of divine objects.[179]

Edwards stirs affection by comparing the work a Christian is called to that of a "soldier," stating the Christian is not called to slumber but to "conflict with principalities and powers and the rulers of the darkness of this world." Thus, the Christian should want the "spirit of a soldier," but not a lukewarm soldier who "won't take strong cities and win crowns and kingdoms." This shows Edwards's focus on rallying and stirring affection for his congregation. He is pushing for his audience to awaken from their "sleep" and to run, fight, and obtain the world for Christ "as it were by conquest."

Edwards begins his application by asking his congregation to examine if they are possessed of that virtue of zeal for good works and then examines (as in *Religious Affections*) how it compares with false zeal. He shows how pious zeal is "according to knowledge" and that those earnestly zealous will first be zealous against their own sin. He uses the metaphor of light and darkness to show the source of true and false zeal.[180] For his exhortation, he charges his audience to again be zealous for religion in a right manner, using the illustrations of light and holy fire. This is compared with the dishonor of having an "indifferent spirit in his service" that is cold and lifeless, which is resented by those who are zealous for God. To be lifeless for God when the world is so zealous for itself is shown by Edwards as a stark contrast. He thus emphasizes his last pointed remark: "Seeing it is thus, how can you expect to be owned as a true disciple, a faithful servant of Jesus Christ, if

[178]Edwards, "Zeal an Essential Virtue," 139–142. Edwards repeats these traits of holy zeal and uses biblical references to 2 Corinthians, Colossians, Numbers, and Matthew. Ibid., 142–143.

[179]Ibid., 143–145. Here again can be seen Edwards's biblical references peppered throughout his points. Ibid.

[180]Edwards, "Zeal an Essential Virtue," 146–150. Edwards again uses biblical reference to Gal 4:18, Prov 8:12, and Ps 112:5.

you are lukewarm, dull, and backward, full of excuses and objections in Christ's service?"[181]

Christ the River[182]

Date: 1742
Key Text: Psalm 1:3 – "And he shall be like a tree planted by the rivers of water, that bringeth forth his fruit in his season; his leaf also shall not wither; and whatsoever he doeth shall prosper."

In this latter sermon, Edwards uses a short, outlined manuscript "made from scraps of fan paper, amounting to three small, irregularly shaped leaves." A different sermon on the same text (Ps 1:3) preached for the Mohicans at Stockbridge is much more thorough (which will be analyzed in the following chapter). This sermon manuscript was also repreached later and featured Edwards's use of the imagery of a river to describe closeness to Christ as a tree planted by a river that flows His "gracious communications" to the saints.[183]

In this manuscript, Edwards forgoes writing out an introductory section and starts with the doctrine that "Christ is to the heart of a saint like a river to the root of a tree that is planted by it." His doctrinal section is an abbreviated outline with eight points that compare Christ's love and communication as flowing freely like water through a river, its abundance (to "answer all varieties of demands"), its constancy, its irresistible and unfailing flow, how it brings the saint near to Christ, how it gives the saint vital union with Christ through communication, and how it gives the "fruits of life."[184] Edwards, in the application, then gives three uses: examination, awakening, and exhortation. His use of examination follows a catechetical manner of asking questions to his audience:

First. Have you seen the grace of Christ to be thus full and free?
Second. Have you been plucked up by the roots, and transplanted?
Third. Does your heart naturally draw that nourishment?
Fourth. Have you experienced that life-giving refreshment?
Fifth. Is Christ your life?

[181] Ibid., 150–155.

[182] Edwards, "Christ the River," ed. Kenneth P. Minkema, *Jonathan Edwards Sermon Index* (Sermon 693c), (New Haven: Jonathan Edwards Center, Yale University), 1–5.

[183] Minkema, "Christ the River," 1–2.

[184] Edwards, "Christ the River," 2–3.

> Sixth. Does your life and trust remain in time of drought? Or do you dry up?[185]

Edwards, in his use of awakening, explains those not in union with Christ will be "like the barren heath," and their "streams will fail," and their end "will be to be burned." For them, Christ will be a "river of brimstone." Edwards's use of exhortation and direction for his audience is to seek the "great privilege" of communication with Christ and the gift of "fruits of life" and not to uproot from where they are planted in Christ but honor that "river" (Christ).[186]

The Great Concern of a Watchman for Souls[187]

Date: June 8, 1743
Key Text: Hebrews 13:17 – "They watch for your souls, as they that must give account."

Watchman for Souls was preached as an ordination sermon for Jonathan Judd, who was to take charge of a Southampton congregation and was previously under Edwards at Northampton. Edwards preaches solemnly on the great responsibility of serving as a pastor and as a Christian.[188] The sermon starts with a short introduction of what is to be preached from the text, that the "watchman" is charged with caring for the souls of men, and how he is charged with giving an account of this business. For the doctrine, there is not a singular (or even multiple) explicit doctrine to see, but instead, four points. First, ministers have men's souls "committed to their care" by Christ. The second and third points are the purpose of their commission by Christ and how Christ expects them to fulfill this charge. The final point is how they will give an account to Christ for fulfilling this commission.[189]

Edwards intends to prove the special relationship of God creating men's souls and cites several passages from Numbers, Ecclesiastes, Hebrews, Zechariah, Genesis, and Ezekiel. This special creation of souls is given as more intimate and special than even the bodily creation as it is solely

[185] Edwards, "Christ the River," 3.

[186] Ibid., 3–4.

[187] Edwards, "The Great Concern of a Watchman for Souls," *Sermons and Discourses 1743–1758*, ed. Wilson H. Kimnach, vol. 25, *The Works of Jonathan Edwards* (New Haven: Yale University Press, 2006), 59–82.

[188] Kimnach, "Watchman for Souls," 59–61.

[189] Edwards, "Watchman for Souls," 62–63.

the creation of God and not used through "second causes, instruments, or means, or any thing preexistent."[190]

The purposes for the commission of men's souls to the care of ministers are first for those men to fulfill their purpose in glorifying God through their lives and second for their salvation in having everlasting life. Edwards shows how they are made for eternity, how Christ has saved them for eternity, and how ministers are charged with caring for their souls so that they will be with Christ for eternity.[191]

This was a charge Edwards took responsibility for himself. Next, Edwards references passages from Song of Songs, Isaiah, and Nehemiah to show the care by which ministers should care for the flock "through a great and howling wilderness;" Edwards illustrates this "wilderness" is filled with "hungry wolves and roaring lions." Edwards finishes with the serious charge that ministers will give an account of what happened to the souls that were given to their care and how their eternal state was "owning to their faithfulness or unfaithfulness in that care and watch that was appointed to them." Edwards then, for his application, first speaks directly to Judd, whom he commends as given "how great an honor he does" by the very souls God saved through his death and resurrection. He calls Judd his "co-worker with him, and should commit precious souls" to his care to provide passage to everlasting life and to be charged for his service in this work.[192]

Along with this serious charge for Judd and other ministers, Edwards also shows the joy found in seeing those for whom they have faithfully cared led to the "promised land." Finally, Edwards exhorts the congregation to take ownership as members of the church and to Christ and His salvation. He charges them to support Judd both spiritually and physically (citing Proverbs, Deuteronomy, Philippians, Matthew, Haggai, and Malachi). Edwards closes the sermon with two contentions he would warn the congregation to avoid. The first is over temporary issues. Second (forecasting Edwards's own issues to come with his congregation at Northampton) is over church discipline. The obvious parallel with Edwards's own weakened efficacy at Northampton is seen in his explanation that if those at this congregation become contentious with their minister, it will effectually weaken his ability to minister and care for them. He concludes on an optimistic note that if they live in peace with their pastor, their pastor, themselves, and their church will

[190]Ibid., 63–66.

[191]Edwards, "Watchman for Souls," 67.

[192]Edwards, "Watchman for Souls," 67–72.

"flourish and prosper with all manner of prosperity" with Christ dwelling among them (John 4:36).[193]

The Sovereignty of God's Mercy[194]

Date: August 1746
Key Text: Exodus 33:19 – "And will be gracious to whom I will be gracious, and will show mercy on whom I will show mercy."

In a sermon directly related to the political events of the Jacobite forces under "Bonnie" Prince Charles Stuart and their defeat by the army under the Duke of Cumberland in the Scottish Highlands, *Sovereignty of God's Mercy* (subtitled "Thanksgiving for Victory over the Rebels"), was preached in the same month Massachusetts Governor William Shirley established a day of thanksgiving (August 14, 1746). The sermon was re-preached in Stockbridge eight years later during the beginning of the French and Indian War in the Colonies.[195]

The sermon is outlined more than previous sermons examined with shorter sentences. Instead of a title for doctrine, the doctrinal section has a title, "Subject," which is "The sovereignty of God's mercy." Doctrinal points are what the audience should understand of God's mercy, how those mercies differ from God's sovereign judgments, and how God's sovereignty is bestowed in His practice of bestowed mercies. The first point by Edwards shows God's sovereign mercy, for the second point, Edwards fills in with more body as he notes God, in His judgment, fulfills His role as "judge, and not as a sovereign." This includes His appointing "the subordinate rule of judgment, ... leaving" sinners to act sinfully in exposing themselves to punishment by the rule of judgment and withholding mercy on those He judges. In His acting as a sovereign, Edwards notes God is free to go beyond His limits as a judge and "the prescribed rule," namely the Law. In showing mercy, God as a sovereign gives exercises of mercy to sinners without merit and with the limitations or direction of a declared rule. Edwards ends this point by recapping that God is sovereign in His exercising mercy both in a

193 Edwards, "Watchman for Souls," 74–82.

194 Edwards, "The Sovereignty of God's Mercy," ed. Kenneth P. Minkema, *Jonathan Edwards Sermon Index* (Sermon 833), (New Haven: Jonathan Edwards Center, Yale University), 1–12.

195 Minkema, "Sovereignty of God's Mercy," 1–2.

negative aspect (withholding or not withholding judgments) and positive (executing punishment in light of that judgment withheld or kept).[196]

Edwards's third point is the lengthiest of his doctrinal section. He uses this section to show how God is sovereign in the exercises of His mercy to mankind (general), particular persons, people, and times. The period of probation given to mankind to live and potentially be saved is given as an example (by way of Ps 145:9) of his mercy shown to mankind. Where one is placed temporally on the earth, and the advantages (or disadvantages) is a sovereign merciful act of God, according to Edwards's second subpoint. These placements and advantages distinguish one person from another (citing Ezek 16:46–48 and 23:11 as his prooftexts for this point). He shows this particularity includes sinners at their conversion and after.[197] He also shows the distinction made when God bestows temporal mercy on a nation He chooses (Israel) though they are a "very wicked people" through using the history of Israel in the wilderness, and the instances of David slaying Goliath, and victories for wicked kings such as Jehoram.[198]

Compared to the lengthy discourse on God's mercy on nations, his final point is succinct: God's mercy is shown in specific times, noting, "The day of the Gospel is more remarkably a day of mercy, than the time of the Old Testament. God brought on that dispensation when he pleased."[199] His application is also brief and outlined in giving the "use of information" that the sermon had shown the audience "the glory of God's mercy," how both he and his audience are "absolutely and universally" dependent on God for their salvation (with a caution not to assume God will show mercy in the encouragement of their sin). He finishes with an exhortation to seek out being recipients of God's sovereign mercy, to be thankful for the mercy they are given, and to be "excited and encouraged" to pray for God's sovereign mercy on their "public societies" to which they belong, and mankind in general.[200]

[196]Edwards, "Sovereignty of God's Mercy," 3–5. Edwards uses Rom 9:8 as his prooftext for this point. Ibid.

[197]Ibid., 5–9.

[198]Edwards, "Sovereignty of God's Mercy," 9. This is another example of Edwards's "peppering" of scriptural illustrations to demonstrate a point. Ibid.

[199]Ibid., 10.

[200]Ibid., 10–11.

The Holiness of God[201]

Date: August 1747
Key Text: Isaiah 6:3 – "And one cried unto another, and said, Holy, holy, holy, is the Lord of hosts."

A sermon preached a year after *Sovereignty of God's Mercy*, *The Holiness of God* is even more outlined (showing the progression of Edwards's outlining methodology later in his preaching ministry). It has parallels to his *Miscellanies* entries 1077, 1080–82, and 1084, which all deal with the end of creation, God's glory, and the glory of God being the end purpose of creation. Minkema notes his "Blank Bible" note on the key text of Isaiah 6:3; Edwards translates it as "His glory is the fullness of the whole earth."[202]

Like *Sovereignty of God's Mercy*, Edwards has titled his doctrinal subject "The Subject," and with two points, he would first "endeavor" to explain God's holiness and then show the evidence of the holiness of God. The bulk of what is written out in Edwards's manuscript focuses on the first point of explaining the holiness of God through what God's holiness is and how "God in his holiness is distinguished from all other beings." Edwards explains the difference between moral and natural holiness and evil. Moral evil or good is based on the intellectual will of the being whose quality is based on their "will or heart, and its acts and exercises."[203]

God is supremely holy due to being both naturally and morally excellent. Because of this, Edwards explains, God's nature disposes Him to, and He "delights in everything that is morally excellent, and opposes everything that is morally evil." For biblical references, Edwards begins by referencing the quality given by John in his first epistle (1 John 4:8), which is that God is love. This sets up Edwards as he notes the "holiness of men consists in love." Edwards then shows the union of love between God the Father and the Son and mankind due to their reflection of His love worked out in their creation and redemption. This love is also holy in its abhorrence of sin and wickedness (citing Exod 15:11).[204]

With his second point, Edwards's sermon begins taking on a more outlined form as he uses brief statements about what distinguishes God's holiness from other created beings' holiness. He begins by referencing 1 Samuel

[201]Edwards, "The Holiness of God," ed. Kenneth P. Minkema, *Jonathan Edwards Sermon Index* (Sermon 872), (New Haven: Jonathan Edwards Center, Yale University), 1–10.

[202]Minkema, "The Holiness of God," 1–2.

[203]Edwards, 'The Holiness of God," 3–4.

[204]Edwards, 'The Holiness of God," 4–5.

2:2 and Revelation 15:4 to show His holiness is far set apart from others. This shows that there is no comparison between God's holiness and others. He also adds a biblical reference to Job 15:5 and 25:5. Edwards states how God is holy in origin, in juxtaposition to the creature with their holiness derived *from* God. God is also unchangeable and independently admirable.[205] Having shown God's holiness as unique, Edwards finishes his doctrinal section with evidentiary statements of God being "thus perfectly and infinitely holy."[206]

What follows next in his application is also given in outline form. Here, he adds to his sermon's application with biblical citations of 1 Samuel 6:20 and 1 Corinthians 10:20 to show the "great privilege" Christians have in their God being holy. And secondly, Edwards writes of the acquaintance God's people have with God and His holiness. Third, Edwards notes proper worship to be given to God (who is holy), giving biblical citations of Psalm 29:2, 96:9, 93:5, and 1 Chronicles 16:29. He cites Matthew 5:8, Psalm 5:4, and Revelation 21:27 to show how necessary holiness is to abide with God, and Habakkuk 1:13 to show the danger in presuming to sin before a holy God. Malachi 3:2, Isaiah 10:17, and Hebrew 12:29 are given for his final points that emphasize God's judgment, man's need for a mediator, and the terrible fate of the ungodly. His final use of exhortation is given without notes other than it is about self-examination.[207]

Dreadful Fear Will Seize the Hearts of the Wicked[208]

Date: August 1747
Key Text: Proverbs 10:24b – "The fear of the wicked, it shall come upon him."

Before preaching *Holiness of God*, Edwards preached a short two-sermon series on Proverbs 10. These sermons, along with a four-part sermon series from Acts, and another three-part sermon series from Proverbs will be examined next to observe how Edwards advanced short sermon series in comparison with the short sermon series format that will be observed in the next chapter among Native Americans in Stockbridge.

[205] Ibid., 5–7.

[206] Edwards, 'The Holiness of God," 7.

[207] Edwards, 'The Holiness of God," 7–9.

[208] Edwards, "Dreadful Fear Will Seize the Hearts of the Wicked," ed. Kenneth P. Minkema, *Jonathan Edwards Sermon Index* (Sermon 870), (New Haven: Jonathan Edwards Center, Yale University), 1–19.

The first of Edwards's sermon series on Proverbs 10 was *Dreadful Fear*. Edwards initially preached the sermon as stated in 1747, and repreached the sermon in 1751.[209] To begin the sermon, unlike many others, Edwards begins without an exposition of the key text, and instead states the text and gives the first proposition. Minkema proposes Edwards could have extemporized an exposition before giving the key text and proposition.[210]

If the proposition was the first thing given after the key text it is a stark warning to his listeners "dreadful fear" will seize their hearts either at the first, or at the last. Edwards explains the heart of many "wicked men" are hardened from fear, though they have great cause to be fearful. These men can go about their days "drinking and eating" without care, yet there is a fear that will eventually catch up with them. For those who are fortunate in God's providence, this "dismal fear" in God's "terrible dispensation" are given while they are in "life and health." Edwards illustrates these "terrible fears" in looking at the Israelites in the wilderness when God descended on Mt. Sinai (referencing Num. 16:34), and later those who had inhabited the promised land (notably Rahab) before God reclaimed it (referencing Ex. 15:13–15, and Joshua 2:9–11).[211]

Edwards looks at those who facing their death (especially those who were under "the clear light of the gospel") are "seized with amazing fears." Edwards then goes beyond those still living to propose those departed from life will still have amazing fears of "what judgement lies ahead." This includes the bleak futility of having the same "carnal, corrupt hearts" prone to idolatry and lusts never "gratified any more" and "never have any comfort in any respect."[212]

Replacing comfort and fulfilled craving will be the "terrible effects of the wrath of God" and "the cruelty of devils." Edwards notes those approaching death and fearful of their future were observed to have "affrighted, amazed, ghastly countenances." Edwards uses the following illustratory language in describing their misery:

> The misery that the wicked at the day of judgment will fear, will be so great, that they would account death, the most terrible death that should put an end to their beings, a most joyful refuge.

[209]Minkema, "Dreadful Fear," 1–3.

[210]Minkema, "Dreadful Fear," 1–3.

[211]Edwards, "Dreadful Fear," 4–5.

[212]Ibid., 5–6.

> [They will] run to the caves and rocks, {and cry} to be crushed, as men run to a refuge when afraid of some dreadful enemies. It would seem terrible to be crushed to death by the weight of rocks and mountains; but the wicked at that time will esteem the weight of rocks and mountains to be light in comparison.[213]

This misery, according to Edwards, will cause them to desire total destruction of their existence over further pain. This includes even the great unholy beasts including 'roaring lions and leviathans" and inquires if such "great spiritual Goliaths" are melted under such fear how "will sinful worms support themselves."[214]

Edwards explains (in a similar fashion to *Religious Affections*) how this fear will be apprehended by the sinner through their "natural conscience" though they are not regenerate. They will have a natural fear of God, though they will not spiritually attain a knowledge of His beauty. Edwards delves into visualizing for his audience the terrible amazement of the second coming and judgment of Christ. He pictures this through references to biblical prophecies of the destruction and remaking of the heavens and earth found in Psalms, Isaiah, Nahum, 2 Thess., 2 Peter, and Revelation.[215]

The imagery from those prophecies then leads into his second proposition of how those fears of the ungodly "shall come upon them." The fears of God's wrath for them will be realized with "no agreeable disappointment." And this fulfillment of their fears will not be unfamiliar according to Edwards stating Jesus as he comes as the "Judge" has not come in the Bible to appear "as a frightful bugbear" to terrify them with expectations of wrath to later be realized with terrible fulfillment.[216]

Edwards then closes the sermon with application giving three uses on how the fears in the "natural conscience" explained above will not save one from hell. Second, those who have gotten over those fears are still in danger of those fears being realized. And third, to let "sinners be hence warned not go on in wickedness." He gives warnings to take heed of the means of warnings over their danger, to not rush in on "acts and ways of sin," to not backslide after being stirred up in the fear of the Lord, to "fly for refuge unto Christ," and finally to not "rest fearless in some false confidence" by

[213]Edwards, "Dreadful Fear," 6–8.

[214]Ibid., 8.

[215]Edwards, "Dreadful Fear," 8–12.

[216]Ibid., 12–13.

temporal affections and "illuminations" that are common but are not a "real change of your nature, and the temper of your heart and course of your life."[217]

The Desire of the Righteous Shall Be Granted[218]

Date: August 1747
Key Text: Proverbs 10:24c – "The desire of the righteous shall be granted."

The second part and "counterpoint" to *Dreadful Fear*, *Desire of the Righteous* gives a juxtaposition to the fate of the wicked. *Desire of the Righteous* was also repreached later by Edwards.[219] The sermon begins with a "handling of the doctrine" which is the key text that the "desire of the righteous shall be granted." The handling of the text by Edwards will be to explain the desires of the righteous and show "that they shall be granted."[220]

In explaining the desire of the righteous, Edwards observes what they are, how far they extend, and closes with the circumstances of these desires. These desires are first beyond human desires and are of what Edwards states "the desires of the new nature." In explaining how the original good nature of desires was corrupted and became self-internalized, Edwards relates the ideal of "disinterested benevolence" that would define those who followed such as Samuel Hopkins and his Edwards, Jr. This is shown in his words here:

> But a spiritual nature enlarges his appetites and desires to, and causes them to extend to, something vastly greater and more important than self-interest or private good: the glory of God, and the good of the world of mankind, especially the church of God. Spiritual desires are from an higher principle than self-love, strictly so-called; [they are from] a principle of proper benevolence, [and a] love to God, that is not at all founded in a principle of self-love. So that spiritual desires extend to that which is entirely diverse from private interest. Self is denied for God's sake; God is placed highest, and man places his happiness in God's

[217] Ibid., 13–17.

[218] Edwards, "The Desire of the Righteous Shall Be Granted," ed. Kenneth P. Minkema, *Jonathan Edwards Sermon Index* (Sermon 871), (New Haven: Jonathan Edwards Center, Yale University), 1–19.

[219] Minkema, "Desire of the Righteous," 1–2.

[220] Edwards, "Desire of the Righteous," 3.

> being glorified, and so on the prosperity of that holy society that stands in a special relation to God, even the church.[221]

Godly desires, Edwards explains, also include godly honor, spiritual food, holy habitation, union with God, God's elect, that God be glorified "in every respect," God's commands obeyed, God be glorified everywhere, and "sinners may be converted." These desires, for the believer, are all good and "to as high a degree" as possible for them to conceive, and to eternity in their thinking forward of these desires.[222]

In giving his final observations on the desires of the righteous, he states grace doesn't diminish but increases godly desires. Next, Edwards moves on to how the desires of the righteous will be granted, first in this life (to a degree), and second, as an end to "all uneasiness in a future state (to some degree). In the future state (at the day of judgment) Edwards shows the sharp distinction for the believer and the condemned (as seen in *Dreadful Fear*). Where unending fear and torment are the consequence for the "wicked," complete satisfaction of holy desire is the reward for the believer. Those lesser degrees of the fulfillment of godly desire are whole for the faithful in "every faculty, the use of every enjoyment, and in all respects possible."[223] This shows the purpose in Edwards's sermon series, to warn of the horrors of hell in *Dreadful Fear*, and then reach the affections of his audience in showing the glorious beauty of fulfilled holy desires in *Desire of the Righteous*.

After showing the desires of the righteous and how they will be fulfilled in the future state, Edwards moves to his second proposition of showing God will fulfill these desires. First, is how God has given the righteous these desires. These desires are righteous because of this (third point), and they are given for a purpose (fourth point). This is also proved through seeing the fulfillment for those with unholy desires (fifth and sixth points) of leaving them unfulfilled and how God's wrath comes upon those with them. Finally, holy desires are fulfilled because unlike human desires they are not vain.[224]

In the application, the phrase by Edwards that "you are at an age wherein natural desires and expectations are commonly at their greatest height"

[221] Edwards, "Desire of the Righteous," 3–6.

[222] Edwards, "Desire of the Righteous," 6–9.

[223] Ibid., 9–11.

[224] Edwards, "Desire of the Righteous," 11–14.

points to the possibility of a younger audience for Edwards's audience.[225] Edwards concludes somberly in noting the wrath of God for carnal desires in the first version of this sermon manuscript. However, in a revision for the version that was repreached, Edwards does include a return to the purpose of this message in showing the beauty of God's grace in granting holy desires and offering the Gospel through quoting Rev. 3:20 "If you will hear my voice, and open the door, I will come unto you and sup with you, and you with me."[226]

This two-part sermon series shows the heart of Edwards's desire to go after the affections of his listeners and visualize for them the danger of not pursuing God, His Word, and righteousness, and the joys of holy desires fulfilled in attaining godliness and sweet affection for God and His Word.

Turned From Darkness to Light[227]

Date: November 1747
Key Text: Acts 26:18a – "To open their eyes, and to turn them from darkness to light."

In this second sermon series studied from 1747, Edwards preached four sermons from Acts 26:18. They are connected by the doctrine and content. Minkema notes they are a series on "the nature of saving conversion that plays on the distinctions of spiritual darkness and light."[228] The key text for the sermon series (the whole of Acts 26:18) is from Paul's defense to Agrippa on Paul's mission to the Gentiles.

Edwards will use this key text to preach on how the sinner who is converted has their eyes opened from blindness and darkness to turn from their past darkness into light (*Turned From Darkness to Light*); how converted sinners are turned from the power of Satan to God (*Turned From Satan to God*); how converted sinners' sins are forgiven (*Turned From Wrath to Forgiveness*); and have an inheritance from those who are sanctified (*Turned From an Alien to an Heir*). Edwards gives at the beginning of *Turned From Darkness to Light* the steps of conversion instigated by the voice of Christ in reproving the sinner, declaring Himself, declares the "business" the sinner is

[225]Ibid., 15. Noted by Minkema in the introduction to the sermon. Minkema, "Desire of the Righteous," 1.

[226]Edwards, "Desire of the Righteous," 15–18.

[227]Edwards, "Turned From Darkness to Light," ed. Kenneth P. Minkema, *Jonathan Edwards Sermon Index* (Sermon 883), (New Haven: Jonathan Edwards Center, Yale University), 1–9.

[228]Minkema, "Turned From Darkness to Light," 1.

now called to, promises His support and defense, and declares the success and effect of this work.[229]

The doctrine stated by Edwards is sinners in saving conversion have their eyes opened (from blindness) and are turned from darkness to light. This blindness is given in three accounts due to their ignorance, delusion, and misery. Like with *Dreadful Fear* (and ultimately stated in *Religious Affections*) Edwards argues that "nothing is known aright [spiritual sight]." Their delusion and misery are also represented by Edwards as similarly limiting their spiritual sight without Christ. Edwards explains the process of the converted's spiritual eyes being opened and brought into a "happy state" (Ps. 97:11), and "glorious morning" (Ps. 30:5, Amos 5:8).[230]

For his application, Edwards charges his audience to examine themselves as to not be deceived by Satan's impressions, mistake "common illuminations" for "special illuminations," or be deceived by those above working together. Edwards exhorts his audience to have their eyes opened and turn from darkness to light. They should note the darkness they are in as Edwards explains the light they are being called to is: "great" (Is. 9:2), "true" (John 1:9, 1 John 2:8), "heavenly" (Luke 1:78, Acts 9:3 and 26:13), "marvelous" (1 Peter 2:9, "most precious" (Rev. 21:11), "of life" (John 1:4 and 8:12), and "Christ's" (Ps. 36:9) which is explained in two ways as Christ's glory (Is. 2:5 and 60:20), and the Sun of righteousness (as a light that Christ enjoys Himself). Edwards goes further in stating they will be children of light as God's children. Because of this Edwards directs them to conform to the "light of reason," "beg of God" to have their conscience be like His "candle," and follow the example of the blind man in Mark 10:46 and cry out for God's mercy. Edwards closes by explaining how Christ is the light."[231]

Turned From Satan to God[232]

Date: December 1747
Key Text: Acts 26:18b – "and from the power of Satan unto God."

The doctrine of this second sermon on Acts 26:18 is sinners converted are turned from the power of Satan to God. Edwards has three propositions

[229]Edwards, "Turned From Darkness to Light," 2–3.

[230]Edwards, "Turned From Darkness to Light," 3–5.

[231]Edwards, "Turned From Darkness to Light," 5–8.

[232]Edwards, "Turned From Satan to God," ed. Kenneth P. Minkema, *Jonathan Edwards Sermon Index* (Sermon 884), (New Haven: Jonathan Edwards Center, Yale University), 1–15.

that sinners that are unconverted are under the power of Satan, when they are saved they are turned from his power, and when they are saved they are turned to God. Under Satan's power, sinners are both his servants, and his "portion and prey." Edwards argues they are his servants through sin's dominion of their hearts, and they are his prey through the guilt of this sin, and its condemnation.[233]

In similar thought again to *Religious Affections*, Edwards explains how the sinner's servanthood to Satan is by their blindness that causes sin to have a "reigning power and influence" over them. He argues their faculties are governed and places the influence as having "the chief command, the highest influence." He adds "no good principles have any equal power; sin possesses the throne. The objects of lust have their choice, [their] highest affection."[234]

This reign of sin in the heart of the sinner is absolute, which will "not suffer men to exert any one act of virtue." This is even to the detriment of the sinner's interest according to Edwards. Edwards argues this is the cause of "things so horrid, filling the world so full of sin, so extinguishing the light of nature, leading mankind into such gross delusions, absurd practices." Finally, this rule of sin leads to the sinner's condemnation through the Law, sentenced Edwards argues, to be Satan's prey.[235]

Edwards moves to his second proposition that sinners are turned from this power of Satan and are no longer under the dominion of sin. While sin can still influence, it has no "reigning power" anymore for the converted. Satan is "turned out of his throne," according to Edwards, and are no longer "governed" by sin and its influence in committing sinful acts. Edwards then explains how the sinner is turned to God. Edwards explains this happens in six respects. This happens first in their heart, they are brought into a "spiritual union" with God, this conforms their nature to God, they go from being Satan's portion to God's, God also becomes their portion, and they go from being under the dominion of Satan to being under God's rule and service.[236]

Where before sin had the chief possession of the sinner's heart, grace and mercy then rule over the converted where the "power of sin there [is] broken." The delusions and spiritual blindness are "scattered" where

233 Edwards, "Turned From Satan to God," 2.

234 Ibid., 2–3.

235 Edwards, "Turned From Satan to God," 3–4.

236 Ibid., 5–7.

the converted now has "true apprehensions." Like with *Turned From Darkness to Light*, Edwards then moves to the application and begins with self-examination. It is to examine whether one was turned from Satan to God with sin's dominion argued by Edwards as the first test, the turning to what end as the second, the forsaking of all for Christ as the third, coming to Christ as God (as the fourth), having a God-like temper, and finally to see if in times of trial what "prevails" in the heart.[237]

In his exhortation section Edwards explains they may not understand the control Satan has over them, but when they turn, all enemies will have no power as God will cause them to triumph over their enemies with Christ, will have perfect liberty, they will have a godly happiness, and the grace God gives in this "importunity does God counsel" them to turn for their "own sake." They are given then directions to turn for all ways of external sin, to see their "miserable bondage," that they are at fault if they will not turn, to earnestly seek God to turn them to God before quoting Jeremiah 3:21–23.

Turned From Wrath to Forgiveness[238]

Date: December 1747
Key Text: Acts 26:18c – "That they may receive forgiveness of sins."

The shortest of the four sermons on Acts 26:18, *Turned From Wrath to Forgiveness* is theorized by Minkema as given in an informal setting (such as a private meeting) instead of the sabbath service.[239] Edwards begins by noting how Paul had become an instrument of delivering the Gospel of grace to others, which he "made the subject of." The doctrine is simple, when sinners are converted, they are forgiven. There are also two simple points of emphasis as well. To explain the nature of forgiveness of sins, and to show why when the sinner is converted, their sins are forgiven by God.[240] Edwards gives a definition of the forgiveness of sins:

> It is a gracious act of God towards the sinner, setting him totally and finally free from God's displeasure towards him for his sin, and his obligation to suffer the punishment of it.[241]

[237]Edwards, "Turned From Satan to God," 7–12.

[238]Edwards, "Turned From Wrath to Forgiveness," ed. Kenneth P. Minkema, *Jonathan Edwards Sermon Index* (Sermon 885), (New Haven: Jonathan Edwards Center, Yale University), 1–5.

[239]Minkema, "Turned From Wrath to Forgiveness," 1.

[240]Edwards, "Turned From Wrath to Forgiveness," 2.

[241]Ibid., 2.

Edwards cites Ps. 7:11, John 3:36, and Ps. 85:4 to explain that while God's anger towards sin never ceases, the sinner who is converted is reconciled to God and there is peace instead of wrath. Edwards follows up by stating how the sinner is set free from the punishment of sin and is "totally and finally set at liberty."[242]

Next, Edwards moves to his second point of explaining why a sinner is forgiven when he is converted. This is explained as from God's "free grace and good pleasure" (citing Rom. 3:24, 5:20, and Eph. 1:7). This is in God's sovereign will as Edwards explains as God "gives 'em the qualifications by which they are interested in the sacrifice." This forgiveness is also procured through the atonement of Christ. Edwards closes with short notes for his application (which is as Minkema explains could be where Edwards preached extemporaneously) to tell the unconverted to earnestly seek converting grace by noting how miserable they are without forgiven sins, and what "great ground of comfort have they, that have good evidence that their sins are forgiven."[243]

Turned From An Alien to An Heir[244]

Date: December 1747
Key Text: Acts 26:18d – "And inheritance among them that are sanctified."

More lengthy than *Turned From Wrath to Forgiveness, Turned From An Alien to An Heir* concludes the Acts 26:18 series. The sermon shows the inheritance of the converted (in juxtaposition from the sorrowful state of those unconverted in *Turned From Satan to God*). In the doctrine Edwards notes the inheritance is shared with those others who are sanctified. In the sermon Edwards will show three observations of what the communion of the inheritance is, the inheritance itself, and the title "given 'em to this inheritance."[245]

Before giving the above observation he will preach, Edwards shows how those who are unconverted are aliens from God's "commonwealth" and are "far off" (citing Acts 8:21 and Neh. 2:20). The implications (assumptions) of those who are have the shared inheritance is given by Edwards. It is that

[242] Ibid., 2–3.

[243] Ibid., 3–4.

[244] Edwards, "Turned From An Alien to An Heir," ed. Kenneth P. Minkema, *Jonathan Edwards Sermon Index* (Sermon 886), (New Haven: Jonathan Edwards Center, Yale University), 1–11.

[245] Edwards, "Turned From An Alien to An Heir," 1–2.

they are converted (and sanctified), they are children of God, through being children of God they are then heirs (citing Rom. 8:17).[246]

Edwards explains what the inheritance is. This is first all the goodness God "is possessed of" so far as the converted are "capable of enjoying it." This is summed up as God Himself and His kingdom by Edwards. The converted are united with God through His Spirit. And this is a perfect union with Father, Son, and Spirit. Citing 1 Peter 1:3–4 and Rev. 22:11, 22:14, this includes "all the blessings of the heavenly Canaan" and the right to the "river of life" and the "tree of life." They also have an inheritance to the "crown of glory, "kingdom of glory," "throne of glory," "God's palace," and "eternal triumph over enemies."[247] Edwards though, explains why even if the unconverted were to receive it, they are incapable of having any part in it due to not having a spiritual interest in it.[248]

Edwards moves to how the converted are brought "to a title to this inheritance." For this section, Edwards explains first how the Law was given to adjudge the inheritance of life for perfect obedience. After the fall of Adam, this title was given partly through the covenant God the Father made with Christ (in appointing him as the converted "surety"). This was given partly to the converted through their covenant of grace made between them and Christ (in getting the title to Christ Himself and His benefits). This is explained that though there was a covenant with Adam (as humanity's federal head), it is a "subordinate rule to the covenant made with Christ." This explained by Edwards means the sinner who is converted is thus justified by Christ, and have further privileges as God's children.[249]

For application, Edwards first calls on his audience to examine whether they are converted and hate sin and are possessed of God's Spirit to love all divine things including God's Word, and God's people. Next, he exhorts those who are unconverted to consider how bad their state is and to consider how they could have the inheritance of God if only they would choose and accept it finally citing Rev. 22:17.[250]

In Edwards's "Turning" series from Acts 26:18, it is clear how Edwards is speaking to an audience that understands the Bible and is appealing to them to become more engaged with it. The sermons Edwards spends the most

[246] Ibid., 2–3.

[247] Edwards, "Turned From An Alien to An Heir," 3–5.

[248] Ibid., 6.

[249] Ibid., 6–8.

[250] Edwards, "Turned From An Alien to An Heir," 9–10.

time in (*Turned From Satan to God*, and *Turned From An Alien to An Heir*), are spent by Edwards in illustrating how terrible it is to be under Satan's rule, and how great it is to be an heir of God through Christ. He appeals to their affections (in using visualization for sin and glory), and he appeals to their understanding of doctrine (in explaining the process and benefits of God's inheritance). By preaching in the manner illustrated above, Edwards shows a familiarity of his audience, and a drive to reach them in the best homiletical method he knows.

Grace in Lively Exercise of Excellent Benefit to Men as a Guide to Direct and Conduct Them in Their Way[251]

Date: January 1750
Key Text: Prov. 6:22a – "When thou goest, it shall lead thee; when thou sleepest, it shall keep thee; when thou awakes, it shall talk with thee."

Grace in Lively Exercise is one of three sermons Edwards preached at the beginning of 1750 on Proverbs 6:22. On the manuscript is a reproaching notation for Feb. 1752.[252] In February of 1752, Edwards was already settled as the pastor of the dual congregation at Stockbridge is family moved there that month. It is unclear if this sermon was preached to the colonial congregation, the Native, or a mixed audience. The manuscript was not revised. On Dec. 26, 1749, less than a month earlier than the first preaching of the manuscript, the preliminary council at Northampton had met to consider the controversy between Edwards and the Northampton church which eventually lead to his dismissal.[253] The sermon begins by explaining the benefit of "thy father's commandment" and the "law of thy mother" as the guide to "direct and conduct" oneself on their way. What way it leads in, and how it guides and leads is what Edwards will explain as his points of explanation. First, Edwards will explain the qualities of the way and its qualities.[254]

In explaining the way, Edwards explains it is a way of duty that leads in the way of true virtue, to the business God "hath made us," in the way

[251]Edwards, "Grace in Lively Exercise of Excellent Benefit to Men as a Guide to Direct and Conduct Them in Their Way," ed. Kenneth P. Minkema, *Jonathan Edwards Sermon Index* (Sermon 948), (New Haven: Jonathan Edwards Center, Yale University), 1–15.

[252]Minkema, "Grace in Lively Exercise," 1–2.

[253]Minkema, "A Chronology of Edwards' Life and Writings" (Jonathan Edwards Center at Yale University).

[254]Edwards, "Grace in Lively Exercise," 3–4.

of truth and righteousness, agreeable to right reason, agreeable to the will of God (acceptable to Him), mortifies and removes corruption, enlightens the mind, and prevents men from going into sin. Instead of leading to the way of sin, it leads in the way of safety, the "narrow way" as referenced in Matt. 7:14. Edwards follows with scripture references to this way of safety (1 Pet. 3:13, Is. 33:15–16, 34:9, 40:13, Prov. 3:23, Ps. 91:11–12, 91:3, and Eccles. 9:12) and how those who walk it are safe from snares, beasts, enemies, poison, and the "arrows of God's wrath. Instead they are kept "close to God" and "out of the reach of innumerable calamities that others are exposed to."[255]

Edwards finishes this first point by showing how the way leads in peace and pleasantness. Edwards explains the way of grace is a way of the peace of conscience in troubling times. It gives the one who follows it a "pleasant prospect" of the future. This is because (and as a set up for his second point of the first explanation) the way of grace leads to an excellent end (future). This end results in the one following it living out what they were created for (worshipping God). Those who follow it to its end are satisfied, with an "enlightened, awakened conscience."[256]

The ways in which grace maintained in lively exercise are guided is given next. This includes deliverance from spiritual blindness and delusion, awakening of the mind to God's way, rectification of one's spiritual taste for goodness, singleness of focus on God's way, an enlightened mind to understand God's Word, beyond that the inclination to relish God's Word, and an interest in God's promises and guidance. This final point of being interested in God's promises and guidance is followed with scriptural references to Isaiah 42:16, 49:10–11, 57:18, 2 Cor. 5:7, and Heb. 12:2 (closing with the charge to look "unto Jesus the author and finisher of our faith").[257]

Edwards moves to his application. In reviewing the information he has given Edwards notes that "this may lead us to the true reason why some, that we have reason to think are true saints, are so much out of the way of their duty, and fall into so much mischief" (a probable direct reference to the controversy he was facing with regards to open communion, church membership, and discipline). He explains the "mischief" is due to not

[255]Edwards, "Grace in Lively Exercise," 4–6.

[256]Ibid., 6–9.

[257]Ibid., 9–10.

maintaining grace in lively exercise.[258] Edwards continues by showing the path of darkness followed by those in sin without any grace in their lives:

> Let such as are in this condition, consider what wretched guides they follow. You are led by your enemies. [You are] lead by your lusts. They are deceitful and fatal guides. [You are] lead by evil spirits. [You are] lead by a view to carnal objects; those you are constantly pursuing, and they are the devil's baits. [They are] held up before you in the way that leads to hell, to entice you on. [You] are lead blindfold. [You are] under constant delusion. If you knew who lead you, and knew where they were leading you, you would not go on so boldly, so securely, so obstinately against all that is said to reclaim you. You would be surprised. You would not dare to go forward a step further. If your eyes ben't opened now, hereafter they will be opened, and you will see your error.[259]

Next, Edwards gives more illustration to depraved the way is through showing how they are ensnared like a bird for a fowler, or the end of journey where there "is no way, no passage, from hell to heaven" (ref. Luke 16:26). Edwards explains there will be no guide, voice, star, compass, "glimmering of light," or Bible "containing rules" to lead them back to safety. This is followed up with an observation that there may be many "under great difficulties" wanting to know what to do, before Edwards transitions to his exhortation to "earnestly seek that you may live in the constant and lively exercise of grace."[260]

He closes by mentioning how through his sermon he has explained how great is his audience's need for a guide (the Word), how excellent of a guide the Word is, how "no other guides will avail with this" (the Word), and finally how this is a blessed guide (the Word) to lead them as they are walking "through the valley of the shadow of death" which he closes in visualization:

> [You will] not stumble in that dark valley. [You will] not be swallowed up and left in the darkness. [You will walk] in a path of light. [That light will be] like the pillar of cloud and fire to

[258] Edwards, "Grace in Lively Exercise," 10–11.

[259] Ibid., 11.

[260] Ibid., 11–13.

> Israel in that dark and stormy night, when passing through the Red Sea. [You will walk] in the right way to [the] gates of the celestial paradise, where you shall come to your home, your rest, and the blessed end of your wearisome journey.[261]

Grace Maintained in Lively Exercise is a Continual Safeguard to a Person[262]

Date: January 1750
Key Text: Prov. 6:22b – "When thou sleepest, it shall keep thee."

The second of the three sermons on Prov. 6:22, the manuscript for *Grace Maintained* was half the length of *Grace in Lively Exercise* (24 duodecimo leaves to 12). Like the first sermon, Edwards noted it too was repreached in 1752.[263] The key text from Prov. 6:22b is explained first as showing the benefit ("it shall keep thee") along with the circumstances ("When thou sleepest"). This is followed by the doctrine that the grace seen in the previous sermon, when maintained not only guides, but safeguards the follower continually. Edwards lays out what he intends to show in the sermon as the evils this grace "guards against" and "preserves from," how (and the means) it guards, and how it does so continually.[264]

The evils it safeguards are the corruption, Satan (citing Eph. 6:11), the "snares of an evil world" (citing Is. 40:31), the evil of "wicked men" (citing Eph. 6:16), "divine displeasure," spiritual darkness, the sting of temporal afflictions, anxiety over the world (citing Ps. 127:2), and fear over future evils (citing Heb. 2:15, Ps. 112:7, Is. 32:17, and 1 Cor. 15:55). Edwards then moves to his second point in showing the ways grace maintained is a safeguard by "natural influence," and by engaging "the watchful eye and mighty power of god to be our guard."[265]

The engagement of God (and His heart) in being the follower's guard is what Edwards emphasizes as he cites Ps. 11:7, 45:11, and Cant. 4:9 before referencing Noah, Joseph, and the patriarchs of the Old Testament from Gen. 15:11, 35:5, and Ps. 105:12. He references God as the pillar of

[261]Edwards, "Grace in Lively Exercise," 14.

[262]Edwards, "Grace Maintained in Lively Exercise is a Safeguard to a Person," ed. Kenneth P. Minkema, *Jonathan Edwards Sermon Index* (Sermon 949), (New Haven: Jonathan Edwards Center, Yale University), 1–10.

[263]Minkema, "Grace Maintained," 1–2.

[264]Edwards, "Grace Maintained," 3.

[265]Edwards, "Grace Maintained," 3–4.

cloud from Ex. 13:21 before noting the "virtue of God's promises" further citing Ps. 31:19–20, 33:18–19, 121, Prov. 16:7, and in noting the angels' participation in this protection cites Cant. 3:7. This leads to his final point of explaining how first it is a continual safeguard under all circumstances and through all changes. Edwards then shifts to how grace is the safeguard when followers are under most duress explaining each of the following points with several Old Testament Scripture references to highlight how they are guarded: when the follower is most opposed, when enemies are most numerous, when most "powerful and malignant enemies threaten," when assaults are "most violent," when they are most vulnerable and the enemy thinks "the day is their own, when others perish (noting Noah and Lot), and when they are most desperate with "no other hope of salvation."[266]

Edwards follows up with his application to those without grace to "seek the grace of God" noting how unsafe they are and how they are in real danger of sin, death, hell, Satan's rule, and God's wrath. For the godly, "to seek the lively exercises of grace," and to note the "calamities" of those without grace and "how visible are the benefits" of the exercises of their grace.

A Gracious Person is Never Alone But is Entertained with the Conversation of a Most Excellent Companion[267]

Date: January 1750
Key Text: Prov. 6:22c – "When thou awakest, it shall talk with thee."

In this third and final sermon on Prov. 6:22, *A Gracious Person is Never Alone* builds upon Edwards's first two discourses on what keeping "thy father's commandment" or knowing the Law and God's Word benefits those that do so. In this sermon which is slightly longer than *Grace Maintained*, Edwards offers the remembered Word as a constant companion for those that have maintained a "lively exercise" and have kept it in their heart. It goes with them, and converses with them as "an inner companion" especially during times of solitude. Like with the first two sermons, Edwards would preach this too at Stockbridge (in March of 1752).[268]

[266] Edwards, "Grace Maintained," 4–6.

[267] Edwards, "A Gracious Person is Never Alone But is Entertained with the Conversation of a Most Excellent Companion," ed. Kenneth P. Minkema, *Jonathan Edwards Sermon Index* (Sermon 950), (New Haven: Jonathan Edwards Center, Yale University), 1–13.

[268] Minkema, "A Gracious Person is Never Alone," 1–3.

God's Word maintained in the heart seen in *Grace Maintained* was a constant safeguard, in *A Gracious Person is Never Alone*, it is an eager companion prompting the follower to "have their first thoughts on divine things." This is because, as Edwards notes in his doctrine, the person is "entertained from within himself" in conversation with a "most excellent companion" when they are alone. As points of explanation Edwards offers that grace maintained in the person allows the companionship, that entertains the person's mind with "most desirable conversation," constantly and especially when they are alone.[269]

In explaining how grace communicates within the person it is maintained in, Edwards notes that it "excites affections" in the person as it were a "friend conversing with us." This is "Christ in the soul by his Spirit" speaking to the person who answers in "holy breathing" and ecstatic "prayers and praises." The "desirable conversation" this produces for the follower is profitable and pleasant. This is because the grace is a "divine light" enlightening the mind of the follower and instructing them "about the most important and excellent things." And further it is a perfect companionship with Jesus Christ:

> By this means, a person is brought to converse with Christ as an intimate friend. There is no jar or discord; nothing to spoil or mar the intercourse. But Christ appears clothed not only in glory, but in love, instructing the soul in the like friendly manner as he anciently instructed the disciples. John 15:15, "I have called you friends." This is the best companion under affliction. Conversing in such a manner doth most effectually support and comfort the mind, and assuage grief and drive away clouds of darkness.[270]

Edwards moves on to explain the constancy of the companionship of grace citing Rom. 10:16 to illustrate how grace will go with the person who maintains it wherever they go, and in whatever they do as it is in their hearts, and is faithful even when earthly friends fail. The final point of explanation is how grace is especially with the follower when they are alone, noting how "the most remarkable instances" of "saints favored with" conversation with God was when they were alone (referencing Abraham, Jacob, Moses, Elijah, Elisha, and Mary).[271]

[269]Edwards, "A Gracious Person is Never Alone," 4–5.

[270]Ibid., 5–7.

[271]Edwards, "A Gracious Person is Never Alone," 7–9.

For his application, Edwards first notes as way of information those who do not employ themselves in this conversation and contemplation are most likely not maintaining a connection to God's grace. Next, he exhorts his audience to seek out grace as a companion because it is first what Christians do, and they are very lonely in a dark wilderness without it. Third is it will make other company "profitable and pleasant," and fourth is it will "fit them for heavenly society."[272]

Edwards then closes with direction that would apply to the controversial situation with youths causing mischief at Northampton. First, he directs his audience to examine the company they keep and "take heed" as they can be a cause of "great temptations," can keep "grace very low," and that during evil times bad company is "very infectious." Instead, they should retire for the purpose of maintaining grace in "religious exercises" as Edward's second direction before his final direction to care for how they spend their time alone.[273]

In this series on the principles of knowing God and His Word through meditating on it and keeping it as a constant companion, one can see how Edwards sought to respond to what he saw as a culture crisis among his congregation at Northampton. His prescription was for them to stop being so enamored with the things of the world. He desired them to again be awakened to see the value and necessity of God's Word to restore his congregation in faithful fellowship.

In observing his notes that he then repreached the sermons to his new congregation at Stockbridge (whether it was his colonial, Native, or combined congregations), it is noteworthy he chooses these sermons to set the foundation for how they should build this new culture he is seeking to establish at Stockbridge. It will be one built on the Bible as the foundation for their fellowship and growth. This shows the contrast of his purpose in reawakening affections to God and His Word among his Northampton audience, and possibly his choice to start as a building block for awakening his Stockbridge congregations.

[272]Ibid., 9–12.

[273]Ibid, 12.

Great Encouragement for Young Persons to Seek Christ Earnestly and Early[274]

Date: August 1756
Key Text: Proverbs 8:17b – "I love them that love me; and those that seek me early shall find me."

Great Encouragement was a sermon preached by Edwards at a catechizing of English children at Stockbridge in August of 1756. While the title may be long, the sermon manuscript itself was shorter than *Sovereignty* and *Holiness of God,* written on two octavo-sized leaves made from a discarded letter cover. It does feature two doctrines and an application and encourages the children to embrace piety and the love of Christ in conversion.[275]

The sermon is wholly in outline form, written by Edwards to give himself the main points to emphasize to his audience. It begins with two points of introduction of the text; he notes there is a privilege (God's love to those that love Him) and how to obtain said love (seeking Him early). The first doctrine (labeled Doctrine and not Subject, unlike *Sovereignty* and *Holiness of God*) is the happiness of those who love Jesus Christ and are loved by Him.[276] He first notes those who truly love Christ (which gives an example of his outline format):

1. They [are they] that see him to be more excellent than all.
2. [They] are brought in their hearts to choose him above all.
3. [They are brought] to place their greatest delight in him.
4. [They are brought] to be willing to give themselves wholly to him.
5. [They are brought] to follow and serve him as long as they live.[277]

Secondly, Edwards notes those who do love Christ "certainly depend" on Christ loving them in His death for them, His reconciliation with them, His prizing of them, His delight in them, and His seeking after their good. Third is why Christ loves those who love Him and are undeserving of His love, loved first by Him, loved by Him through grace freely given, give love to Him, and are delightful to Him because of the "beauty he himself has put upon them." For his second doctrine, Edwards notes those who earnestly

[274]Edwards, "Great Encouragement for Young Persons to Seek Christ Earnestly and Early," ed. R. Craig Woods, *Jonathan Edwards Sermon Index* (Sermon 1171), (New Haven: Jonathan Edwards Center, Yale University), 1–6.

[275]R. Craig Woods, "Great Encouragement," 1–2.

[276]Edwards, "Great Encouragement," 2–3.

[277]Ibid., 3.

seek Christ early in life will find Him. His only notes for this second doctrine are given (as another example of the brevity of said notes):

> [If persons will] seek him earnestly, and see[k] him early, they have great advantages.
>
> *First*. What evidence [there is] of this.
>
> *Second*. Reason.[278]

After this second doctrine, Edwards finishes with his application, which includes the "infinite importance" of seeking Christ, the rarity of the opportunity to seek Christ, the uncertainty of how many opportunities there will be to seek Christ, the waste of throwing the opportunity away, the disadvantage of delaying seeking Christ, and "how much sorrow will be prevented."[279] Edwards closes by giving himself notes of what to relate to his audience of his personal experience of those who did not seek Christ and the joy of finding Christ:

How you will probably lament it hereafter.
When old. I have heard.
On a deathbed. I have heard.
At the day of judgment.
Forever.
Eighth. How much rejoicing it will be an occasion of.
[There shall be] joy in heaven [Luke 15:7].
Angels [Luke 15:10].
Jesus Christ.
God.
You yourself.
[You will] rejoice at the day of your conversion.
[You will] rejoice all your life.
When you come to die.
When you meet Christ and the saints in heaven.
[When you] meet angels.
[When you] meet all the saints and angels together at day of judgment.
[There will be] no end of the joy.[280]

[278] Edwards, "Great Encouragement," 3–4.

[279] Ibid., 3–4.

[280] Edwards, "Great Encouragement," 4–5. Of note are the biblical references to Luke 15 and how the outline reads like a verse in a poem or song with abbreviated, staccato statements to engage Edwards's audience. Ibid.

In this last portion of the sermon is Edwards's earnestness of invitation and argumentation for repentance for those in his care (in this case, children). He presents them in this section with the options of lamenting not seeking Christ or the joy and benefits of seeking Christ.

Observations from Edwards's Colonial Preaching

Throughout Edwards's colonial ministry, his preaching has a recurrent theme: the movement from the "plain style" of preaching to the stir of affections beyond knowledge and routine. Edwards's purpose was shown to be moving his congregations (and, at times, especially those youths therein) to live wholeheartedly for Christ. Edwards would want to pursue his audience with the thematic application of his key texts. This had at its foundation that "plain style" of tethering his sermons to biblical references peppered through his doctrinal sections to explain further and illustrate each sermon's thematic vision.

In *The Value of Salvation*, Edwards uses rich biblical imagery to capture the terror of judgment and the beauty and joy of eternal salvation to help a biblically literate audience grasp the value of their salvation. Both *The Value of Salvation* and *Poverty of Spirit* were lecture-driven sermons, with Edwards showcasing his ability to relate deep points of doctrine to his audience. In *Poverty of Spirit*, Edwards shows the poverty of life before Christ and the replaced glory of heaven afterward to give his audience a sense of the beauty of God and His Salvation again.

In *Christ, the Light of the World* and *Light in a Dark World, a Dark Heart*, Edwards shows his emphasis on moving beyond explaining the key texts of John 8:12 and 2 Peter 1:19 and moving his listeners on the journey of understanding the qualities of Christ being the light of the world, and their benefit in having Christ as the light to overcome the darkness of the world. He reinforces this by showing their spiritual blindness and the glory of Christ awakening them to glorious sight (affection). *Christ the Light of the World* showcases Edwards's rich metaphysical language of dark blindness and glorious light. Edwards does the same with *Our Present and Immediate Business* in contrasting eternal misery and happiness in light of faithful response. Edwards's use of reason and rhetorical repetition of logic is showcased in *All God's Methods*. Then again, Edwards's illustrative language of feasting is given through his sacramental sermon, *The Spiritual Blessings of the Gospel Represented by a Feast*.

In *The Spiritual Blessings of the Gospel Represented by a Feast,* Edwards again uses visualization to persuade his audience of the rich feast of salvation that awaited them. *The Spiritual Blessings of the Gospel Represented by a Feast* and *Receiving the Blessed Fruits* also show Edwards's emphasis on giving the context of the key text he would preach. In *Receiving the Blessed Fruits,* Edwards also emphasizes abiding affection for God and His Word.

Through *Receiving the Blessed Fruits* and *The Pure in Heart Blessed,* Edwards's passion for awakening drowsy congregants uninspired by God's Spirit and His Word is seen in his call to urgent action. In *The Pure in Heart Blessed,* Edwards exhorts his audience to become pure in heart by showing again the beauty and sweetness of God's pure blessing for them. This is even more evident in *Honey from the Rock,* where Edwards uses the image of honey and stone foundation to show his audience the sweetness and firmness of God's salvation. Purpose and pleasure in God's service are the biblical themes given by Edwards in *Serving God in Heaven,* as Edwards again shows his ability to illustrate heaven's beauty and pleasure.

In *All God's Methods,* Edwards shows his ability to logically argue for a point of doctrine to a biblically literate audience (on the necessity of compulsion). He also demonstrates his logical arguments in the same sermon by showing the reasonableness of following God's command because of His infinite authority and being.

The focus of *Self-Examination and the Lord's Supper* shows Edwards's intention on his audience and their context. He preaches to an audience who are familiar with the Lord's Supper and presses them to evaluate themselves and whether they have taken it for granted. This is in line with examining whether the Lord's Supper, God, and His Word have become something devalued in their hearts instead of having an earnest affection and reverence for them.

In *East of Eden,* Edwards goes beyond informing his audience about the Fall but illustrates the weight of the Fall and what it meant to be cast out of Eden, to be corrupted by a sin nature after the Fall, and to be at enmity with God. *The Time of Youth* is another good example of logical argumentation (in this case, for attaining piety in one's youth before hard-heartedness).

The hope and strong foundation of the Gospel to build upon and to replenish the arid soil of apathy and dryness is seen through *Honey from the Rock* and *Foundation of a Good Hope,* while the illustration of desolation at being cut off in the Fall was given by Edwards in his *East of Eden* sermon. In *The Time of Youth* and *Great Encouragement,* like *Receiving the Blessed Fruits,*

Edwards highlights the need for urgent action he saw as necessary for the youth of his congregation.

God is the People's Portion showed how Edwards would go beyond explaining a passage to explaining what it means (like *East of Eden,* though in the case of *God is the People's Portion* explaining what it meant to be an inheritor of God). Like with *The Value of Salvation, Tis Not Inconsistent* showed Edwards's ability to illustrate the terror and eternality of judgment. *Tis Not Inconsistent* showcases Edwards's ability both to visually illuminate points (the terror and eternality of judgment) and logically argue for God's authority, immutability, and sovereignty.

Edwards's preaching of terrible and pleasant eternal options in *The Sins of Youth,* like *The Value of Salvation,* shows Edwards's care in presenting biblical argumentation for his audience familiar with the Bible. *The Lord's Supper* shows Edwards's purpose in stirring affection in his audience not only in "memory" but in their practice.

God is the People's Portion is a sermon custom-fit for a biblically knowledgeable audience to show the richness and blessing of their inheritance in Christ, challenging them to appreciate and not squander it. Likewise, *Zeal an Essential Virtue* stirs up zeal in the midst of an apathetic congregation. Another sermon highlighting Edwards's targeted homiletics to an audience influenced by Enlightenment thought is *Tis Not Inconsistent,* given as a response to the philosophical dismissal of the eternality of condemnation for the unregenerate. In line with *Tis Not Inconsistent* is the sermon *The Sins of Youth,* targeting those in Edwards's audience who might have thought to dismiss the seriousness of living worldly lives.

Light in a Dark World is another sermon showing Edwards's ability to illustrate the beauty of God's redemptive light (in a similar manner to Heaven is a World of Love). *Foundation of a Good Hope* has a similar theme to *Honey From the Rock*: Christ, the foundation for all hope. It also features Edwards's passion in stirring affections from apathy. Like *Foundation of a Good Hope*, the final exhortation in *Mercy and Not Sacrifice* shows Edwards's passion for his audience to have not only biblical knowledge but also pious action. This is similar to his stirring of affections in *Zeal an Essential Virtue* in rallying his audience to awaken from their slumber and awaken to obtain the world for Christ "as it were by conquest."

Christ the River has a section structured in a catechetical manner for his audience to think about the Gospel and whether they have accepted its benefits. *Sovereignty of God's Mercy* is another sermon noted for Edwards using biblical references to argue for a doctrine (God's sovereign mercy). *The*

Holiness of God shows Edwards's progression of outlining his manuscripts while maintaining robust biblical references and arguments. The catechetical sermon *Great Encouragement* is an example of Edwards's earnest preaching of invitation and argumentation for repentance for children in his care. In the sermon, he presents them with the options of rejecting the Gospel (leading to lament) and of seeking Christ (leading to "no end of joy."

In analyzing *Watchman for Souls*, the sermon gets at the heart of Edwards's view of his homiletical duty: to care for the souls of his audience. *Watchman for Souls* showed Edwards's serious responsibility for those under his ministry, which he then related to Jonathan Judd.

Of special note should be the three short sermon series preached by Edwards. The first was the two-part sermon series on Proverbs 10. *Dreadful Fear* and *Desire of the Righteous* show Edwards's purpose in visualizing the horror of God's wrath in hell in *Dreadful Fear*, and then the beauty of fulfilled righteous desire in *Desire of the Righteous*. The eternality of fear and torment of hell (juxtaposed with the complete fulfillment and peace of heaven) are the purpose for Edwards, to stir the affections of repentance in an apathetic audience in need of a fresh understanding of the stakes of salvation.

Second was the four-part series from Acts that showed how Edwards could build upon a central theme of regeneration and repentance in first showing the spiritual blindness of the sinner (in *Turned From Darkness to Light*) before salvation to their spiritual sight being restored in conversion. The second sermon (*Turned From Satan to God*) again visualizes the horror of being subjugated under the dominion of Satan to the glorious freedom of God. In his final two sermons (*Turned From Wrath to Forgiveness* and *Turned From an Alien to an Heir*) from Acts Edwards then visualizes what forgiveness and inheritance mean for the converted sinner. Throughout the Acts series it is clear Edwards places a premium on being engaged with the Word and appealing to his audience to become more engaged with the Bible.

In the three-part series from Proverbs 6:22, it is an especially poignant series to examine as it was during the transition of Edwards being dismissed from Northampton and moving on to Stockbridge. Edwards shows in this series his desire to minister to the end to what he sees as a wayward congregation. The series is focused on the "lively exercises" Edwards believes will serve his audience the best. To be committed to the Word, and to prayer, and to fellowship with other believers is the greatest desire Edwards hopes his audience will have. Edwards believes this commitment will lead to the betterment of the culture for the congregation.

The desire for his congregation to be focused on the Word and prayer is culminated through his third and final sermon (*A Gracious Person is Never Alone*) which offers the Bible as the best companion to safeguard oneself and to have their "most excellent companion" to enrich and guide their lives in true worship and beauty. This series is then repreached as a bedrock for his congregation at Stockbridge. This shows a threaded centrality for Edwards in both congregations to be built on the foundation of God's Word to guide his preaching and ministry.

Through the foundation of the "plain style" of preaching under which Edwards learned to preach, Edwards moves to observing and reacting to the felt needs of his audience to have vital affection for God and His Word. Through a variety of homiletical methods (rhetorical repetition, topical imagery, and affectional urgency, among others), Edwards responds to what he saw as the open avenues of delivering the Gospel message for his audience. As will be seen in the following chapter, these homiletical methods had to be altered in light of a vastly different audience with a different level of biblical literacy and cultural demographic. Edwards would respond to this opportunity and give an example of adaptableness for preachers to follow.

CHAPTER 4: EDWARDS'S HOMILETICS AT STOCKBRIDGE

Background on Native American Missions in Colonial America

> Perhaps the wonder is not that Europeans found it so difficult to evangelize Native Americans, but that any of the Indians took the Christian message for themselves.[1]

Mark Noll writes the above in *The Old Religion in a New World: The History of North American Christianity,* and it speaks to the swirling obstacles that missionaries from England and elsewhere in the New World faced. In moving to Stockbridge, Jonathan Edwards joined ranks with many others who had come before (some with pure intentions, others with less noble aims) for mission and ministry among the Mahican and varied Native American tribes of New England.

In the 17th century, only the Puritans initiated missions on any notable scale in New England. A decision the earlier Puritans evaluated, and which Edwards later advocated for, was the instruction and use of the English language among the Native Americans. Earlier in the 17th century, John Eliot had advocated for using the native languages and translating the Bible and catechisms into them.[2]

[1]Mark A. Noll, *The Old Religion in a New World: The History of North American Christianity* (Grand Rapids: Eerdmans, 2002), Loc. 420–421, Kindle.

[2]Hugh Amory and David D. Hall, ed., *A History of the Book in America: The Colonial Book in the Atlantic World* (Chapel Hill, NC: University of North Carolina Press, 2007), 15. Eliot brought assumptions about biblical literacy and knowledge for those wanting to be candidates

However, by 1710, Cotton Mather would see differently as he wrote the New England Company, stating, "The best thing we can do for our Indians is to Anglicize them in all agreeable instances; and in that of language as well as others."[3] Mather wrote this as part of a response to ordering a third edition of the Eliot Indian Bible in 1710. He hoped "that by good English schools among the Indians, and some other fit methods, the grand intention of Anglicizing them would be soon accomplished."[4] It is important to note both Mather's denigration of the Native languages in calling it a "barbarous lingo" and his concern about the varied differences in dialect. Mather also noted there was an issue with Eliot's translations, which he observed was a "grief to" Native Americans, who could not understand Eliot's translation. His final argument is in line with the desire for Native Americans to be educated in biblical literacy:

> Such a knowledge in their Bibles, as our English ordinarily have in ours, they seldom any of them have; and there seems to be as much difficulty to bring them unto a competent knowledge of the Scriptures, as it would be to get a sensible acquaintance with the English tongue.[5]

Monaghan notes, in contrast to earlier views, the imposition of English linguistics as "coercive cultural change," wherein the missionary is seen as a "cultural revolutionary," is condemnable as the limitations for response for the Native Americans. She notes the new opinion among scholars is of the Native American defense of their culture in adapting to the new imposition of European influence:

> This new view suggests that in order to evaluate missions from the Indian point of view, we must consider whether or not the Indians' acceptance of Christianity helped them to preserve their ethnic identity and even facilitated their survival as a people. From this point of view, the missions, in introducing the Indians

for church membership. This included knowing the Bible, Christian doctrine as outlined in a catechism, the ability to testify to their spiritual experience, and virtues in line with Christian morality. Ibid.

[3] Letter reprinted in George Parker Winship, *The Cambridge Press 1638–1692: A Re-examination of the Evidence Concerning the Bay Psalm Book and the Eliot Indian Bible* (Freeport, NY: Book for Libraries Press, 1968), 175.

[4] Winship, *The Cambridge Press 1638–1692*, 175.

[5] Ibid., 175–176.

to literacy, are said to have provided them with a "practical technique" that helped them adjust to a new world.[6]

In his article, Silverman argues the Wampanoags of seventeenth-century Martha's Vineyard would have an "impressive knowledge of Puritan doctrine" through a process of "religious translation" as an acknowledgment that native and Christian beliefs were "analogous at several critical points." This religious translation would occur on Martha's Vineyard in three overlapping stages: first with an invitation as a response (in the mid to late 1640s) to an argument Thomas Mayhew and his assistant Hiacoomes crafted and relayed of God being the "source of the Indians' spiritual power" and protecting them from disease; second (in the 1650s and 1660s) Mayhew and other mainland missionaries translating and dissecting Christian concepts into meaningful Wampanoag words and ideas for native audiences; and third (following King Philip's War of 1675–1676) Wampanoags leading in their own indigenized mission movement.[7]

The emphasis on literacy was "an essential component of Missionary activity," especially in the Protestant culture of biblicism, noted earlier by passing legislation related to biblicism in Massachusetts, Connecticut, and New Haven (then a separate colony). Like with "white New Englanders," reading was seen as "an essential literacy skill which both boys and girls had to acquire in order to become good Christians." John Eliot, who pastored in Roxbury, Massachusetts, translated the Bible into the native dialect. The translation was called the *Indian Bible*.[8]

Monaghan views Experience Mayhew's *Indian Converts* (1727) as helpful for seeing the missionary work among Native Americans done in the colonial Massachusetts area from a Native American perspective. *Indian Converts*, published through an intermediary, the earlier *Tears of Repentance* by Thomas Mayhew and John Eliot (1653), and Samson Occom's autobiography (the first Native American to publish in English), give a picture of the response to the mission work preceding Edwards's undertaking at Stockbridge (and in Occom's works during and after).[9]

[6] E. Jennifer Monaghan, "She Loved to Read in Good Books," *History of Education Quarterly* 30, no. 4 (Winter 1990): 494.

[7] David J. Silverman, "Indians, Missionaries, and Religious Translation: Creating Wampanoag Christianity in Seventeenth-Century Martha's Vineyard," *The William and Mary Quarterly* 62, no. 2 (April 2005): 146.

[8] Monaghan, 494–497.

[9] Amory and Hall, *History of the Book in America*, 23.

Thomas Kidd notes it was Christian Native Americans who had proved effectual in both conserving distinct Native identity and through resistance to assimilation into the "dominant English society," creating their own "distinct forms of evangelical Christianity."[10] As noted above, examining the three works gives insight into the response to earnest Christian mission among Native Americans in New England during the 18th century. This insight is crucial to seeing the importance of what will be examined at Stockbridge, especially in Edwards's ministry therein.

John Eliot and Thomas Mayhew's *Tears of Repentance* (1653)

Tears of Repentance, published in 1653, is a first-hand narrative of the mission at present-day Martha's Vineyard (called Nope in the work by the Indians living there).[11] It begins with several addresses by Thomas Mayhew, John Eliot, and Richard Mather. In one of the first addresses, written on October 22, 1652, Mayhew relates that the Indians (to which he names "about 30 Indian children" at the school in 1651) were "constant attenders of the Word of the Lord, and some of them (I hope) conscionable seekers after the knowledge of God."[12] He adds the eagerness of those in the area of sending more to the school as they are "apt to learn." Following the addresses are testimonies collected from oral "confessions" members gave before the church elders at Martha's Vineyard. The confessions are similar to those recorded by Thomas Shepherd, as related in chapter three of the present work.

Of note in the first confession from Totherswamp is his conviction that being out of the will of God caused him to fear "that I do so, when I teach the Indians, because I cannot teach them right, and thereby make the Word of God vain. Again, Christ said *If the blind lead the blind they will both fall into the ditch*. Therefore I feared that I am one blind, and when I teach other Indians I shall cause them to fall into the ditch."[13]

[10]Kidd, *The Great Awakening*, 190.

[11]Laura Arnold Liebman, ed., *Experience Mayhew's Indian Converts: A Cultural Edition*, (Amherst, MA: University of Massachusetts Press, 2008).

[12]John Eliot and Thomas Mayhew, *Tears of Repentance: or, a further Narrative of the Progress of the Gospel Amongst the Indians in New England* (1653; repr., Ann Arbor: *Early English Books Text Creation Partnership*, 2008).

[13]Eliot and Mayhew, *Tears of Repentance*. Included in this confession is a quote from Matt 15:2–3, 14.

The confessions are given in two parts, the first before they were converted and the other after. In testimony of his life before, Monequassun (who was the schoolmaster at the mission) said in wanting to stay at Cohannet, he would offer false prayers, "but desired a little to learn the Catechism on the Lecture days, and I did learn the Ten Commandments, and after that, all the points in the Catechism."[14] Like in Totherswamp's confession, Monequassun quoted from several scriptures, including James 1:5. He also showed his desire to know God's Word (biblical literacy) is tied with education and literacy in general.[15]

Another member named Ponampam referenced several scriptures in his confession; however, he tied each scripture remembrance (most notably for himself, the creation account from Genesis) to the Catechism he knew from childhood. This confession shows the instruction and Bible memorization that had taken place in his education. In his confession, Nookau is recorded as understanding the difference between the Catechism and the Bible itself: "I believe the Catechism we learn to be the (sic) according to the Word of God, but the writings of the Bible are the very Words of God."[16] One of the final confessions recorded is by Owussumag. He is recorded as stating that he "hated instruction by the Word of God" at first but later "feared when I heard the word read and taught, and I was glad to hear the Word of God."[17]

Experience Mayhew's *Indian Converts* (1727)

At the beginning of his narrative on the work done in colonial New England, Experience Mayhew advises readers that those being ministered to (the Native tribes) were "a great measure destitute of those advantages of literature, which the English and many other nations enjoy."[18] He adds that a considerable number learned to read and write, though they had fewer written works in their languages, and few read or wrote well in English. He explains this is why there were not many written accounts from the Indians in America about their own experiences. Mayhew's purpose in his work is to "keep as much, as may be to the very words of the Indians themselves, that

[14]Eliot and Mayhew, *Tears of Repentance*.

[15]Ibid.

[16]Eliot and Mayhew, *Tears of Repentance*.

[17]Ibid.

[18]Experience Mayhew, *Indian converts: or, Some account of the lives and dying speeches of a considerable number of the Christianized Indians of Martha's Vineyard, in New-England* (London: Samuel Gerrish, 1727), xxiii.

the simplicity of their intentions may, by their own simple expressions, the better appear; since it is not the learning of any, but the piety of some, that is here designed to be discovered."[19]

Mayhew starts with accounts from several ruling pastors, ruling elders, and deacons who were accounted as "godly persons." The first account is from Hiacoomes, who is identified as "the first Christian Indian, and minister on the island of Martha's Vineyard." Mayhew then references Thomas Mayhew's goal in ministering to Hiacoomes during his ministry. Experience Mayhew relates how Thomas Mayhew ministered daily to Hiacoomes as the latter had a "disposition to hear and receive instruction," which led him to increase daily in knowledge and eagerly want to "suck in the instructions given him."[20]

Mayhew records that, though he faced opposition from those in his tribe (especially a grievous blow from one named Sagamore), Hiacoomes "earnestly desires to learn to read and having a primer given him, he carried it out with, till, by the help of such as were willing to instruct him, he attained the end for which he desired it."[21] Hiacoomes's desire again shows the reaction and willingness of those receiving ministry to learn to read for knowledge tied with the desire for biblical literacy. Through his perseverance in the face of persecution from his brethren, Mayhew relates that Hiacoomes was asked by many of the Indians to preach to them, which he did along with Thomas Mayhew. Mayhew notes this marked the first public preaching to the Indians of that area. Those taught by Hiacoomes would then meet together; Mayhew called them the *praying Indians*.[22]

Indians associated Europeans initially with spiritual power (*manit*) due to their technology (ships, fire-arms, knives, magnifying glasses, etc.), though they did not consider them (or as will be seen with Hiacoomes) as "being a spirit." When they would shout "*manitou, manitou*" at the Europeans, it was, in essence, saying, "You have *manit*" (spiritual power) rather than "You are a god." At first, they didn't see Europeans or native Christians as intrinsically different than the *Pawwaws* (spiritually potent native shamans).[23]

[19]Mayhew, *Indian Converts,* xxiv.

[20]Ibid. Also found in Mayhew, *Indian Converts: A Cultural Edition*, 95–96.

[21]Mayhew, *Indian Converts: A Cultural Edition*, 97–99.

[22]Mayhew, *Indian Converts: A Cultural Edition*, 99–100.

[23]David J. Silverman, *Red Brethren: The Brothertown and Stockbridge Indians and the Problem of Race in Early America*, (Ithaca, NY: Cornell University Press, 2016), 12.

Mayhew writes one of the Pawwaws (who were against Hiacoomes and the *praying Indians*) was a converted *Sachim* (tribal leader) who, in his "confession," noted he prayed to his god (who appeared to him in the form of a snake) to kill Hiacoomes for seven years, but, after seeing his prayers as ineffectual, converted to Christ and abandoned praying or "employing" the former god in anything again.[24] In the face of a similar challenge from a Pawwaw, Hiacoomes declared all the Pawwaws on the island could do all they could against him, and he would "without feare set himself against them."[25]

Mayhew gives this story and others as examples of the health of the praying Indians before 1650, at which time Hiacoomes was first afflicted with the death of his son. Hiacoomes, however, showed his faithfulness and abandoned his former Native funeral rites for a newfound Christian practice of mourning.[26] Silverman writes about the Wampanoags' reform of their "death ways" and burial rites, forsaking their traditional and "taboo" native practices and "promoting the faith among their own kind."[27]

Hiacoomes was the first minister to the Indians at Martha's Vineyard and became the first ordained Indian pastor in North America, along with another Indian, Tackanash, who became the first ordained Indian teacher.[28] Later, a "Mr. Japhet" was given charge by Hiacoomes (who had reached a "great age) after the death of Tackanash. During this time, John Mayhew (Thomas Mayhew's son and Experience Mayhew's father) was also ordained and preached to the Indians at Martha's Vineyard.[29]

Tackanash is recorded by Mayhew as receiving a charge to plant a second church on the island to reach more of the inhabitants with the Gospel. Mayhew describes Tackanash like Hiacoomes, wanting daily to grow in knowledge and understanding. Mayhew writes, "To this end he not only followed his study and reading closely, allowing himself, as I am credibly informed, but little time for such diversions" for further instruction and understanding.[30]

[24]Mayhew, *Indian Converts: A Cultural Edition*, 100–102.

[25]Silverman, "Indians, Missionaries, and Religious Translation," 156.

[26]Mayhew, *Indian Converts: A Cultural Edition*, 100–102.

[27]Silverman, "Indians, Missionaries, and Religious Translation," 165.

[28]Mayhew, *Indian Converts: A Cultural Edition*, 100–109. Also in Silverman, "Indians, Missionaries, and Religious Translation," 163.

[29]Ibid., 100–109.

[30]Mayhew, *Indian Converts: A Cultural Edition*, 108–111.

Mayhew esteems Wunnanauhkomun as one who "constantly read the Scriptures," sang parts of Psalms in the morning and evening, and "very frequently and diligently instruct his children and household in the things of God ... [he] used also frequently to catechize the children of the town, yea and some that were grown up likewise."[31] Janawannit is given as another example of a minister who was diligent in biblical study and daily singing of Psalms to his family. Paul (also called Mashquattuhkooit), a deacon of an Indian church at Martha's Vineyard until he died in 1688, likewise is shown as one who diligently read Scriptures, sang Psalms, and catechized his children.[32] These examples show not only the initial individual reaction to the ministry but also the system employed and passed on in catechizing, discipling, and building a culture of biblical literacy through education within this Native Community. Catechizing and discipling are shown by Mayhew as the assumed responsibilities of the head of the households within the community in the testimony of Assaquanhut, a ruling elder on the island.[33]

Assaquanhut's testimony shows the importance of individualized instruction that would be crucial to Edwards's ministry vision at Stockbridge. Mayhew notes one Abel Wauwompuhque, who after the "Psalter was printed for the use of the Indians in 1709 ... delighted much to read and meditate therein; he therefore carried it about with him wherever he went to work, and whenever he sat down to rest him, he would look into it."[34] Those printed works dedicated to the ministry among the Indians were well responded to, as can be seen through the testimony of Samuel Coomes (the youngest son of Hiacoomes), of whom Mayhew writes, "[He] also read the Scriptures, and frequently sung Psalms in his house, and was careful to instruct his children in their catechisms, and bring them up in the nurture and admonition of the Lord."[35] Significantly, Coomes was not called a minister, deacon, or elder but was still expected to lead and instruct the members of his household, even as a lay member of the church.

[31]Ibid., 112–113.

[32]Ibid., 113–119.

[33]Mayhew, *Indian Converts: A Cultural Edition*, 122–124.

[34]Mayhew, *Indian Converts: A Cultural Edition*, 162–164. Mayhew was actually the translator of the bilingual *Massachuset Psalter* of 1709. Monaghan, "She Loved to Read in Good Books," 521.

[35]Mayhew, *Indian Converts: A Cultural Edition*, 182–186. Mayhew notes Coomes's one fault was his reticence of receiving the Lord's Supper due to Coomes's self-evaluation of being "not well qualified for the enjoyment of so high a privilege." Ibid., 188–189.

After the section on religious men (non-preachers, elders, or deacons), Mayhew then writes about religious women giving their testimonies. One such testimony was of Abigail Kesoehtaut, who, Mayhew writes, "loved to read in good books," and, after being married and having children, "did herself teach them to read, and did otherwise carefully instruct them" though she had not received schooling.[36] In writing of her desire to reach others with the Gospel, Mayhew writes:

> Having thus obtained peace in believing, she opened her mouth in the praises of God to others. She told those that were about her, that what she had formerly heard of the power and mercy of God, she did now find and experience to be true . . . she then earnestly called on her relations and friends, to choose God for their portion, and love, fear, and obey him all the days of their lives.[37]

In the testimony of Abiah Paaonit, Mayhew mentions the instruction given to her by her parents, Jonathan and Rachel Amos. They "took care to teach her to read when she was a child, and did otherwise well instruct her; so that she was a person of good knowledge in the things of God."[38] Jonathan and Rachel's instruction shows again the communal charge in religious upbringing instilled in those in the church and surrounding missions at Martha's Vineyard.

In another picture of the positive response by those at Martha's Vineyard to the resources provided to them, one Sarah (named as the wife of Japheth Hannit) is reported by Mayhew as not highly literate, yet still "read frequently in such books as she could make the most advantage by: and Mr. Perkin's *Six Principles of Religion*, translated in to the Indian tongue, was what she took great delight in reading of."[39] Mary Coshomon is an example of someone who was given printed resources, though there was not a school for instruction nearby. Due to this, Mayhew writes "she was a diligent instructor of her children; and one little girl in particular, which she

[36] Ibid., 234–239.

[37] Mayhew, *Indian Converts: A Cultural Edition*, 238–239.

[38] Ibid., 248–249. It is also notable in Mayhew's testimony of Abiah that he does not shrink from also pointing out faults as he states "only one failing she was guilty of, she was too apt to be offended, and to resent any injury which she received higher than she should have done; but then she would be easily satisfied, and reconciled to the person that wronged her, or which she supposed to have done so." Ibid.

[39] Ibid., 258–259.

could not send to school because there was none near, she did herself teach to read, and say her Catechism competently well by that time she was six years old, and did otherwise well instruct her."[40]

In giving the testimony of Elizabeth Urquat, Mayhew shows the assumed link between literacy, biblical literacy, and salvation by noting Urquat, while young, was "put to an English master on the mainland, who neither taught her to read nor took care to instruct her in the principles of the true religion, the knowledge whereof is necessary to life eternal."[41] Mayhew's next example, Margaret Osooit, shows the converse as Osooit was raised to be literate and knowledgeable about God. He notes she, like others, would "often read the Word of God" and other books translated into the Indian tongues. She would utilize those resources not only for herself but also to train her children in reading and biblical knowledge. Mayhew writes of her children, "Several of them with tears told me what pains she used to take with them, as by teaching them their Catechisms, and also reading the Scriptures to them, and pressing them to the duties mentioned in them."[42]

Mary Manhut, given as another example of one who was instructed to read and catechized, shows the desire of many at Martha's Vineyard to be immersed in the Bible, even as they were dying. Mayhew writes that as she was dying, she "earnestly desired" to hear the preaching of the Word. Her father, Hosea Manhut (a pastor), was the one who would preach from John 4:42. Hosea would also sing the fourth Psalm with her and pray. Another woman Hosea would comfort at the time of her death was Rachel Wompanummoo, who had learned to read not only Indian books but also English ones and would read at every opportunity. [43]

In writing of three youths who had passed at 16 years old (Abigail Kenump), 17 years old (Jedidah Hannit), and 18 years old (Jeremiah Wesachippau), Mayhew notes they took advantage of the ministry of their parents in educating them in literacy and the knowledge of God. He writes that all three earnestly desired to read and learn more about God through the Bible and their catechisms.[44]

[40]Mayhew, *Indian Converts: A Cultural Edition*, 270–271.

[41]Ibid., 281–282.

[42]Ibid., 285–286.

[43]Ibid., 298–299.

[44]Mayhew, *Indian Converts: A Cultural Edition*, 316–320. He notes especially for Kenump, who, when sickness caused her to lose the ability to go to church, appeared "careful to spend her time well at home; and reading and meditation was now a great part of her employment" and

Of Job Tuphaus, who died at the age of fifteen, it is written that, during his sickness, he "shewed a great delight in hearing the Word of God read; and sometimes desired his mother to read in the book of the Psalms to him; and Psalms of prayer he was most desirous to have read in his hearing."[45] Mayhew writes he would raise his hands as able in worship and would join in singing Psalmody.[46]

In writing of one Laban Panu, who had died at ten years old in 1715, Mayhew shows how ingrained the catechesis lessons had become to those they were offered to.[47] Desire for biblical knowledge and literacy grabbed hold of Panu and the children Mayhew mentions above. It was a culture that fostered and encouraged growing deep in the understanding and knowledge of the Bible. This culture demonstrates the missiological method of indigeneity whereby missionaries fulfill the Great Commission in raising indigenous disciples who then advance the Gospel and Great Commission among their people group.[48]

Sarah Coomes, great-granddaughter of Hiacoomes, is recorded by Mayhew as asking her grandmother "*Kukkootammah Mannit* (Teach Me God)," showing her desire to learn about God and the Gospel message. Mayhew adds:

> And as the child increased in knowledge, so she appeared to be more and more affected with a sense of the reality and importance of the truths wherein she was instructed; and would, when the same were at her desire proposed to her, frequently affirm her belief of the truth and certainty of them, saying, that though she could not herself express them, yet she firmly believed them. Nor did this child rest in the bare and naked knowledge of the things she learned, but endeavored also to put the same into practice; and did evidently appear to be influenced thereby in her life.[49]

also asked others when they visited her that she knew could read to "read some portion of God's Word to her." Ibid., 320–322.

[45]Ibid., 325–326.

[46]Ibid., 326–327.

[47]Ibid., 330–331.

[48]International Mission Board, *Foundations*, Version 4 (International Mission Board, 2002), 55–58.

[49]Mayhew, *Indian Converts: A Cultural Edition*, 343–344.

Coomes died at six years old on March 10, 1723, five days before Reverend Samuel Pierpont, Sarah Pierpont Edwards's brother, would drown in the Connecticut River. As Coomes lay sick and dying, Mayhew writes:

> When she drew near her end, she desired her grandmother not to be too much grieved for her; for, said she, I am now going to the House of God, and when you go to God's House also, we shall again see one another with joy; and we shall there see others also, who are gone before us, leaving us sorrowful here behind them; and then we shall be where there is everlasting joy.[50]

These testimonies given by Mayhew show the response to the Gospel mission at Martha's Vineyard and the indigenous advancement of that mission when resources and guidance were provided. Just like with the colonial awakening and revival, which would become labeled the Great Awakening, a missional awakening and biblical culture was being formed among the Indian tribes of Martha's Vineyard. It was a self-growing movement that would grow naturally through the propagation of those who was converted and were then spreading the mission and biblical education among their tribes.

It was a movement that surprised even the English missionaries as they would be bombarded with deep theological questions such as whether to take Matthew 5:29 literally and physically remove one's eye, or whether Judas should be punished if God ordained his betrayal or further questions that challenged Puritan beliefs on paedobaptism or the move of the Sabbath from Saturday to Sunday.[51] This shows the effectiveness of catechesis and the religious ministry among the natives at Martha's Vineyard as their biblical literacy and desire for further biblical knowledge grew. However, as will be seen through the next primary source, war and exploitation would hinder much of the goodwill and Gospel advancement among the Mohegans and other tribes in colonial America.

Samson Occom's Writings and Autobiography

In the foreword for the 2006 published volume of Occom's work, Robert Warrior explains the tension for the modern reader of Occom due to his "insistent

[50] Ibid., 344–345.

[51] Silverman, "Indians, Missionaries, and Religious Translation," 161.

piety" and his nuanced leadership in the face of societal tensions between an invasion of European Christendom and protection of the Mohegan people and their culture. Warrior remarks many of his students (especially those of his "Native students") remark about Occom as a "dupe of his Christian handlers."[52]

Warrior, though, commends the newly published work as showcasing Occom's trusted leadership and complex thought in balancing the aforementioned tension of his time. The many writings are also previewed as having invaluable context for the struggles Occom faced in traversing New England and across the Atlantic to Great Britain. Occom's commendableness is shown not only among the many varied Native tribes but also from all he met.[53]

Warrior also notes the fondness and camaraderie that comes through in his writing while spending time with Native communities and Christian Indian leaders as they struggled through a lack of material means and overwhelming political barriers. The work and resilience of Occom and those who would follow him have left a lasting foundation for the Mohegan community, which still thrives as "one of the most culturally and politically intact groups of Natives in New England, and Dartmouth" after what Warrior describes as "Wheelock's betrayal of Occom and subsequent neglect of the education of Native students."[54]

Occom was born to Sarah and Joshua Occom at Mohegan in 1723. As mentioned above, Occom sought college-preparatory instruction from Congregational minister Eleazar Wheelock. When Wheelock abandoned his commitment to Native education, Occom broke with Wheelock and spent the rest of his life with the foremost goal of Native education. In the fall of 1751, Occom married Mary Fowler (Montaukett). They would have ten children together, including their tenth, who was born in 1774. Occom died in New Stockbridge in 1792.[55] Kidd notes Occom as the "most influential Native American Evangelical convert in the eighteenth century."[56]

[52]Robert Warrior, foreword to Samson Occom, *The Collected Writings of Samson Occom, Mohegan*, ed. Joanna Brooks, Leadership and Literature in Eighteenth-Century Native America (New York: Oxford University Press, 2006), v.

[53]Warrior, "Foreward," v-vi.

[54]Ibid., vi-viii. Eleazar Wheelock was who Occom studied under before terminating his studies in 1747. Ibid., xxi.

[55]Joanna Brooks, "The Indian World: An Introduction to the Writings of Samson Occom," *Collected Writings*, xxi-4.

[56]Thomas S. Kidd, *American Colonial History: Clashing Cultures and Faiths* (New Haven: Yale University Press, 2016), 220.

Occom begins his autobiography by stating he was "born a heathen and brought up in heathenism till I was between 16 and 17 years of age."[57] This is the first statement of apprehension for those critiquing his autobiography for the connection to European Congregationalist Calvinism. Occom states his parents, like "all the Indians" at Mohegan, "lived a wandering life," which was "strictly maintained and followed" through their customs and Native religion. The interaction between Occom and Christians would come, as he notes, "once a fortnight" during the summer when a minister would bring blankets, which caused the Indians to attend and hear their sermon.[58]

According to Occom, there was also a "sort of" school kept, though he advises he knew of no one who "ever learnt to read any thing" at the school. When he was ten, there was also a man who would go about the "Indian Wigwams" and would make any Indian child he could find read. He notes the children (including himself) would avoid the man and only learned some letters due to his insistence. At sixteen years of age, Occom and other Natives "heard a strange rumor among the English" of those going from place to place preaching; they would not see them until the summer of that year. This was the beginning not only of them hearing preaching when they came but also when they started going to the churches to hear preaching. It was during this time that Occom began learning to read through a primer.[59]

After six months of "a trouble of mind" and through learning to read through the use of a primer (no doubt centered on Christian knowledge and biblicism), Occom discovered "the way of salvation through Jesus, and was enabled to put my trust in him along for life and salvation."[60] After this, Occom had become literate enough to "read in the New Testament without spelling" and further had "a desire still to learn to read the Word of God" while also having a desire of being capable "of instructing my poor kindred, I use to think if I could once learn to read I would instruct poor children in reading."[61]

He continued in his desire to become biblically literate through his nineteenth year of age. At this time, he desired to be under the tutelage of

[57] Occom, "Autobiographical Narrative, Second Draft (September 17, 1768)," *Collected Writings*, 52.

[58] Ibid.

[59] Occom, *Collected Writings*, 53. Brooks notes in 1723 a school at Mohegan was established by John Mason, supported by the colony and missionary societies, and "a school house for Mohegan children was built in 1727." Brooks, "The Indian World," fn. 30.

[60] Brooks, *Collected Writings*, fn. 30.

[61] Ibid., 53–54.

Wheelock. Brooks notes before Occom, Wheelock would prepare colonial British youth in the classical languages and theology. Through seeing success with Occom, Wheelock established Moor's Indian Charity School in 1754 and connected with David Brainerd (the missionary nursed by Edwards's daughter Jerusha before his death in 1746 and whose biography was written and published by Edwards) about recruiting students. These students would receive training in English (along with classical languages) until 1762 when "one of his sponsoring missionary societies discourages this course of study as unnecessary and inappropriate."[62]

When Occom departed from Wheelock, he writes he went to Montauk and established a school there where he taught 30 students. Occom notes they met three times for worship "every Sabbath" and once on Wednesday evening. He read scripture to them and then preached on a passage in his own tongue. He also did the pastoral work of visiting the sick and attending "their burials" for two years until he was married. He found after marriage the demands necessary for ministering to and educating those there required more than he could give, so he communicated with Samuel Buell and Wheelock, who "represented" his circumstances to the commissioners who agreed to give him fifteen pounds a year sterling.[63]

Now sponsored as a missionary at Montauk, Occom also served as a judge in civil matters and was later licensed to preach, acting as the sole minister after the departing minister Azariah Horton recommended Occom succeed him. The mission at Shenecock, at which Occom notes Horton spent the majority of his time while ministering at Montauk, would have resident Indians send their children to Occom for education. Occom gives insight into how he would train and educate the children by use of the *Shorter Catechism* and primers. When they became literate enough, Occom notes his method further in religious training, which includes the use of the "plain style" of exposition.[64] This shows the faithful adaptation of Puritan instruction in biblical knowledge and literacy.[65]

Occom closes the second draft of his autobiography by relating his meager pay and larger responsibilities. He illustrates the perception of his inexperience and performance by using the example of an Indian child who was beaten for not driving a plow well enough since he could only "drive"

[62] Occom, *Collected Writings*, 54n33.

[63] Ibid., 54–55.

[64] Occom, *Collected Writings*, 56.

[65] Ibid., 56–58.

(in Occom's case, minister, educate, and serve in administrative functions) as well as able, but is more likely due to his being Indian. He writes:

> So I am ready to Say, they have used thus, because I Cant Instruct the Indians so well as other Missionaries, but I Can assure them I have endeavored to teach them as well as I [know] how—but I must say, I believe it is because I am poor Indian. I can't help that God has made me so; I did not make myself so.[66]

This is the lament of many Indians who sought to serve God in the context of their colonial supervisors. In a letter he sent to his wife Mary, Occom encourages her to pray with and for their children and to "instruct our children in the fear of God as well as you can, and send them to school as much as you [think] advisable if the school continues."[67] This encouragement demonstrates Occom's earnest faith and desire to see his wife and children live in and practice their Christian faith and for his children to grow in their faith through religious education. In two letters sent to Robert Keen in September of 1768, Occom notes the financial needs of the school and the added issue of the Dutch and French who were "trying all they can, to prejudice the minds of the Indians against the school and the English."[68]

In a letter to Benjamin Forfitt written March 4, 1771, Occom notes the books donated by Forfitt were disbursed among the Indians and "have been of great use and benefit to the Indians, and they continue to come to me from all quarters for books, even to the distance of 60 miles – the Indians are greatly delighted and edified with singing."[69] Singing was a "beloved activity" where it "served as a ritual of community celebration and reconciliation." In 1774, Occom would even publish a volume of hymns he wrote titled *A Choice Collection of Hymns and Spiritual Songs*.[70]

In response to Wheelock's attitude of abandoning Indian students and focusing on white students reflected in his *Continuation of the Narrative of the Indian Charity School* (1771), Occom wrote a scathing letter adding he was quite willing to volunteer to be a "gazing stock, yea even a laughing

[66]Ibid., 58.

[67]Occom, "To Mary Fowler Occom 1767," *Collected Writings*, 81.

[68]Occom, "To Robert Keen," *Collected Writings*, 82–84.

[69]Occom, "To Benjamin Forfitt," *Collected Writings*, 94.

[70]Brooks, *Collected Writings*, 94n56.

stock, in strange countries to promote your cause" adding they had sold their donors on how they were "begging for poor miserable Indians" and instead were educating many more colonials instead.[71]

Wheelock's abandonment of Indian students for colonial whites would lead to the founding of Dartmouth College. Occom's disgust would be over this and his negligence of caring for Occom's wife and children during Occom's trip to England to raise money for the school. Occom would find his wife and children "nearly destitute" though Wheelock had given a promise to look after them.[72] George Whitefield, whom Occom noted as a "tender father to us," had actually predicted Wheelock's abandonment, noting Wheelock would use Occom as a "fine tool" for getting money, but would then be set "adrift."[73]

In a letter sent to Andrew Gifford dated October 19, 1772, Occom notes his brother-in-law Jacob Fowler's work of education "among the Pequot Tribe of Indians" and requests a copy of "Mr. Benj French's Book on Metaphor" (which Brooks notes is referring to Benjamin Keach's *Tropologia: A Key to Open Scripture Metaphors* first published in 1682) as it was "the best book for the instruction of the Indians of human composure I ever saw."[74]

Writing against the consequences of the American Revolution and the divisions created by it, along with an indictment of Wheelock's abandonment of the Indian mission, Occom penned a letter to John Bailey in June or July of 1783, noting the Revolution had been the "most destructive to poor Indians of any wars that ever happened in my day."[75]

Occom wrote Bailey again in 1784 with worse testimony of the consequences of the American Revolution (which he calls "this family contention of the English") among Native American missions, stating that it became "a besom of destruction to sweep them (Indians) from the face of the Earth, there are but few remaining among the English." He adds those still there were living "very careless" and had hardened their hearts to the Gospel. Further, Occom notes all the schools among the Indians "are all ceased and there is not one missionary among them all that I know of." The letter

[71]Occom, "To Eleazar Wheelock," *Collected Writings*, 98–99.

[72]Kidd, *American Colonial History*, 220–221. Silverman notes this betrayal of Occom was in line with other experiences of Indians in southern New England for decades preceding the founding of Brothertown. Silverman, *Red Brethren*, 71.

[73]Thomas S. Kidd, *George Whitefield: America's Spiritual Founding Father*, (New Haven: Yale University Press, 2014), 244.

[74]Occom, "To Andrew Gifford," *Collected Writings*, 101.

[75]Occom, "To John Bailey (June or July 1783)," *Collected Writings*, 120–121.

goes on to again blast Wheelock's Institution as a "sham" and "altogether unprofitable to the poor Indians."[76] This bitter disappointment from Occom was in response to what he saw as the exploitation of Natives for the benefit of Wheelock's institution under the guise of ministering to them.

In June 1790, Occom wrote to Jedidiah Chapman and advocated for some from the "Stockbridge Indians." These were from those who were originally settled in the mission township of Stockbridge, Massachusetts but had moved to New Stockbridge in New York. They came from the families that were ministered to before by John Sergeant and Jonathan Edwards. In the letter, Occom notes a "young man" and a "boy with the young man" who both desired religious instruction and education. He further notes the "Stockbridge Indians in particular were very glad, and thankful that there was such benevolent opening, for the instruction of Indian youth, they hope, that this may be a door of great and a lasting good to the poor Indians."[77]

The furtherance of faith of those who were at Stockbridge and carried their faith to New Stockbridge shows the lasting impact of earnest missions among the Native Americans. Those who received both ministry and a benevolent opportunity to learn desired it for themselves and their brethren. Amongst the Stockbridge Indians, the promise of ministry and education was a "spiritual light and life" amongst "very great discouragement and gloominess of mind." It was also a potential "extraction from our gloomy state" sustained among them from the abandonment of those like Wheelock.[78]

Due to the American Revolution and the damage it caused among the Indians, Occom believed there was a "very great prejudice against the white people." He was thus convinced "the Indians must have teachers of their own color or nation" because he also believed "there seems to be agreeable prospect opening amongst the western tribes to introduce civilization and Christianity . . . when they shall beg to Jesus Christ for his inheritance and the uttermost parts of the Earth his position."[79]

Occom also kept a journal throughout his life, which provides intimate insight into his day-to-day ministering. In writing on the sabbath of June 14, 1761 (a sabbath he was advised not to go into the city due to smallpox), Occom notes his surprise at finding the worldliness among the English. He

[76]Occom, "To John Bailey (1784)," *Collected Writings*, 121.

[77]Occom, "To Jedidiah Chapman," *Collected Writings*, 130.

[78]Occom, *Collected Writings*, 130–131.

[79]Occom, "Indians Must Have Teachers of Their Own Coular or Nation (Nov. 1791)," *Collected Writings*, 133–134.

notes how many were riding and working on the sabbath; others were drunk and "staggering in the streets" or "tumbling off their horses," with the most notable "practice of these people" the vulgarity of their language.[80]

In an entry for Sabbath August 14, 1774, Occom records "Mr. Kirkland preached" while later Occom "put a question to them, which was this, what is it that make a Christian or who is a Christian" noting a number of them responded well.[81] Brooks notes this was a form of pedagogy Occom learned at the school in Montauk. This pedagogy aligns with the applicatory follow-up sessions seen before in typical Puritan and colonial churches of the time.[82]

In an entry for the sabbath on April 16, 1786, Occom records having spoken to a mixed congregation of Native and English congregants at a church near Lanthorn Hill. He notes the "word fell heavy upon" them such that they "attended, like criminals under sentence," hearing the sermon from Ecclesiastes 1:15.[83] This is noteworthy as Occom is speaking of revival for both the English and Native hearers who attended. Throughout his journal, Occom repeatedly notes the solemnity and attentiveness of his audience as he preached. This is one of the clearer notes he makes specifically regarding a mixed audience who had heard his preaching.[84] Such is the case on August 23, 1786, during a Wednesday evening service at Jacob Fowler's church. Occom records speaking to the group from Proverbs, praying, and "exercising" with his Christian cards as "they were awed with the various texts of Scripture ... there was one Stockbridge girl ... there was one English girl, and they also chose each of them a text, and they concluded with singing several tunes" he writes.[85]

A common vein runs through these primary works seen above. When presented with earnest Christian missions, there was a great response by those ministered to. Even in the face of exploitation and broken faith, there is still the desire to adhere to and propagate the Gospel among the Native Christian community (not only in public vocation but intimately in households). This response shows the effect of earnest, Christian mission and

[80]Occom, "Personal Journal (Sabbath, June 14, 1761)," *Collected Writings*, 260.

[81]Occom, "Personal Journal (Sabbath, August 14, 1774)," *Collected Writings*, 277.

[82]Brooks, Fn. 74, *Collected Writings*, 277.

[83]Occom, "Personal Journal (Sabbath, April 16, 1786)," *Collected Writings*, 334–335.

[84]Occom, "Personal Journal (Sabbath, April 16, 1786)," 334–335.

[85]Occom, "Personal Journal (Wednesday, August 23, 1786)," *Collected Writings*, 340.

the influence of education and biblical literacy in developing an indigenous Christian culture. Next, the specific mission at Stockbridge will be analyzed.

Background on the Mission at Stockbridge

In the introductory chapter of her dissertation on the Housatonic Indians and missions, Rachel M. Wheeler notes that, at first, a mutual necessity bound the Mahicans and those settling in the frontier mission village of Stockbridge. Soon, however, disappointments from both parties led to the town becoming "like any other New England town – which meant a town without Indians."[86] Wheeler adds it was "Indian relations guided by *realpolitik* and not ideals of Christian benevolence" that caused the failure of colonial missions among the Mahicans. However, a new identity, both Mahican and Christian, would emerge among the tribes who eventually moved westward to New Stockbridge (in New York) and even further into the Midwest frontier.[87]

The self-identity of the Mahicans as peacekeepers and "cultural brokers" initially fueled the founding partnership and mission at Stockbridge. Through their "covenant chain of friendship ... lively trade" had begun for the outnumbered European settlers in 1609. The betrayal of this "covenant chain of friendship" by the Dutch, who later sided with the Mohawk, became a recurring theme from those who exploited the Mahican culture's earnest intentions, which valued loyalty and friendship.[88]

Indigenous people would define the relationship in the 16th century in the context of their extension of friendship when they were at their strength and the colonists at their weakest, and the colonists' betrayal when the natives were at their weakest and the colonists their strongest.[89] Warfare, disease, and exploitation would be the three forces that would disrupt the mission among several tribes in colonial New England.

However, the Mahicans' cultural adaptability proved to be a force that allowed them to maintain community; "despite the merges and dislocations, a distinctive Mahican identity persisted, whether in the adopted homes of

[86]Rachel M. Wheeler, "Living Upon Hope, 13–14. As Wheeler's dissertation details Edwards's ministry at Stockbridge and the background therein more extensively, it is used in this work along with her published volume *To Live Upon Hope*.

[87]Wheeler, "Living Upon Hope," 14.

[88]Wheeler, "Living Upon Hope," 15–19.

[89]Silverman, *Red Brethren*, 12.

the Miamis or closer to their homelands."[90] Wheeler notes that "cultural accommodation and creative adaptation" were the defining components of Mahican identity through the 17th and 18th centuries.[91]

Two years after attending a meeting at Albany with Mahican leaders Konkapot (chief of the Housatonic-Mahican village of Wnahktukook) and Umpachenee (chief of the village of Skatekook), John Stoddard (an influential politician in Massachusetts, and the uncle of Jonathan Edwards) would convince twenty-one Mahican men (including Konkapot) to sign a deed granting "a certain tract of land lying upon Housatonack River, allias Westonook." This deeded land would later comprise the towns of Great Barrington, Sheffield, and Stockbridge.[92]

One Mahican traditional belief that possibly "paved the way for belief in the myth of a man named Jesus, son of a heavenly father and earthly woman" was one relayed by Ebenezer Poohpoonuk to John Sergeant of a man-god who "came down from heaven on snow shoes and cleared the country of monsters."[93] This man-god would also teach the people about the heavenly customs, marry a woman, and have children (one of whom the man-god left when he departed "with the smoke through a wigwam).[94]

The openness to Christianity among the Mahicans could be primarily due to a cultural revitalization in response to the idea of their "routes of communication with manitou" failing. This failing would be in response to game reserves depleting in light of European over-hunting and trapping and the inability of their healing practices to help stop the ravages of "epidemic diseases brought by the Europeans." Wheeler writes that, in response, the Mahicans "chose to seek out the Christian God, thinking perhaps he would listen when the manitou did not."[95]

Stoddard spearheaded a secular mission to grab land and settle on the frontier and led the charge for mission among the Housatonic tribes. He proposed to Massachusetts Governor Jonathan Belcher (and the New England Company) in the 1730s a mission to the Housatonic. New England divine Benjamin Colman (a supporter of mission work), disillusioned with a mission among the Iroquois traders, agreed with Stoddard on the benefits of

[90]Wheeler, "Living Upon Hope," 19–22.

[91]Ibid., 22.

[92]Wheeler, "Living Upon Hope," 26–27.

[93]Ibid., 32.

[94]Ibid., 32.

[95]Wheeler, "Living Upon Hope," 35–36.

the mission among the Housatonic. The difference between the mission to the Iroquois traders and the Mahicans was the Mahicans were not influenced by French Jesuits, nor were they as nomadic and disconnected as the traders. The missionaries to the Mahicans could not only connect with the men of the tribes but also with their families.[96]

The Deerfield Conference in 1735 marked the inauguration of the mission at Stockbridge. Belcher's ideal was that the Mahicans would receive "an education in Christianity and English agriculture and governance" and "symbolically become 'children' of" the Massachusetts colony. Wheeler's quote of Belcher's assurance to the Mahican delegates ("I look upon you as my children, and hope you are good subjects of King George")[97] echoes the patriarchal attitude brought out in John Lowe's dissertation of slavery seen as a "loving" familial relationship with the slaves as an extension of the family or "*pater familias*" adopted by Puritans such as Cotton Mather who took the concept from William Perkins's *Christian Economy, or the Ordering of a Family According to Scripture Christian Economy*.[98] It is a familial responsibility to those viewed in subservience under one's care. Under the best of intentions and through the best of examples, the attitude of responsibility could be considerate, coming from one accountable for those under their self-identified charge. More often, it proved exploitative and selfish.[99]

Joseph Sewall, along with others, would give charges as they spoke at ordination services that the land was "given" by God so that they would "gift" the inhabitants with Christianity. The Gospel was their gift, and they saw the land as given to them with this mission and responsibility to spread the Gospel. Wheeler also notes it was the fear of God's use of the Indians (similarly to God's wrathful use of the Babylonians) as a consequence of not Christianizing the Indians. Increase Mather and Solomon Stoddard would

[96]Ibid., 37–38.

[97]Ibid., 40–42.

[98]John Thomas Lowe, "'The Practice that Prevails,'" 41–43.

[99]Thomas Kidd notes white missionary agencies' "patronizing attitude" (described above) along with their "neglectful policies" would lead those like Samson Occom and other native Christians to dissolve their partnerships with white evangelical sponsors. Kidd, *Great Awakening*, 212. Silverman notes this breaking from the "English yoke" would surprise those colonists who saw a weaponized form of Christianity as a method of colonization become an "expression of autonomy." Silverman, *Red Brethren*, 48–52.

both see King Philip's War "as punishment for New England's sins, especially worldliness."[100]

Most of the funding, though, for the mission at Stockbridge would come from overseas, as Wheeler notes Isaac Hollis, a businessman from London, provided the initial grant of 300 pounds. Other funds came from the England-based New England Company. John Sergeant, chosen by the Massachusetts Commissioners of the New England Company as the minister and resident instructor for the school, came to the Housatonic in 1734. Wheeler notes later in her book *To Live Upon Hope* that Sergeant had studied under Edwards, which most likely helped secure him the position at Stockbridge.[101]

Stockbridge became incorporated in 1739. The goal for the Mahicans was their spiritual direction and acquisition of literacy (an "essential skill for survival in this new world," according to Wheeler). Alcohol regulation was a pressing concern for the Mahicans from the beginning of the mission through its course as a mission. Finding a means of living beyond traditional hunting and agriculture (threatened by the use of the Europeans) and as laborers on neighboring Dutch and English farms was a final goal for the Mahicans.[102]

Wheeler notes two events in 1739 that caused a shift from the equal partnership between the English and the Mahicans to more of an exploitation of them. The first was the incorporation of the town, the arrival of more English families, and the marriage of John Sergeant to Abigail Williams. The Williams clan would become the greatest stressors to and exploiters of the mission at Stockbridge. Jonathan Edwards, writing to Secretary Andrew Oliver in 1752, would note, "They say that Mr. Sergeant did very well till he married her; but that afterwards there was a great alteration in him and he became quite another man."[103]

In the initial meeting between Indian leaders and the Massachusetts Commissioners for Indian Affairs, Wheeler notes that the two leaders (Konkapot

[100]Wheeler, "Living Upon Hope," 42–44.

[101]Wheeler, "Living Upon Hope,", 45–47; Wheeler notes in *To Live Upon Hope* Sergeant's valedictory address at Yale was "an obsequious tribute to his university mentor, Edwards." Rachel M. Wheeler, *To Live Upon Hope,* 46n73.

[102]Wheeler, "Living Upon Hope," 45–47. Silverman notes it was Konkapot who would see the need for his people to be equipped to deal with colonial society by approaching the colonial leaders in starting the mission. Silverman, *Red Brethren*, 34.

[103]Wheeler, "Living Upon Hope," 47–48. Quote by Edwards as found in Edwards, *Letters and Personal Writings*, 424.

and Umpachenee) were cautious in dealing with missions due to what they saw as backsliding among the English. Wheeler writes about Konkapot:

> Further, he continued to be perplexed that so many professed Christians did not adhere to the precepts of their religion. He explained to the commissioners that "he did not know how to think well of the Christian Religion, because the Christians lead immoral lives."100 Umpachenee, now and throughout the rest of his life, harbored graver reservations about a religion whose professors so often violated its basic precepts.[104]

Silverman notes the term *praying-Indian* (seen by the Indians themselves as relating to their spiritual practice in similitude with Methodism's methodological identification) had become a derogatory term for those who were "almost, but not quite" at the spiritual and social level of white colonists. This is brought into view through the questioning of a Christian Wampanoag who asked why they were not welcome to rest with whites, which would be a violation of Christian fellowship principles in juxtaposition to the native culture's emphasis on courtesy towards even strangers.[105]

Wheeler observes that literacy and education (as noted, a primary desire for the Mahican leaders for their children) would draw settlers (both Mahican and English) to Stockbridge. John Wauwaumpequunaut came to the mission for this reason, and he planned to utilize his education to know God. By the spring of 1741, Sergeant would report forty scholars in attendance in his classes. Literacy would become a prerequisite for leadership among the Mahicans, especially in light of the abuse and exploitation endured through contracts unknowingly signed that gave their land away. Literacy would be a means for Mahican leaders to protect their tribal lands.[106]

In January 1736, as many as ninety would attend Sergeant's services, held at Umpachenee's longhouse. Word of mouth from new converts during trade would effectively proselytize the bound native communities. In 1734, the Indian population at Stockbridge was 218, of which 129 were baptized, and forty-two regularly took communion. Between thirty-five and fifty-five students attended Timothy Woodbridge's school. Throughout his time at Stockbridge, Sergeant remained cynical about affecting true change from the Mahicans and notes in the end, "The 'soil' of Mahican souls had proved

[104]Wheeler, "Living Upon Hope," 48–49.

[105]Silverman, *Red Brethen*, 16.

[106]Wheeler, "Living Upon Hope," 51–53.

more difficult to till than he had imagined."[107] Sergeant would get an illness, including a fever and throat canker, and die in mid-1749 at the age of thirty-nine.[108]

During the first celebration of communion for Jonathan Edwards as pastor of the mission at Stockbridge in August 1751, he chose Psalm 1:3 as his text for the 150 congregants present. The sermon titled "He shall be like a tree planted by the Rivers of Water" had as its doctrine, "Christ is to the heart of a true saint like a river to the roots of a tree that is planted by it." Following the sermon, Cornelius and Mary Munneweaunummuck came forward to profess their faith in Christ. Cornelius also resolved to "give up my life to the service of God and to follow Christ in all his ways and ordinances." Their names were signed at the bottom of Edwards's sermon manuscript.[109]

Wheeler notes the change in style of Edwards's sermon from Psalm 1:3 as "chosen with care to resonate with the presumed sensibilities of his audience and with the rich, metaphorical cast of native rhetorical styles."[110] Wheeler, however, judges the sermon's tone as a departure from the characterized trope of Edwards as a "fire and brimstone" preacher. On the contrary, Edwards was concerned with sparking the affections of his listeners through rich imagery (whether negative, as seen in "Sinners" or beatific, as seen in "Heaven is a World of Love"). Of note are the metaphorical language and illustrations used to reach a new audience with a differing sensibility and biblical literacy.

Wheeler notes the neglect of scholars in analyzing the sermons from Stockbridge and how, in looking at the Stockbridge sermons, one can see "the workings of Edwards' mind and the shift in rhetorical style necessitated by a change in audience."[111] Edwards would also instruct the Indian children at Stockbridge once a week and employ new pedagogy methods during those lessons. He would "overhaul catechetical methods in order to better reach his audience."[112]

[107]Ibid., 65–74.

[108]Marsden, *Jonathan Edwards*, 378.

[109]Wheeler, "Living Upon Hope," 133–135.

[110]Ibid., 135. Wheeler notes Edwards's metaphorical imagery and abandonment of his dogged exposition seen at Northampton identified him closer with Moravian preachers than with his previous sensibilities. Ibid., 134–135.

[111]Wheeler, "Living Upon Hope," 137.

[112]Ibid., 138.

When Edwards arrived at Stockbridge in 1751, there were approximately 250 Housatonic Mahicans and some Mohawk Indians. The English population numbered Thirteen families. Fifty-five students attended Woodbridge's school, while another boarding school was set up under Sergeant's time and run by Captain Martin Kellogg (who was connected with the Williams family). Because of his ties to the Williams family, Kellogg had received funding for building a boarding school without regard for Woodbridge's plans for a boarding school. Kellogg was also described by Edwards as having "pretty good understanding for one that was being an illiterate man."[113]

While Woodbridge had invested in and trained Mahican youth, Kellogg's school neglected them as Kellogg desired to work with Mohawk's more (as he was fluent in their language during a childhood captivity among them). But even the Mohawk children who boarded with Kellogg were neglected. Adding to the neglect of the educational mission at Stockbridge were false narratives and charges of neglect brought up against Woodbridge by the Williams family, leading to Woodbridge being ordered to Boston to answer charges. His reputation and bond with those at Stockbridge led to many Mahicans traveling to Boston in his defense.[114]

In 1751, Edwards and his family moved to Stockbridge from Northampton, where he was forced out after the communion controversy. At this point, Edwards was forty-six years old, and, with a large family, he worried about supporting them due to his age and limited vocation. He had received an offer to move to Scotland and minister in the Presbyterian church from his friend John Erskine. He would have found a good response in Scotland since his writings on the Great Awakening were published there, making him well-known. Yet, Edwards was unwilling to journey with his family over the Atlantic to the Old World, given the many difficulties they would face in travel.[115]

Edwards's decision to move to Stockbridge was practical as a move of sixty miles west for him and his large family would be easier than moving to Virginia (where he had also received interest) or Scotland (noted above). Edwards's Calvinism would be a deterrent for the congregations in eastern Massachusetts who were helmed by a majority of pastors of Arminian bent. Stockbridge's inhabitants were divided on Sergeant's replacement, with many who followed Woodbridge hoping for Samuel Hopkins, who had

[113]Wheeler, "Living Upon Hope," 139–142.

[114]Ibid., 142–143.

[115]Wheeler, "Living Upon Hope," 144–145.

settled in Great Barrington and was a defender of the New Lights. Those with Williams championed Ezra Stiles, a young Yale graduate who opposed the New Lights. As Hopkins acquiesced to his role at Great Barrington instead, he suggested his mentor Edwards, who was selected against the desires of the Williams clan.[116]

Within a year, Edwards already felt the weight of the heavy conflicts instigated by the Williamses and the dour effect it had on the mission and education of the Mahicans. He wrote to Andrew Oliver, "I expect nothing but perpetual dissensions, undermining, and counterworking of one another among the inhabitants of the town, which probably will soon bring all to the ground."[117] He had also voiced to Oliver (the secretary of the Commissioner for Indian Affairs) the specific threat of the Williamses, who saw him as a "great nuisance here" and would purge him like anything else standing in their way of land and influence.[118]

After the death of the chief sachem of the Mahicans, who had resided in Menanoke (a village on the Hudson), Umpachenee had become the most likely chief sachem, and the headquarters of the River Indians' tribal confederation had moved to Stockbridge. Umpachenee had graver reservations about the English mission at Stockbridge than Konkapot and had communicated considerably with the Moravians, whose mission was at Shekomeko. Naturally, this had also resulted from the land grab by the English (most notably Ephraim Williams and family) and the continued neglect of the Stockbridge schools.[119]

When Edwards arrived, Timothy Woodbridge transitioned from being a schoolmaster to focusing on legal advocacy. This transition meant he needed to be replaced. Gideon Hawley, newly appointed, made a positive impression among the Mahican and Mohawks. They spoke with their feet as the children gathered in greater numbers for Hawley than for Kellogg and Abigail Dwight (the appointed teachers for the Indian girls at Kellogg's school). Hawley taught the children to read and write in English, and this education was naturally tied to Christian knowledge and biblical literacy. Because Hawley was successful and endeared himself to the Mahican and

[116]Philip F. Gura, *Jonathan Edwards: America's Evangelical* (New York: Hill and Wang, 2006), 166–170, Kindle. Also noted in Marsden, *A Life*, 378–379.

[117]Edwards, *Letters*, 428.

[118]Edwards, *Letters*, 428; as noted in Wheeler, "Living Upon Hope," 147n41.

[119]Wheeler, "Living Upon Hope," 148.

Mohawks, the Williamses and Joseph Dwight (Abigail's husband) harassed Hawley and sought to undermine his progress.[120]

In May of 1752, Jonathan Hubbard (a friend of Kellogg's) hit the child of one of the "chief Indians." After Hawley reached out to Edwards for advice on what to do with the situation, which escalated in Indian anger over the incident, and Edwards's declining to intervene, Dwight, who had told Edwards not to interfere in Mohawk affairs ("in no uncertain terms"), physically and verbally abused Hawley for three hours in front of Mohawk children who thought Hawley would be killed. Abuses such as this would eventually lead to Mohawk disillusionment with the mission and Hawley's departure for the mission at Onohquaga in the summer of 1753.[121]

Edwards wrested control away from the Williamses, Dwights, and Kellogg in the spring of 1754, only after the damage to the relationship between the mission and the Mohawks.[122] Only one child, who was staying with Edwards, remained. Edwards recorded an entreaty by the native Stockbridge residents for the Mohawks to stay, stating, "We have but a little time to continue here. Let us give diligent heed to the instructions that we have and do our utmost to practice accordingly, and it may be, if we do so, we may hereafter meet together in heaven."[123]

The loss of the Mohawks was not only dire for the mission at Stockbridge but, as Edwards saw and noted, was a dire strategic blow in losing those tribes making up the Six Nations to the French since land offered in Canada and the Jesuit proselytization drew their allegiance away from the English and Protestant alliance. She adds that while, ultimately, the Mohawk departure was a loss for Edwards, he found consolation in the loyalty he had among the Mahican and Mohawks who had remained in support of his ministerial efforts.[124]

Edwards preached (most times separately for the English and Indian congregants) 226 times from January 1751 to January 1758 (averaging about 2.8 times a month when discounting Edwards's absence from the Stockbridge pulpit from March to July 1751). Wheeler notes he would use

[120]Wheeler, "Living Upon Hope," 152–153.

[121]Marsden, *A Life*, 399.

[122]Wheeler notes in *To Live Upon Hope* that several petitions were made against the Williams faction, including one "signed by forty-one Stockbridge Indians, including Umpachenee, Konkapot, Ebenezer Poohpoonuk, and Paul Umpeatkow." Wheeler, *To Live Upon Hope*, 210.

[123]Wheeler, "Living Upon Hope," 153–154. Marsden notes Dwight would use blame the departure of the Mohawks on Edwards. Marsden, *A Life*, 405.

[124]Wheeler, "Living Upon Hope," 155–160.

more metaphorical language that spoke to the Mahicans, including sowing seed, fishing, trees by rivers, and "briars and thorns that impeded a traveler's way." She notes this abandonment of "narrative scaffolding" and infusion of metaphor and imagery was an attempt not to "reach the heads of his listeners, but their hearts."[125]

Edwards, in the twilight of his preaching career, had grown less bound to sermon manuscripts, and this process of becoming less and less of a manuscript preacher showed physically through his use of small outline manuscripts written on duodecimo leaves. This shift refutes again the image of Edwards as the stoic, bound, monotone manuscript preacher. John Wauwaumpequunaut, who was baptized in 1740 by Sergeant, would serve as Edwards's interpreter.[126] Hawley comments on Edwards's preaching to the Indians at Stockbridge that "he was a plain and practical preacher; upon no occasion did he display any metaphysical knowledge in the pulpit. His sentences were concise and full of meaning; and his delivery, grave and natural."[127]

Wheeler notes Tracy, in examining Edwards's preaching at the end of his ministry at Northampton, had become "more disillusioned and frustrated," which resulted in less "fire and brimstone" preaching and a shift to "preaching the 'sweet reasonableness' of religion and the love of God."[128] She notes this shift caused him to preach less of an active, immanent God at work, but rather one more passive and withdrawn. This emphasis is juxtaposed with a

[125]Of the 226 sermons, sixty-eight were taken from the Old Testament, and 156 from the New Testament. Wheeler, "Living Upon Hope," 163, 167n97. While this is one of the main arguments of Wheeler's dissertation, the assertion of this work is that Edwards was more intent on conveying understanding and affection for those at Stockbridge (reaching their head and hearts) through imagery and metaphor that spoke to their experience, while his aim was to do the same at Northampton (to an audience more biblically literate whose "affections" would need to be raised). Thus, the disagreement with Wheeler is that Edwards did not change his focus (reaching the head and hearts of his audience), only his homiletical methodology. She alludes to this before making the statement on his singular focus on the hearts of his listeners at Stockbridge. Wheeler notes and shows agreement with Edwards scholars Wilson Kimnach and Patricia Tracy of Edwards's evangelical preaching both at Northampton and Stockbridge, She writes "To both audiences, he was a practical preacher urging his congregation toward the experience of saving grace." Ibid. In her published work based on her dissertation *To Live Upon Hope*, released nine years after her dissertation, Wheeler re-asserts Edwards's change in style to reach the hearts of those at Stockbridge. Wheeler, *To Live Upon Hope*, 214.

[126]Wheeler, "Living Upon Hope," 163–165.

[127]Gideon Hawley, "A Letter from Rev. Gideon Hawley of Marshpee, Containing an Account of His Services among the Indians of Massachusetts and New-York, and a Narrative of His Journey to Onohoghgwage," in Massachusetts Historical Society, Collections ser. 1, vol 4 (Boston: Massachusetts Historical Society), 51. Noted in Wheeler, "Living Upon Hope," 165.

[128]Wheeler, "Living Upon Hope," 169.

sermon from Stockbridge on Revelation 3:20 preached in February of 1751, where Wheeler notes the similarities in language with the earlier "Sinners" sermon on the torments of hell.[129]

Wheeler notes that this emphasis on condemnation for sinners and the most notable sins characterized Edwards's preaching mostly during his first year at Stockbridge. She suggests his focus shifted after seeing improvement in actions by those at Stockbridge to align with Christian practice. From preaching on the damnation of hell, Wheeler notes Edwards began preaching on the hope of salvation."[130]

Some of the most notable contents of Edwards's vast library are the professions of faith written by Edwards and signed by the Indians who had given them. Wheeler advises they should be considered authentic for a number of reasons, including Edwards's strict standards for communion, the fact they are written in his shorthand almost illegibly and for private noting (not for publication), and the varying lengths of the written professions (though with notable similarities in the conversion experience theme). To this should be added the tradition of journaling these professions, as seen in those recorded by Thomas Shepherd (in chapter three), Thomas Mayhew, and Experience Mayhew (seen in this chapter).[131]

A New Congregation with a Different Biblical Literacy

In a letter sent to Benjamin Colman on August 1, 1743, John Sergeant proposes introducing the English language to them as something intertwined with piety.[132] Sergeant saw the introduction of the English language and, with it, English piety, marking out the "most effectual Manner change their whole Habit of thinking and acting."[133]

Sergeant advises that carefully instilling in their minds the "principles of virtue and piety" would make a lasting impression and advance the introduction of the English language to them. Those who would be part of the program were those between the ages of ten and twenty. The design Sergeant had to accomplish this program was to mark out two hundred

[129] Ibid., 173–174.

[130] Wheeler, "Living Upon Hope," 175–177.

[131] Ibid., 199–200.

[132] John Sergeant, *A Letter From the Rev. Mr. Sergeant of Stockbridge, to Dr. Colman of Boston* (Boston: Rogers and Fowle, 1743), 1.

[133] John Sergeant, *A Letter*, 3.

acres of land and build a house under the care of two masters who would educate and manage those working at the house. Those educated would work to alleviate any ideas of "idleness." Their labor was to help raise funds for the mission while also helping to raise them in farming and industry.[134]

Sergeant hoped this mission would not only encourage piety among those in the area but also lead them to carry the message of "Christian Knowledge" and the "Principles of Virtue" to even the "remotest tribes."[135] Sergeant's design was also to take in both boys and girls and train them in a "manner suitable to their sex."[136] Significantly, Sergeant saw the incorporation of piety, virtues, "Christian Knowledge," the English language, and manners as something to "root out" what he saw as their 'vicious habits" and to "change their whole way of living" to benefit them from what he saw as their "foolish, barbarous, and wicked customs."[137]

Sergeant, in his letter, charges his sole aim was "the good of the Indians" and saw no "expectation of any personal benefit at all" other than the "mere satisfaction" of his being instrumental in promoting Christ's Gospel and the virtues entailed in piety. He adds while there was discouragement in previous attempts, he saw his approach as having a greater chance of success. Sergeant also responded to those who viewed the project as meaningless and those he attempted to reform as "ungrateful" by showing his desire that all the more they should have "humanity" promoted among them and "shews the need there is of cultivating a soil so barren, or rather a soil so overrun with hateful weeds, and prickling thorns."[138]

Moreover, at this time, Sergeant includes Edwards (or Northampton) as among those who should be charged with receiving and disbursing the money for the school. In his response to Sergeant's letter and request, Colman explained how Sergeant was going about serving the youth at the mission and how the introduction of the English language and education was tied to biblical literacy.[139]

In his letter to Pepperell (quoted in the first chapter), Edwards was aware of the limitations of his new Congregation's biblical literacy even

[134]Ibid., 3–4.

[135]Ibid., 4.

[136]Ibid., 15.

[137]Sergeant, *A Letter*, 4–6. Sergeant saw the failures of past attempts at education and reformation as due to a lack to encouraging labor and industry. Ibid.

[138]Ibid., 5–7.

[139]Ibid., 12.

after the efforts detailed in the above quote. Edwards desired that while the children were given lessons on reading in Psalters, Bibles, and catechisms, they learned not only to regurgitate sounds but be pressed on the meanings of "*things*" as well as "*words*." This instruction would stir their desire for knowledge and lead them to see the benefit of what they would be reading (religious texts).[140]

Making a common culture of biblical thought and conversation is seen in Edwards's letter to Pepperell as the aim of instruction of Native children at Stockbridge. Edwards sees personal instruction and ownership of thought as the bridge to reaching the goal of children attending to the Word. As they become familiar with the ideas and basics of biblical knowledge, Edwards relays to Pepperell that they learn biblical history and the overarching story of redemption (which Edwards would endeavor to give in his unfinished *History of the Work of Redemption*). He sees the relaying of biblical events and then further events since the time of the Bible until their day as an "obvious" avenue to make "the story so much the more distinct and entertaining."[141]

Edwards further explains the foundation of their whole endeavor at the Stockbridge school (promotion of "the salvation of the children") be built on public worship, daily familial worship in the home, catechism in school, and individual instruction and an emphasis on the "duty of *secret prayer*."[142] Marsden notes for Edwards, "Literacy was a key to effective missions."[143]

Edwards would go from having a negative view of Native Americans through his family's personal tragedy at their hands and his own preconceived notions to seeing them as his congregation and responsibility. As Lowe argues (in part) in his dissertation, Edwards's sermons (as will be analyzed below) were never "dumbed down" but were adapted to fit a new audience who had a different level of biblical knowledge (though the same capacity for understanding when presented well by the preacher).[144]

When approaching the sermons by Edwards for colonials and Native Americans in this work, it was found that instead of making a habit of repreaching or reformatting old sermons from earlier, Edwards was consistent in composing new expositions (even with similar or identical key texts). While Edwards would repreach sermons, this was not consistently

[140]Edwards, *Letters and Personal Writings*, 408–409.

[141]Ibid., 409–410.

[142]Ibid., 410–412.

[143]Marsden, *A Life*, 389.

[144]Lowe, "The Practice That Prevails," 105–106.

done at Stockbridge (and was done throughout his ministry in repreaching both with sermons preached at one colonial congregation and later at another colonial congregation, or to multiple colonial audiences and later to a Native American audience). Many of these sermons analyzed in the next section have identical key texts preached in sermons analyzed in the previous chapter but are wholly new compositions with different objectives in exhortation, instruction, and application based on the different audiences. For this reason, the focus of the sermons analyzed at Stockbridge is those created fresh for this new audience (or for a mixed audience, as will be shown).

A Change in Preaching Method Analyzed at Stockbridge

Seek God in the Days of Your Youth[145]

Date: February 1751
Key Text: Ecclesiastes 12:1 – "Remember now thy Creator in the days of thy youth, while the evil days come not, nor the years draw nigh, when thou shalt say, I have no pleasure in them."

The first sermon to examine from Edwards's ministry to the Mahicans at Stockbridge is *Days of Your Youth*, a sermon probably given in a mixed crowd of colonial English and Native at the mission. Like many of his sermons at Northampton, this sermon calls the youth of his ministry to seek God and be pious in the days of their youth. A line in his outline-form manuscript calls on his audience to "Read. Learn the English tongue," pointing to the significance of a Native presence among his hearers. Of note is the absence of the Exposition, Doctrine, and Application format. The sermon is in Edwards's later outlined form (as opposed to the fuller manuscripts of his earlier preaching ministry) and written on four octavo-sized leaves.[146]

From the start, the sermon has a more explanatory tone (than *The Time of Youth* seen in the previous chapter over the same key text), with Edwards first instructing his audience that God is their Creator and explaining the key text of the sermon. He further explains the command "remember" is given for them to "think much of Him," "seek Him," and "give Him that respect" as their Creator. He explains the phrase "evil days" in the passage refers to the days of old age in comparison to younger days, which he explains are

[145]Edwards, "Seek God in the Days of Your Youth," ed. R. Craig Woods, *Jonathan Edwards Sermon Index* (Sermon 982), (New Haven: Jonathan Edwards Center, Yale University), 1–7.

[146]R. Craig Woods, "Days of Your Youth," 1–2.

"men's best days" because they are the days in which men are "strongest, most active, and most capable of enjoying the good things of this life."[147]

Those best days, Edwards explains, should be given to God instead of the devil. In likeness to the sermons examined in the previous chapter (*The Time of Youth*, *Our Present and Immediate Business*, and *The Sins of Youth*), Edwards notes the lesser ability to seek and find God in older age after "their hearts are exceedingly hardened." Like the use of exhortation in his other sermons, Edwards charges his audience (young men and women) to seek God to the utmost while they are still young and to care about God, their Creator, unless they want to be fooled by the devil (who is "exceedingly busy" in doing "his utmost" to bring them down to the "broad way that leads to destruction"—describing how foolish they would be to go laughing like fools to the "bottomless pit").[148]

Edwards exhorts them (in a manner pointing to his mixed audience) to avoid abusing themselves with strong drink, frolicking (singing and dancing), idleness (citing the fourth command given in Exod 20:8–11), lasciviousness (reminiscent of the bad book controversy in Northampton), and profane speech. The positive exhortations are to be dutiful in secret prayer, keep the sabbath, be devout publicly, read, learn the English tongue (as mentioned above), and be earnest in concern over their souls (in similitude with *Religious Affections*).[149]

Bookending his warning against the broad road to destruction, Edwards cites Luke 13:24, calling them to strive to enter the "strait gate." The end of *Days of Your Youth* reads like a Gospel presentation to not wait and "flatter" themselves in thoughts of living to an old age, but to "make haste" as death "often comes when least expected" (citing 1 Thess 5:3). He finishes with a final Gospel invitation (in contrast to his applicatory exhortations in *The Time of Youth*):

> Christ calls and invites you. He is ready to receive you. He stands at the door and knocks, [and] offers you great things [Rev. 3:18–21]. I am his messenger. [I] pray you in his stead. If you will not hearken, you alone must bear it [Prov. 9:12].[150]

[147] Edwards, "Days of Your Youth," 3.

[148] Ibid., 3–4.

[149] Edwards, "Days of Your Youth," 4–5.

[150] Ibid., 5–7.

The invitation quoted above shows discernment in preaching to an audience he saw as in need of invitation as opposed to the audience of *The Time of Youth,* whom he saw as in need of applicatory exhortation.

Made in God's Image[151]

Date: August 1751
Key Text: Genesis 1:27 – "So God created man in his own image, in the image of God created he him."

One of the first sermons from the recently installed missionary at Stockbridge, *Made in God's Image* was directed wholly at the Mahican and Mohawk audience at Stockbridge. The date of August 1751 coincided with the arrival of Indian Commissioners from Boston on August 10. The sermon is from the creation account of Genesis.[152]

Made in God's Image forgoes a doctrinal section and instead has a two-fold explanation and application structure. It begins with an explanation of Genesis 1 (as the record of the creation of the world) and man's creation, first in God's image with reason and understanding and second in holiness. Edwards explains man's creation with reason and understanding as the capacity to know God (unlike other creatures), right and wrong, the will of God, and one's duty to God. Because of those cognitive faculties, man was set over the rest of creation.[153]

For the second point of explanation of man's creation in God's image, Edwards shows his pedagogical method by explaining how when Adam and Eve were first made, they were "holy, good and upright, and without any sin," and not "full of all manner of wickedness."[154] Later in his application, Edwards shows the results of the Fall of Adam and Eve (reminiscent of the *New England Primer*'s rhymed alphabet that starts with A for "In Adam's Fall We Sinned All").[155] To conclude his explanatory section, though, Edwards instead illustrates the beauty of man's holiness before the Fall using the

[151]Edwards, "Made in God's Image," ed. Kenneth P. Minkema, *Jonathan Edwards Sermon Index* (Sermon 998), (New Haven: Jonathan Edwards Center, Yale University), 1–7.

[152]Minkema, "Made in God's Image," 1–9.

[153]Edwards, "Made in God's Image," 3–4.

[154]Ibid., 3–4.

[155]Ford, *The New-England Primer*, 65.

sun's brightness to show God's holiness and man as likened to a glass, which shines with an image of the brightness of the sun's beams.[156]

For application, Edwards begins with man's "honored" state before the Fall and the "sorrowful alteration ... made in man by the Fall." Edwards explains that through the Fall, man lost "his goodness and holiness" and later adds man lost that "which was his life, and his glory, and his happiness," leaving man a "mean, low, miserable creature." He compares lowly man with the "beasts," stating they are inclined to "drunkenness and lasciviousness, and placing their happiness in eating and drinking and the pleasures of this world."[157]

Edwards presents to his audience that Christ came to "deliver men from their sin, and to restore the image of God in them." That without Christ, they are "dead in sin" and cannot restore themselves "to holiness" but can be restored through Christ who has "wrought salvation and deliverance for men, that they might be again restored to life, and made holy and happy." Edwards follows this Gospel presentation with a denouncement of the "great evil of the sin of drunkenness," relating those who act in drunkenness to having no "more reason than a beast" and behaving in a "beastly manner, like a pig that wallows in the mire." This comparison is set in juxtaposition with the image of man as the "child of God," the "child of the great King of heaven and earth," compared to wallowing in the mire "like the swine" (paralleling the story of the prodigal son).[158]

Of note, both in the section on drunkenness and in the next section on showing honor, Edwards relays to his audience that they have intrinsic worth since they are made in the image of God and that God is calling them to be restored from sinfulness, which has made men "beastly" and dishonorable. But in this section on honoring all men (taken from 1 Pet 2:17), there is an equality of personhood they have in common (Native and colonial), both being made in God's image (specifically in being made with reason and understanding – and holiness before the Fall). Therefore, those who are hateful to each other or who further commit the sin of murder are guilty of a great thing (citing Gen 9:6).[159]

[156]Edwards, "Made in God's Image," 4. Edwards also shows the devil as having understanding but worse off without having any holiness to go with it. Ibid.

[157]Ibid., 5–6.

[158]Ibid., 6–7.

[159]Edwards, "Made in God's Image," 7–8.

Edwards shows the greatness in the restorative work of salvation and the bringing of men "out of darkness into glorious light," wherein the "hateful child of the devil is made the beautiful, lovely child of God." He also uses the images of a "den of serpents" transformed into "a temple of God" and a "toad," "serpent," or "heap of dung" turned into "one of God's precious jewels" fit for heaven, "the country where all that are truly converted do belong, where is their hope."[160]

Edwards closes with a final exhortation to his audience to be converted and have "hearts like God" so that God will "take delight" in them and will "love to behold" them as they are made in His likeness. The benefits Edwards lists of being converted include being safe, having peace, having joy, not being afraid of dying, having further peace at death and the day of judgment, and union with the saints and angels for all eternity. He gives a last charge for his audience to examine if they have had a "great change," love God, love the things He loves, hate the things he hates, and act like Christ.[161] Edwards's explanation of Genesis 1, his emphasis on the Native audience's intrinsic worth as God's creation in His image, and his use of metaphors throughout (such as the "den of serpents" transformed into the "temple of God") show Edwards's focus on his audience and their instruction.

Christ is to The Heart Like a River To A Tree Planted By It[162]

Date: Aug. 1751
Key Text: Psalm 1:3 – "He shall be like a tree planted by the rivers of water."

Christ is to The Heart is a sermon Edwards preached before the Sacrament in August 1751 to the "Stockbridge Indians." It uses the same text (Ps 1:3) as *Christ the River* (preached in 1742 to a colonial audience and examined in the previous chapter). The sermon is written on just two octavo leaves (or a single fold), though it is more written out than *Christ the River*. Instead of focusing on the entire verse as in *Christ the River, Christ is to The Heart* focuses on the beginning of the verse, "He shall be like a tree planted by the rivers of water."[163]

Edwards begins his sermon outline with scriptural references to Jeremiah 17:8 and Isaiah 33:21 (supplementing the doctrine that "Christ is to the

[160]Ibid., 8.

[161]Edwards, "Made in God's Image," 9

[162]Edwards, "Christ is to The Heart Like a River To A Tree Planted By It," *Sermons and Discourses 1743–1758*, 600–605.

[163]Wilson H. Kimnach, "Christ is to The Heart," 600–601.

heart of a true saint like a river to the roots of a tree that is planted by it"). The sermon does not have an introductory section but instead begins with an explanation of the doctrine of the sermon as instruction of the work of Christ in salvation. He explains Christ's love came freely into the world (using the free flow of a river's water as an example) to lay down His life. Then he relates Christ's blood shed as bestowed to His "saints" to water freely running in a river. So, too, are the influences of the Holy Spirit on the saint's heart bestowed freely by Christ "to enlighten and sanctify and comfort."[164]

Using the metaphor of a river was ingenious by Edwards as his Mahican and Mohawk audience were inseparably linked with the Housatonic and Connecticut Rivers. It was the source of their commerce and life, and the Housatonic was linked to the founding of Stockbridge. Edwards further uses the river metaphor to show how Christ's love and grace are abundant like a river. Like a river whose worth is incalculable, Edwards expresses that the happiness Christ gives is infinitely great and valuable. So, too, as a river's water flows unfailingly, Edwards points out "that inward life and comfort that Christ gives the hearts of his saints shall continue to all eternity." Even though death should come or the end of the world, "yet their comforts shall still be like a river that shall not be dried up."[165]

Next, Edwards continues using the river metaphor to show how, like a tree by the river, united to the river whose water enters into its roots, so too does Christ's Spirit come "into the very heart of a saint," making the heart rejoice, keeping it alive, making it grow "beautiful and fruitful." Edwards concludes the sermon with an application for his audience to examine whether they are true saints (reminiscent of *Religious Affections*) who see Christ as "sweeter and better than the sweetest food" and an exhortation for "sinners" to seek Christ lest all of their "streams should fail" (in line with the exhortation in *Christ the River*).[166] This sermon shows Edwards's ingenuity in reaching his audience through metaphors that would strike home for them in their daily life.

[164]Edwards, "Christ is to The Heart," 602.

[165]Ibid., 602–603.

[166]Edwards, "Christ is to The Heart," 603–604.

To the Mohawks at the Treaty, August 16, 1751[167]

Date: Aug. 16, 1751
Key Text: 2 Peter 1:19 – "We have also a more sure word of prophecy, whereunto ye do well that ye take heed, as unto a light that shineth in a dark place, until the day dawn, and the day star arise in your hearts."

To the Mohawks at the Treaty is a shorter manuscript than *Light in a Dark World* (a sermon on the same key text examined in the previous chapter). As the title indicates, it was given during the meeting between government officials and Mohawk representatives. As with *Light in a Dark World*, Edwards uses the metaphor of light that illuminates the soul. The sermon has no headings for doctrine or application but is written as a speech sermon with both the Native and colonial audience in mind.[168]

In the first part of the sermon, Edwards shows how man first had the light (holiness shining in his heart and mind) but lost it during the Fall. This loss would lead to man's heart being possessed by "sin and the devil." Consequently, man fell into "darkness" and worshipped such things as "the sun and moon and stars," "images of gold and silver, brass and iron, wood and stone," and also "serpents and other beasts." Edwards explains they became ignorant, blind, and unable to know how to be "reconciled to Him and obtain His favor."[169]

Edwards moves on to relaying the redemption narrative in God revealing Himself to Moses, sending Christ, and the writing of the Bible. Edwards notes the Bible was made for "all nations, and that all should be instructed of it" as the "great light" given to "teach mankind" about God. Those without the Bible live in darkness with the devil reigning over them. But some who have the Bible are also "perfectly dark" due to their disregard of Scripture. Edwards exhorts his audience (in light of those who disregard the Bible) to seek to know the Bible and "be instructed by it," to receive it into their hearts and put it into practice.[170]

Edwards speaks directly to his Mohawk audience when he says they had lived in "great darkness" for "many ages," and he gives a chastisement for those "white people" who came "over the seas" and neglected their duty to instruct them in the Bible. Edwards ties (as noted throughout this work) the

[167]Edwards, "To the Mohawks at the Treaty, August 16, 1751," *The Sermons of Jonathan Edwards: A Reader*, 105–110, Kindle.

[168]Kimnach, Minkema, and Sweeney, "To the Mohawks at the Treaty," 105.

[169]Edwards, "To the Mohawks at the Treaty," 105–106.

[170]Ibid., 106–107.

natural union between reading in the colonial world and religious/biblical instruction when he writes, "But few of your children have been taught to read. And therefore you know but little of the Word of God, for you ben't able to read it." Edwards notes again the "shameful neglect" of those who have not instructed the Native people of the land in reading for the purpose of knowing the Bible.[171]

Edwards chides that the French (Catholics) gave a pretense of instructing them about God but were, in fact, afraid to actually instruct them in the Word, as they "would know that their ways are not agreeable to Scripture." He also derides English and Dutch colonials who neglected to instruct them and hid the Bible "for the sake of making a gain of you." Edwards proposes a better way based on the earnest course of instruction he had known. He adds:

> But you have been neglected long enough. 'Tis now high time that some more effectual care should be taken that you may be really brought into the clear light, and know as much as the English do.[172]

Edwards instructs his Native audience then to receive the Word as a "wise and happy people," and to think of their children (and consider what is best for them), if they love them, and to "therefore take care for their instruction, that they may be the children of the light, the children of God, and not the children of the devil."[173]

Christ Gave Himself for Us[174]

Date: December 1751
Key Text: Titus 2:14 – "Who gave himself for us, that he might redeem us from all iniquity, and purify unto himself a peculiar people, zealous of good works."

Christ Gave Himself for Us is a fitting sermon to analyze as it shows the contrast in Edwards's methodology in sermon preparation between those he preached at Northampton (in *Zeal an Essential Virtue* from the same key

[171] Ibid., 107.

[172] Edwards, "To the Mohawks at the Treaty," 107–108.

[173] Ibid., 108–110.

[174] Edwards, "Christ Gave Himself for Us," ed. R. Craig Woods, *Jonathan Edwards Sermon Index* (Sermon 1018), (New Haven: Jonathan Edwards Center, Yale University), 1–7.

text as *Christ Gave Himself for Us*) and those to his Mahican congregation at Stockbridge. In *Zeal an Essential Virtue* (examined in the previous chapter), Edwards focuses on the latter portion of the text, the zeal of the "true" Christian. In *Christ Gave Himself for Us*, it is on Christ's sacrifice and the offer of the Gospel that Edwards will spend his energy preaching to this new congregation.[175]

Instead of a doctrine, *Christ Gave Himself for Us* begins with the text and then continues with three points of Gospel exposition taken from the text. The first point is on how Christ gave Himself and exposits the plan and purpose of the incarnation of the sovereign Christ in three subpoints. The first subpoint is how it was planned and agreed upon from "before the world was." The second subpoint is how the Eternal Word came down and became flesh for the salvation of mankind, to be "our Savior." The third subpoint is Christ's fulfillment of His role as the sacrifice through His death on the cross. Edwards instructs this fulfillment was through being wounded, tortured, and placed on a cross, where Christ suffered and died.[176]

Edwards's second main point of Gospel exposition is that Christ "gave himself" to be their savior through his closeness in kind (as a man to suffer and die). His third main point of Gospel exposition is the purpose of Christ's plan, that those He would redeem he would buy (through His death) from God's anger, hell, the power of sin, and corruption of their heart. Edwards explains Christ would buy His people from death, sin, and hell to be then His possession – "sanctified, pure, and holy." Here, Edwards moves to the latter portion of the key text he spent most of his time on in *Zeal an Essential Virtue* and discusses good works, zeal for "His glory," and their happiness.[177]

Edwards concludes with an exhortation to examine what Christ has done for them and to think about how He has redeemed them, how miserable they would have been, and how they should be willing to "be his" and to be "zealous of good works."[178] *Christ Gave Himself for Us* is a good example of Edwards's focus on his Native audience's understanding of Christ's sacrifice and their invitation to the Gospel.

[175]R. Craig Woods, "Christ Gave Himself for Us," 1–2.

[176]Edwards, "Christ Gave Himself for Us," 3–4.

[177]Edwards, "Christ Gave Himself for Us," 4–5.

[178]Ibid., 5–6.

In Remembrance of Christ[179]

Date: January 1752
Key Text: 1 Corinthians 11:23–25 – "For I have received of the Lord that which also I delivered unto you, That the Lord Jesus the same night in which he was betrayed took bread: and when he had given thanks, he brake it, and said, Take, eat: this is my body, which is broken for you: this do in remembrance of me. After the same manner also he took the cup, when he had supped, saying, This cup is the new testament in my blood: this do ye, as oft as ye drink it, in remembrance of me."

In Remembrance of Christ was a sacramental sermon whose brief outline was written on only two octavo-sized leaves, the last nearly blank. R. Craig Woods speculates the Lord's Supper ordinance was observed at Stockbridge twice a month as there is another manuscript for the same month for a sermon on Matthew 26:26–30 (number 1026 in the *Sermon Index*).[180]

Though brief, the outlined manuscript again points to Edwards's purpose in instructing those at the mission in the fundamentals of the faith. He directs himself to show what is meant by the bread being the body and the wine the blood of Christ in the sacrament, as well as their benefit to those who partake. He also directs himself to instruct on what the phrase "broken for" means, what the new covenant is, and how they are to partake in the Lord's Supper. Those explanations of the basics of the Lord's Supper serve as the context Edwards wants his audience to understand before instructing them in the manner of remembering and partaking in the Lord's Supper.[181]

Now, after giving an understanding of what the Lord's Supper is, Edwards instructs that they should remember Christ's sufferings and dying love, be affected by this love of Christ, remember the promises they gave in renewing their friendship with Christ, and show they have received Him. Edwards charges they should often remember Christ and honor and glorify Him. Next is a short application to exhort his audience to prepare for the Lord's Supper and a direction to preach to those "that have offended" and those "that are in good standing."[182]

The clear difference between *In Remembrance of Christ* and *Self-Examination and the Lord's Supper* (examined in the previous chapter) is Edwards's focus

[179]Edwards, "In Remembrance of Christ," R. ed. Craig Woods, *Jonathan Edwards Sermon Index* (Sermon 1024), (New Haven: Jonathan Edwards Center, Yale University), 1–5.

[180]R. Craig Woods, "In Remembrance of Christ," 1–2.

[181]Edwards, "In Remembrance of Christ," 3.

[182]Ibid., 4–5.

on instructing his audience on what the Lord's Supper is before giving a briefer application to examine themselves. Edwards is unsure of what his audience knows about the Supper and its significance, so he instructs before exhorting them in spiritual preparation. Perhaps in light of the reception and after following up with his audience, his next sacramental sermon, *The Lord's Supper is an Ordinance That Represents the Greatest Things,* is given to his audience to instruct them further on the Lord's Supper.

The Lord's Supper is an Ordinance That Represents the Greatest Things [183]

Date: January 31, 1752
Key Text: Matthew 26:26–30 – "And as they were eating, Jesus took bread, and blessed it, and brake it, and gave it to the disciples, and said, Take, eat; this is my body. And he took the cup, and gave thanks, and gave it to them, saying, Drink ye all of it; for this is my blood of the new testament, which is shed for many for the remission of sins. But I say unto you, I will not drink henceforth of this fruit of the vine, until that day when I drink it new with you in my Father's kingdom. And when they had sung an hymn, they went out into the mount of Olives."

The manuscript for *The Lord's Supper is an Ordinance* is written on twice as many octavo-sized leaves (four) as *In Remembrance of Christ*. As theorized above, this could be due to Edwards's goal of giving his audience a basic introduction to what the Lord's Supper is in *In Remembrance of Christ* and then moving on to explaining the significance of the establishment of it by Christ on the night He was betrayed.[184]

Edwards begins by noting that Christ established the ordinance of communion on the night before His crucifixion. Edwards writes the ordinance was established as the first sacrament to represent Christ's great sufferings for His Church. He explains Christ's breaking of the bread with the quote, "This is my body," means the bread represents Christ's body (and the food of the saints). Christ's blessing of the bread means it is for their "spiritual good." The breaking of it also points to Christ's suffering on the cross. His death meant their life, so Edwards says, "When the minister gives (the bread

[183]Edwards, "The Lord's Supper is an Ordinance That Represents the Greatest Things," ed. R. Craig Woods, *Jonathan Edwards Sermon Index* (Sermon 1026), (New Haven: Jonathan Edwards Center, Yale University), 1–7.

[184]R. Craig Woods, "The Lord's Supper is an Ordinance," 1–2.

and wine, this is to signify that Christ offers himself. The minister stands in the stead of Christ)."[185]

Edwards intentionally instructs his audience on what the Lord's Supper is, how it is performed in the church, and its significance. This instruction is given to help them become familiar with the ordinance (and the theological/spiritual implications of its meaning) so they can participate in it with full understanding and purpose. Edwards explains the connection between the wine and the blood of Christ and uses an illustration of a winepress to show the sufferings Christ endured. He further shows how wine (he assures in little portions) gives refreshment to those who are "weak and faint" because of their sin and the sight of "how wicked they be, and what a miserable condition they are in."[186]

Edwards continues that the blood is the seal of the new "testament" or "covenant," which he instructs is like when someone makes a contract ("bargain") with another and seals that contract. Edwards shows the blood was shed for the remission of sins for "some of all nations" and notes God does not desire a second sacrifice but has sufficed it once by Christ's blood. The disciples' partaking in the Supper signifies their acceptance of this covenant. He then repeats his instruction in this ordinance to point to what the Lord's Supper is and what they are doing by partaking in it.[187]

He explains that the phrase "do this in remembrance of" Him meant (citing Luke 22:19 to remember His sufferings) that Christ would "not henceforth drink of this fruit of the vine." This sermon shows how Edwards focuses on explaining the text verse by verse so his audience understands what it means and its significance. After the explanation, he moves to the applications, where he instructs how they "ought to attend on the ordinance of the Lord's Supper." These include renewing their covenant with God, giving themselves to Him, forsaking their sins, praising and loving Him, remembering His love and imitating it, remembering His great promises, and laboring to prepare for the "eternal joy and happiness in heaven, drinking wine with him."[188]

[185]Edwards, "The Lord's Supper is an Ordinance," 2–3.

[186]Ibid., 3–4.

[187]Edwards, "The Lord's Supper is an Ordinance," 4–5.

[188]Ibid., 5–6.

The Poor in Spirit Are Happy Because the Kingdom of Heaven is Theirs [189]

Date: August 2, 1752
Key Text: Matthew 5:3b – "Blessed are the poor in spirit: for theirs is the kingdom of God."

The Poor in Spirit Are Happy is one of three sermons on the Beatitudes from the Sermon on the Mount in Matthew 5 given concurrently to his Stockbridge congregation. This will be the first sermon series given by Edwards examined to see how he built on knowledge of a text or theme to his Mahican and Mohawk audience. The manuscript for this sermon is brief and written on two octavo-sized leaves. The key text has a parallel examined in the previous chapter (*Poverty of Spirit*) given much earlier in Edwards's preaching ministry to a colonial audience.[190]

Instruction is the theme of the first point of Edwards's sermon as he shows what being "poor in spirit" means in the text. He explains it means to not "be lifted up, or trusting in anything of our own" but instead to be humble. Those in the world are most likely to trust in two things: worldly possessions and their "own greatness or goodness." The humble are not like this and will "have the kingdom of heaven," Edwards explains in his second point. They will become "children of the King of heaven." For his third point, Edwards simply writes, "They are happy on that account. How much better (is this) than all earthly things." Edwards's application is just as brief as he explains that humility is what "true religion" is, which men are naturally far from, and that they should pray that they would have a humble heart.[191]

They That Mourn Are Happy Because They Shall Be Comforted[192]

Date: August 1752
Key Text: Matthew 5:4b – "Blessed are they that mourn: for they shall be comforted."

[189] Edwards, "The Poor in Spirit Are Happy Because the Kingdom of Heaven is Theirs," ed. R. Craig Woods, *Jonathan Edwards Sermon Index* (Sermon 1049), (New Haven: Jonathan Edwards Center, Yale University), 1–5.

[190] R. Craig Woods, "The Poor in Spirit Are Happy," 1–2.

[191] Edwards, "The Poor in Spirit Are Happy," 3–4.

[192] Edwards, "They That Mourn Are Happy Because They Shall Be Comforted," ed. R. Craig Woods, *Jonathan Edwards Sermon Index* (Sermon 1050), (New Haven: Jonathan Edwards Center, Yale University), 1–4.

The second of three sermons on the Beatitudes, *They That Mourn Are Happy* is written on two octavo-sized leaves.[193] Edwards uses this second sermon (and key text) to show what mourning is. He notes it is a godly sorrow over sin (of others' and one's own sin). He adds there can be sorrow over "fear from hell," which Edwards states is not godly sorrow, but that which is "mourning from love to God" is godly sorrow that mourns "sin as sin" and "for all sin," not just out of selfish perseverance. Edwards again acts as an instructor here, explaining what godly sorrow is (and what it is not) for an audience who may not understand the idea of godly sorrow.[194]

Edwards's second point is those who have godly sorrow will be comforted. Those who have godly sorrow will have their sins forgiven, will see there is enough in Christ, will live a "life of love to God," will enjoy God's love and favor, will have a "hope of glory," have "deliverance from all trouble," and have eternal joy. Because of the above, Edwards continues with his third point that those who mourn with godly sorrow are happier than those with "worldly comforts," as those with godly sorrow end in comfort while those with worldly comfort end in sorrow.

Edwards further shows the wide contrast since worldly joy is short with no end to its sorrow, while godly sorrow is short with no end to its comfort in eternity. He finishes by imploring his audience to see the world "with eyes open" by seeking after godly sorrow and avoiding "carnal mirth." He adds for them to pray often "with confession of your sins" to have "comfort under affliction," "comfort when all worldly comforts fail," and "comfort when others have sorrow."[195] Humility was the theme in *The Poor in Spirit Are Happy*. In *They That Mourn Are Happy*, Edwards builds upon Jesus's teaching through instructing on godly sorrow and confession.

The Pure in Heart Are Happy Because They Shall See God[196]

Date: August 1752
Key Text: Matt. 5:8b – "Blessed are the pure in heart: for they shall see God."

[193]R. Craig Woods, "They That Mourn Are Happy," 1.

[194]Edwards," They That Mourn Are Happy," 2.

[195]Edwards, "They That Mourn Are Happy," 3–4.

[196]Edwards, "The Pure in Heart Are Happy Because They Shall See God," ed. R. Craig Woods, *Jonathan Edwards Sermon Index* (Sermon 1051), (New Haven: Jonathan Edwards Center, Yale University), 1–6.

The third sermon in the series on the Beatitudes, *The Pure in Heart Are Happy*, again builds on Edwards's theme of what it means to have godly happiness or joy. This sermon has the same key text as the sermon preached twenty-two years earlier by Edwards at Northampton, *The Pure in Heart Blessed* (examined in the previous chapter). This sermon, though, is briefer, written on four octavo-sized leaves (whereas *The Pure in Heart Blessed* is written in a duodecimo booklet with 25 extant leaves).[197]

The stark contrast between the sermons can be seen in the early metaphysical focus of *The Pure in Heart Blessed* on seeing God's glory with one's spiritual eyes instead of one's "bodily eyes." Edwards will briefly talk of spiritual and bodily sight at the end of *The Pure in Heart Are Happy*, but not until he has instructed his audience in what it means to be "pure in heart." Edwards is more gospel-focused and instructive in how one needs to be purified from sin, which "pollutes the soul and makes it more filthy than dung." He explains that the sinner's heart is full of this dung, yet when converted, the converted's heart is "made pure – yet not perfectly in this life – but yet pure."[198]

The converted then hate sin, which no longer has mastery over them. Thus, they should mortify pride, covetousness, drunkenness, and lasciviousness. They should have "holy principles," love what is pure and holy, and love holy things for their holiness (including holy days, exercises, enjoyments, the Bible, God's commands, God's ways, and heaven). Those who are converted, hate sin, and love God and holy things shall be rewarded by seeing God (Edwards's third point). This point is where Edwards (like in *The Pure in Heart Blessed*) explains seeing God not with "bodily eyes" but spiritually. The converted will see the "infinite beauty and loveliness of God." They will also see "the glory of Jesus Christ with bodily eyes" without "any darkness" or "in a dark manner" as here on earth.[199]

Those who are not pure in heart will not see God in the manner he preached above, as they "are not fit to come into heaven, where everything is holy." Their wicked hearts would blind them anyway, according to this third point, but those who can see Him are "truly happy," as his concluding fourth point shows.[200]

[197]R. Craig Woods, "The Pure in Heart Are Happy," 1–2.

[198]Edwards, "The Pure in Heart Are Happy," 2.

[199]Edwards, "The Pure in Heart Are Happy," 3–4.

[200]Ibid., 4.

For his application, Edwards calls them to examine whether they are truly clear or just outwardly showing a false cleanliness and to "endeavor to become more pure." Then he exhorts his audience to seek after a pure heart.[201]

Thus, in the three sermons on the Beatitudes, Edwards's focus on relaying the instructions of Christ in the Sermon on the Mount guides his Native audience in understanding humility, Godly sorrow, and purity, which is seen in this sermon series.

God Invites Men to the Great Feast He Has Prepared[202]

Date: August 1752
Key Text: Luke 14:16–17 – "Then said he, a certain man made a great supper, and bade many: and sent his servant at supper time to say to them that were bidden, Come; for all things are now ready."

Two sacramental sermons Edwards preached to his Mohawk and Mahican audience in January of 1752 were analyzed above (*In Remembrance of Christ* and *The Lord's Supper is an Ordinance*). In November of the same year that Edwards preached the sacramental sermons (above) and those on the Matthean Beatitudes, he gave another sacramental sermon with Luke 14:16–17 as the key text (though he also comments in his sermon on verses 18–21). Edwards's earliest sacramental sermon was given thirty-three to thirty-four years earlier (*The Spiritual Blessings of the Gospel Represented by a Feast* – analyzed in the previous chapter).[203]

In this sermon, Edwards gives five observations of the text before concluding with a short application. The title shows the focus of the sermon (in line with the key text), which relates to something his audience would be familiar with (a great feast). His first observation is that the provision of God by Jesus Christ for the good of men's souls is "like a great feast." He outlines several applications of the provision for man (his audience). The provision is for their deliverance, preservation, defense, being made holy and instructed, having rest and peace, comfort and joy, being made

[201] Ibid., 5.

[202] Edwards, "God Invites Men to the Great Feast He Has Prepared," ed. R. Craig Woods, *Jonathan Edwards Sermon Index* (Sermon 1057), (New Haven: Jonathan Edwards Center, Yale University), 1–6.

[203] R. Craig Woods, "God Invites Men to the Great Feast He Has Prepared," 1–2.

honorable (rich), and having "comfort under all circumstances" even in death and their resurrection.[204]

The provision is also like a great feast (or food) in that it gives life, refreshes, and nourishes. Edwards notes men naturally are poor and without food; therefore, Christ is the bread from heaven (citing John 6:51), and things that are like food are the Word of God, the Bible, preaching, ordinances, holy meditation, the Spirit's influence, and the "enjoyments of heaven." But this provision of food, he adds, was very costly but is provided in abundance in the house of God (the church) and will be in heaven as a wedding feast.[205]

His second observation is that many are invited by God to this feast. Christ is the bridegroom and was sent into the world to invite sinners to the feast. Edwards then quotes Proverbs 8:4 and Isaiah 55:1–3 to show how God invites through His Word. God invites through the preaching of the Word, by His Spirit, from captivity in "service of the devil" to be His friends, His children, to enjoy Christ's peace and joy, and to be with Him in heaven. He invites sinners earnestly, kindly, and "sometimes a great while." This emphasis on the invitational aspect of the Gospel's great feast is expanded even beyond Edwards's sermon on this text thirty years prior, which emphasized the benefits of community after the invitation was accepted.[206]

His third observation is that "God tells sinners all things are ready." Edwards explains that God has made all things ready by appeasing his anger and overcoming what previously stood in the way (men's sin and God's justice and holiness) through what He did in taking "His kingdom not only for Himself, but His people" as "Christ has been made King over all." Ministers, then, are called and sent to invite sinners to the great feast.[207]

The fifth observation is that men are opposed to the invitation (citing Luke 14:18–21 found following the key text). Edwards explains the reasons for their opposition as found in the text. After his final observation is a short application to consider how it was with them, that there must be a great change of heart, and that the old things must be "done away" with.

[204]Edwards, "God Invites Men to the Great Feast He Has Prepared," 3–7.

[205]Ibid., 3–4.

[206]Ibid., 4–5.

[207]Edwards, "God Invites Men to the Great Feast He Has Prepared," 5–6.

Edwards's focus on invitation and regeneration for his Native audience again shows his concern on their behalf.[208]

God is an Infinitely Merciful and Gracious God[209]

Date: January 1753
Key Text: Exodus 34:6–7 – "And the Lord passed by before him, and proclaimed, the name of the Lord: The Lord, The Lord God, merciful and gracious, longsuffering, and abundant in goodness and truth, keeping mercy for thousands, forgiving iniquity and transgression and sin, and that will by no means clear the guilty; visiting the iniquity of the fathers upon the children, and upon the children's children, unto the third and to the fourth generation."

The second sermon series to be examined from Edwards's time at Stockbridge contains doctrinal sermons on the infinite attributes of God (His infinite mercy and grace are seen in this first sermon). *God is an Infinitely Merciful and Gracious God* follows after another doctrinal sermon where Edwards looked at the certainty of God (key text: Ps 14:1b). Edwards uses subsequent sermons in his "infinite" series to look at the strength of God (*God is Infinitely Strong*), and the holiness of God (*God is Infinitely Holy*).[210]

To begin his sermon, Edwards recalls his audience's attention to previous teachings he has given them on how certain God is and how God is wise, powerful, and holy. He then moves on to the purpose of this sermon, which is to relay to them how God is able to do good and is inclined to do so and to give of His infinite happiness. The stating of this purpose sets up his first point that God's "goodness and kindness is great (in many ways)." First, it is because of the great number of people He does good to, including all living creatures, the angels in heaven, man (before the fall), fallen man, great and small, old and young, all nations, and all that "live under the light of the Gospel" (especially those who are "good men"). He then notes that God's goodness is like the sun in its universal abundance.[211]

[208] Ibid., 6–7. There is a note for an exhortation, though it is lost. Woods, "God Invites Men to the Great Feast He Has Prepared," 6–7.

[209] Edwards, "God is an Infinitely Merciful and Gracious God," ed. R. Craig Woods, *Jonathan Edwards Sermon Index* (Sermon 1063), (New Haven: Jonathan Edwards Center, Yale University), 1–6.

[210] R. Craig Woods, "God is an Infinitely Merciful and Gracious God," 1–2.

[211] Edwards, "God is an Infinitely Merciful and Gracious God," 2–3.

Edwards's second point is that God's goodness is great "in the mercy and great gifts" God bestows on mankind (particularly). His illustration for his second point is a river that has overflown its bank, which shows how God's goodness overflows onto mankind. His next five points are given in short succession as follows:

> III. That he shows such great goodness to them that are so much below him, [that are] so little.
>
> IV. In that he is so good to them who are so evil and unworthy.
>
> V. In the great things God has done for such as are so unworthy. [In those great things done] by Jesus Christ. This, above all other things, this opens the heart of God.
>
> VI. In the great good he provides for them.
>
> VII. In that his goodness and mercy last so long.[212]

These attributes are given as instruction for Edwards's Native audience to help them understand the goodness of God. Edwards finishes the body of his sermon by stating God's goodness and mercy are like a perpetually flowing river, returning to his river illustration because of their proximity to the Housatonic River. The application for this sermon is lengthier than those previously examined for his Mohawk and Mahican audience, with nine applicatory points. The first three are written as notes to himself, pointing to how Edwards should tell his audience how "the true God differs from the gods of the heathen" in holiness and goodness, the cause they have to love God (and the great sin of those who do not), and the cause they have to praise him.[213]

Next are exhortations for his audience: to seek after God's goodness and mercy; to seek after God to be their God (and the loss at not seeking after Him); to pray to God for what they may need (with a note to instruct them how to pray);[214] encouragement under "all afflictions and troubles;" a warning not to "abuse and make a bad improvement" on God's mercy and goodness; and finally to "imitate God's goodness and mercy." In this sermon Edwards gives thorough instruction, uses contextual metaphors (of a river

[212]Edwards, "God is an Infinitely Merciful and Gracious God," 3–4.

[213]Ibid., 4–5.

[214]This again shows Edwards's concentration on instruction.

of God's goodness and mercy), and then gives application for his audience to seek out God's goodness in imitation.[215]

God is Infinitely Strong[216]

Date: January 1753
Key Text: Job 9:4 – "He is wise of heart, and mighty in strength."

The second in his "infinite" sermon series, *God is Infinitely Strong,* takes a more narrative tone with Edwards's introduction illustrating God's sight, knowledge, and wisdom before a short doctrine and application. Kimnach notes the sermon shows how Edwards had "fully adjusted his sermons to what he assumed were the capabilities of the Indians" or to what could be relayed through an interpreter. As noted through the previous sermons, Edwards has a purpose solely for this sermon: to show God's infinite sight and knowledge in relation to His infinite strength (to be exposited in the doctrinal section of the sermon).[217]

Edwards begins the sermon by citing Psalm 147:4 to show God's omniscience. He then explains what this means as he relays that God sees over "every man, woman, and child, every beast on earth, every bird in the air, every fish in the sea." He continues by stating not even a gnat is unknown to God, nor anything a thousand miles underground. But beyond seeing the physical realities of what men do or what they speak, Edwards explains that God sees "their hearts and thoughts." So, too, anything from the past, present, and future is beyond God's knowledge and sight. He goes deeper in illustrating this a second time by relaying God's knowledge and sight to His role as Creator in bringing all to its beginning and end.[218] Edwards then concludes this section by speaking on God's wisdom.[219]

Edwards relates to his Native audience here well in showing that all of the wisdom they have of the earth and nature, comes from God. And that God's perfect wisdom goes beyond even their limited knowledge and wisdom. For his doctrinal section, Edwards moves on to God's strength. He notes there is nothing beyond the ability of God, relaying God's creation ex nihilo with the illustration of the creation of the world and great things

[215] Ibid., 4–5.

[216] Edwards, "God is Infinitely Strong," *Sermons and Discourses 1743–1758*, 641–646.

[217] Kimnach, "God is Infinitely Strong," 641–642.

[218] Edwards, "God is Infinitely Strong," 643–644.

[219] Ibid., 644.

and "making 'em out of nothing" while "all the men in the world can't make one grain of sand." God illustrates his power not only through creation but also through God's upholding of the universe, "managing the sun, moon, and stars." Another image Edwards uses in direct context for his audience is the strength and appearance of God's strength displayed in thunder and lightning, the wind, and through earthquakes.[220] He finishes by showing all the mighty displays of God seen in the Bible and foretold within:

> Many things the Scripture gives an account [of]: [a] flood of waters; [God] divided the sea; [the] sun stood still. [In the New Testament are] Christ's miracles, [who] raised the dead. [Some day God will] bring the world to an end; roll [all] together, [make the] stars fall from heaven, [and] set all on fire. [God will] raise all the dead, overcoming all his enemies, great kings and their armies. [Meanwhile,] all the devils are held back by him. [God] must be strong, for he gives all others all their strength.[221]

Edwards's application is simply for his audience to fear and trust in God and to be humble as there is "no getting away from God, no hiding" as it is miserable "to have God to be their enemy." His final exhortation is to fear God and not sin against Him as he "sees your heart" and "remembers all," but to come to him to be saved "from the devil" as God is able "as a strong man comes and takes a lamb out of the mouth of a bear."[222] This again shows Edwards's focus on natural metaphor his audience would have related to, to invite them to God's Word and the Gospel.

God is Infinitely Holy[223]

Date: January 1753
Key Text: Isaiah 6:3 – "Holy, holy, holy, is the Lord of hosts."

The third sermon in Edwards's "infinite" series has Isaiah 6:3 as its key text. Edwards again goes back to his more outlined form of manuscript,

[220] Ibid., 644–645.

[221] Ibid., 645.

[222] Edwards, "God is Infinitely Strong," 645.

[223] Edwards, "God is Infinitely Holy," ed. R. Craig Woods, *Jonathan Edwards Sermon Index* (Sermon 1065), (New Haven: Jonathan Edwards Center, Yale University), 1–9.

though one with many points and subpoints.[224] Edwards begins by recalling their memory to previous sermons they heard him preach, where he taught on the certainty of God and God's wisdom and strength. Now, his first point of this sermon explains "what I mean by God's being infinitely holy" (the doctrine of his sermon). Edwards uses language to speak to the level of his audience, as a teacher would with a pupil.[225]

Edwards explains which attributes of God determine Him as infinitely holy. These attributes include the purity of His heart ("no evil disposition") and the impossibility of Him sinning or doing any evil. He illustrates God's holiness by stating that God is as far from sin and evil as the "sun is from darkness" (citing 1 John 1:15). He then cites Deuteronomy 32:4 before using Deuteronomy 4:24 to state how much God hates sin (infinitely). Third, Edwards notes God is full only of "good inclination" and even "delights in everything that is good, wherever he sees it" (point four). Finally, Edwards concludes his explanation of God's infinite holiness by citing Psalm 145:17 to prove his final explanation that God "always acts holily."[226]

For the second point of his sermon, Edwards doubles down and advises he will now show how "plain that it must be so" that God should be perfectly holy and unable to be otherwise. For this point, he has two subpoints. The first is that God is not able to be "inclined" to sin or do evil because there is none who can "incline" God to do so. He compares this with man, who has every inclination to evil as they "hope to get something by it," referencing drunkenness (pleasure), cheating and stealing (profit), being prideful (greater honor), and hating their neighbor (fear of being hurt); all of which God cannot be inclined by as he has no need for those things and cannot be hurt. Edwards illustrates this by way of God's omnipotence, explaining how God can create anything He would hypothetically need (bread, silver, rum, or wine). Even the devil could not tempt God, though Edwards explains their "first parents" and "mankind" were.[227]

For his second, shorter subpoint, Edwards notes God "must love all that is right and good." This subpoint highlights God's infinite wisdom and knowledge. As God knows and understands all, He sees holiness and love as "excellent," whereas man is blind and thus loves sin. His third and final point is that it "appears that God is holy in the things which he has done,"

[224]R. Craig Woods, "God is Infinitely Holy," 1–9.

[225]Edwards, "God is Infinitely Holy," 3.

[226]Edwards, "God is Infinitely Holy," 3–4.

[227]Ibid., 4–6.

including making man (who at first was holy), His commands and laws, His Word, His justice in punishing sin (and rewards for doing "what is right"), Jesus Christ, the way of salvation by Christ, and the "holiness of heaven."[228]

Edwards concludes with nine applications, including the care they should take in keeping themselves from sin (the first application). The second and third are their need for repentance and a Savior to die for them. The fourth and fifth are the certainty of His hearing their prayers and negatively how "none will go to heaven that live in any wickedness." That there will be a day of judgment is the sixth, leading to the seventh in the certainty of God's Word (which they should not be afraid to trust in), and the eighth states how they should learn to accept affliction as being in God's goodwill. He concludes with an exhortation to examine whether they are holy in hating sin, living holiness, and loving God because "He is holy."[229]

In examining *The Holiness of God* in the last chapter (preached by Edwards five years earlier on the same key text), Edwards concludes *God is Infinitely Holy* with more of an emphasis on instructing his audience on what it means to repent, their access to God's prayers, the trust they can place in God's Word. For both audiences, he concludes with an exhortation to self-examination in light of God's holiness.[230]

Persons' Speech Shows What Fills Their Heart[231]

Date: August 1753
Key Text: Luke 6:45c – "Out of the abundance of the heart the mouth speaks."

Persons' Speech is the first of three sermons preached by Edwards at Stockbridge on the same key text (Luke 6:45). This first sermon sets up the following sermons by showing how outward speech shows what fills a person's heart. The following two sermons (*The Good Man's Treasure* and *The Wicked Man's Treasure*) dive deeper into the desires of those whose hearts are either filled with goodness or wickedness. This first sermon is a brief outline manuscript composed on only two octavo-sized leaves.[232]

[228]Edwards, "God is Infinitely Holy," 6–7.

[229]Ibid., 7–8.

[230]Edwards, "God is Infinitely Holy," 7–8; "The Holiness of God," 7–9.

[231]Edwards, "Persons' Speech Shows What Fills Their Heart," ed. R. Craig Woods, *Jonathan Edwards Sermon Index* (Sermon 1088), (New Haven: Jonathan Edwards Center, Yale University), 1–9.

[232]R. Craig Woods, "Persons' Speech," 1.

Edwards begins this outline by stating his doctrine: "The speech of their mouths will show that which their hearts is full of." This is a simple sermon giving a basic understanding of the wickedness in the speech of "wicked men" and the goodness in the speech of those who are good. He first lists what is in the speech of "wicked men," including lying, swearing, taking the Lord's name in vain, mocking religion, calling others "bad names," reviling, cursing, quarrelsome speech, "talking against others," and conversation about worldly things on the Sabbath. The good things spoken by "good men" include prayers, praises, good things, promotion of religion, "speaking for the good" of neighbors, and love and kindness.[233]

For his application, Edwards first tells his audience to "get a good heart, that your heart may speak right things." Next, he exhorts them not to let their hearts speak evil but rather good by avoiding lies and praying (citing Jas 1:26 and Matt 12:37).[234] This sermon on what comes from within will set up his following sermons on the consequences of a holy or wicked life.

The Good Man's Treasure[235]

Date: August 1753
Key Text: Luke 6:45 – "A good man out of the good treasure of his heart bringeth forth that which is good; and an evil man out of the evil treasure of his heart bringeth forth that which is evil: for of the abundance of the heart his mouth speaketh."

In his first "treasure" sermon (and second preached from Luke 6:45), Edwards briefly outlines what the "good man's" treasure is.[236] The sermon has two brief points. The first is that the good man has a good treasure that not only shows outwardly in profession (as seen in *Persons' Speech*) but also in knowledge, wisdom, and "holy dispositions." The second point is this treasure will bring "forth good things in his life and conversation." Not like those who pretend they are good. But through holy principles, Edwards notes, good men "tend to holy practices." There is then a note by Edwards to tell his audience how they will be answerable for their behavior. Those

[233] Edwards, "Persons' Speech," 2.

[234] Ibid., 3.

[235] Edwards, "The Good Man's Treasure," ed. R. Craig Woods, *Jonathan Edwards Sermon Index* (Sermon 1089), (New Haven: Jonathan Edwards Center, Yale University), 1–4.

[236] R. Craig Woods, "The Good Man's Treasure," 1.

who have "love shining in them" will have it shine out of them and won't live a "wicked" or "idle life."[237]

Edwards gives two applications for this sermon. The second is to bring out the "good things" from their heart. The first is for his audience to seek "that treasure in your heart." He adds they must have a new heart, broken with repentance, for a treasure that is better than all the precious metals in the world since they will be precious to God and His treasure. Then they will have treasure in heaven, where God and Christ will be their treasure. Noteworthy is Edwards's point that they "are taught how to get this treasure out of that excellent book, the Bible," showing the tie again to biblical literacy and affection for God's Word.[238]

The Wicked Man's Treasure[239]

Date: August 1753
Key Text: Luke 6:45 – "And an evil man out of the evil treasure of his heart bringeth forth that which is evil."

The final sermon in the trio of Luke 6:45 sermons now shifts the focus to the "wicked" treasure of the "wicked man."[240] In his two points, Edwards has a bit more to say about the wickedness from a dark heart than he did in his previous sermon. His first point is that the "wicked man" has a "treasure of evil" in his heart since it is full of "all manner of evil," darkness, blindness, unbelief, "folly," pride, hatred of God and good things, selfishness, worldliness, and covetousness (subpoint one). These are things that lead the heart and mind to be "beastly," loving that which "beasts" love, including eating and drinking, being drunk, "fornication," dishonesty, injustice, hatred of each other, and contention.[241]

He continues that this "evil treasure" is very great since sinful actions are not only a great evil but are also plentiful. Edwards would have seen several "evil" events (based on the above list) at Stockbridge that year that would have surely come to mind, including the mysterious burning of the Indian schoolhouse in February and the murder of Waumpaumcourse, a

[237] Edwards, "The Good Man's Treasure," 2.

[238] Ibid., 2–3.

[239] Edwards, "The Wicked Man's Treasure," ed. R. Craig Woods, *Jonathan Edwards Sermon Index* (Sermon 1090), (New Haven: Jonathan Edwards Center, Yale University), 1–9.

[240] R. Craig Woods, "The Wicked Man's Treasure," 1.

[241] Edwards, "The Wicked Man's Treasure," 2.

Schaghticoke Indian in Stockbridge by two horse thieves (leading to the end of the Mohawks' treaty with the British on June 16). His next points about great blindness, pride, and worldly-mindedness are again tied to those events and correlate with his following statement that the "hearts of all alike" are sinful.[242]

In further preaching on how that "evil treasure" of "wicked men" appears, Edwards notes that it comes to be when God leaves them to their sin and manifests in the "dreadful effects" of the world being full of that wickedness (noting wars especially). Edwards then gives a subpoint about the Fall, how man at first was good but then "provoked God" to leave him to his wickedness and "the devil." He concludes with his second main point: the "wicked man" brings about the "evil treasure" in his "life and conversation," and even while some do good things, "they don't do in a right way," but instead do them in hypocrisy and "for the wrong ends." The main points then set up his five applications: to understand why God punishes sin with "afflictions" and death, how man cannot save himself, how great God's mercy is, the need for a "new heart," and how "great a work" the conversion of the sinner is. Edwards concludes with an exhortation to "seek to have that evil treasure taken away. You do but treasure up misery."[243]

With God and the Lamb in Heaven[244]

Date: November 1753
Key Text: Revelation 22:3–5 – "And there shall be no more curse: [but the throne of God and of the Lamb shall be in it; and his servants shall serve him: and they shall see his face; and his name shall be in their foreheads. And there shall be no night there; and they need no candle, neither light of the sun; for the Lord God giveth them light: and they shall reign for ever and ever]."

One of three consecutive sermons from Revelation 22, *With God and the Lamb in Heaven* presents a positive picture of heavenly fellowship with Christ. The manuscript is written with eleven numbered heads that detail the blessings of life in heaven.[245] Edwards uses the points of his sermon

[242] Ibid., 2–3.

[243] Edwards, "The Wicked Man's Treasure," 3–4.

[244] Edwards, "With God and the Lamb in Heaven," ed. R. Craig Woods, *Jonathan Edwards Sermon Index* (Sermon 1098), (New Haven: Jonathan Edwards Center, Yale University), 1–5.

[245] R. Craig Woods, "With God and the Lamb in Heaven," 1.

to explain and then elaborate on the text, instructing his audience on the contents of the text. An example is the first point, taken from Revelation 22:3a, which states, "And there shall be no more curse." Edwards's first point, "[in heaven, there shall be] no more misery or sorrow, darkness, spiritual trouble, outward affliction [or] death," explains what it means that there is no longer the curse of the Fall. Points two and three (taken from the key text) explain the Father and Son (Lamb) shall be there reigning as "their King."[246]

Points four through six explain how those in heaven will be God and Christ's "dear people," God's servants, who will serve Him faithfully and be able to see His face. As will be seen in examining the application of *With God and the Lamb in Heaven,* Edwards's previously examined sermon to colonials (*Serving God in Heaven*) had as its focus stirring the hearts of his congregation from apathy to service of God. Here in this sermon, the focus is entrance and invitation to become members of the family of God. Edwards goes on to explain to his Mahican congregation that they will not only serve but "be as kings" (taken from Rev 22:5b that they shall "reign for ever and ever") and have no want of the "good things of this world." There will also be "no night" there, but all will be lit through God and Christ, who "will be instead of the sun in heaven" (again taken from the key text). He concludes the section by stating their "glory and happiness shall continue forever and ever."[247]

Edwards's application includes four observations and ten exhortations (directions) for his audience. His observations include not setting their heart on "this world" but seeking "after heaven" (citing John 16:33). He reiterates the message that in this world, there is the curse and "wickedness," "contention," and "night;" but in heaven there is God's light, fellowship with Him, and no more death. His second observation is that they can seek after heaven then. The third is how foolish they will be not to hear of this Gospel opportunity, and the fourth is the misery that awaits if they do not go to heaven.[248]

For directions, he starts by saying that they must be convinced of "their miserable condition" and that, because of their sin, they "don't deserve heaven." The third, fourth, and fifth exhortations are to trust in Christ only and to have their heart changed (which must happen in heaven). The

[246]Edwards, "With God and the Lamb in Heaven," 2.

[247]Ibid., 2.

[248]Edwards, "With God and the Lamb in Heaven," 2–3.

seventh is to be willing to serve God and Christ as their servant and to "love Christ better than the light of the sun" (sixth). Finally, they must seek heaven by all the "means God has appointed" (tenth), pray much that God would "fit" them for heaven (ninth), and think often of heaven (eighth). The "means" Edwards gives for his tenth point of exhortation are keeping the Sabbath, listening to sermons, reading the Bible, and "coming to the sacraments."[249]

What Men Are When They Die, They Will Be to All Eternity[250]

Date: November 1753
Key Text: Revelation 22:11–12 – "He that is unjust, let him be unjust still: and he which is filthy, let him be filthy still: and he that is righteous, let him be righteous still: and he that is holy, let him be holy still. And, behold, I come quickly; and my reward is with me, to give every man according as his work shall be."

The second of his sermons on Revelation 22, *What Men Are When They Die* is a potentially charged sermon in light of a dispute between Edwards's Native American congregation and those with whom they had a dispute (the previously mentioned Ephraim Williams Jr., Jonathan Devereux, Josiah Williams, Abigail Williams, Sergeant Dwight, and Judith Williams who had dissented from, and was absent from the church due to their disagreements with Edwards and the church and fear they would be censured). The sermon's theme is the justice and judgment of God. A note at the end ("Church Meeting") points to the above situation and that it was likely preached to a mixed congregation. The manuscript is written on six octavo-sized leaves.[251]

The sermon begins with the doctrine: "The time will come that, as men are at that time, whether good or bad, so they will be to all eternity; they never will change," pointing again to the probability of its preaching in a mixed-audience setting. There are two doctrinal points for the sermon. The first is that while "men" are in the world, they can change from bad "men" to good. Under this point, Edwards relays how, in the Fall, men went from being good to bad but are given a chance to change back (unlike devils,

[249] Ibid., 3–4.

[250] Edwards, "What Men Are When They Die, They Will Be to All Eternity," ed. R. Craig Woods, *Jonathan Edwards Sermon Index* (Sermon 1099), (New Haven: Jonathan Edwards Center, Yale University), 1–8.

[251] R. Craig Woods, "What Men Are When They Die," 1–2.

who were once angels). Edwards explains that some went from very bad, or the least (Paul), to good. Others, he notes, were "drunkards," or were partly changed, or appeared outwardly changed (but not "in their hearts"). Men cannot change others, but "God awakens them," opens their eyes, and transforms them from being "captives of the devil" into "children of God." He concludes his first point that men have this opportunity in their lifetime, even unto their deathbed (like the "thief on the cross").[252]

His second point is simple: the "opportunity won't last always" (citing the key text). There is no changing after this life. Edwards preaches that if some are wicked in life, they will be so in their afterlife and resurrection at the Final Judgement. And those who are holy will "always be so. They will not fall, as Adam did."[253] Woods notes in Edwards's application, which is not ordered as his other sermons with points of improvement, observation, or exhortation, Edwards could be referring to the Williamses and those in their "clique" when he writes, "Therefore, now make haste. Some of you have been wicked a great while. [God has waited] long enough. 'Tis high time [to end your delay]."[254]

His application fits his sermon, to not delay repentance, to "make haste" (citing Matt 25:11), and to make note of "the means" appointed to have their heart "made better," referring to his previous sermon *With God the Lamb in Heaven,* namely keeping the Sabbath, sermons, reading the Bible, and going to the sacramental services.[255]

Christ Will Come Quickly to Judge All Men[256]

Date: November 1753
Key Text: Revelation 22:12b – "And, behold, I come quickly; and my reward is with me, to give every man according as his work shall be."

The briefest of the three sermons Edwards preached in November 1753 to his Native congregation, *Christ Will Come Quickly* was written on two octavo-sized leaves.[257] It is on the part of the same verse as *What Men*

[252]Edwards, "What Men Are When They Die," 3–4.

[253]Edwards, "What Men Are When They Die," 4–5.

[254]Woods, "What Men Are When They Die," 5.

[255]Edwards, "What Men Are When They Die," 6–7.

[256]Edwards, "Christ Will Come Quickly to Judge All Men," R. Craig Woods, ed., *Jonathan Edwards Sermon Index* (Sermon 1100), (New Haven: Jonathan Edwards Center, Yale University), 1–5.

[257]R. Craig Woods, "Christ Will Come Quickly," 1.

Are When They Die (Rev 22:12) and begins with the doctrine "Christ will come quickly to judge men for what they do in the world," applying the same textual point of judgment for the actions in one's earthly life. The sermon has three straightforward points taken from the text. First, Christ is appointed as the Judge of the world by the Father. Second, an implication of the first (and taken too from the key text) is the certainty that Christ will return to "judge all men." Unlike the first (which is given without any elaboration), the second point is the most explained point of the sermon. Edwards lingers on this point to explain the certainty, dreadfulness, and reason for Christ's judgment of "all men."[258]

After explaining the certainty of Christ's judgment, Edwards makes his final point that Christ's second appearance (and judgment) will "quickly come." This sermon has no formal application since this second point acts as an application. This coming judgment can come in two ways, according to Edwards, either by the quickness of one's mortality or by the quickness of Christ's Last Judgment at "the end of the world" (citing Ps 90:4 and 2 Pet 3:8). Edwards ends by stating a thousand years is "nothing in comparison" with eternity. Though it looks long on earth, it will seem short "in another world."[259]

A Good Man Walks in a Holy Way[260]

Date: March 1754
Key Text: Psalm 119:1–6 – "Blessed are the undefiled [in the way, who walk in the law of the Lord. Blessed are they that keep his testimonies, and that seek him with the whole heart. They also do no iniquity: they walk in his ways. Thou hast commanded us to keep thy precepts diligently. O that my ways were directed to keep thy statutes! Then shall I not be ashamed, when I have respect unto all thy commandments]."

A Good Man Walks in a Holy Way is one of two sermons Edwards preached in March 1754. While still in Edwards's later outline form, the sermon is packed with eleven heads on a manuscript written on two octavo-sized leaves. Woods advises that the brief following sermon, *Men Ought to Be Much in Thinking of Their Own Ways* (examined below from the same chapter

[258] Edwards, "Christ Will Come Quickly," 2–3.

[259] Ibid., 3–4.

[260] Edwards, "A Good Man Walks in a Holy Way," ed. R. Craig Woods, *Jonathan Edwards Sermon Index* (Sermon 1112), (New Haven: Jonathan Edwards Center, Yale University), 1–5.

in Psalms), could be a sermon that followed as an applicatory sermon to this one.[261]

The sermon begins with the first point taken from the text that a "good man" walks in a "holy way." Edwards's Congregational doctrine of baptism then comes out as he states the "good man" not only professes but "is baptized, being of godly parents." He then cites Matthew 12:33 (and his previous sermons, *The Good Man's Treasure* and *Christ Will Come Quickly to Judge All Men*) in stating if a man has a good heart, "they will live a good life" and serve God, for "we shall be judged according to our works."[262]

Edwards's second point is also taken from the key text as he adds those who walk in a holy way "must walk in that way that God's law requires." This way includes keeping God's Word and seeking God with their whole heart. Edwards preaches that men know who God is and His holiness, will, and works (especially Christ's). His second subpoint is they must seek God wholeheartedly, desirously, and with continual prayer. His fourth point is that those who live holy are happy, and if they are truly holy, they will not live "in any way of wickedness" but "keep all God's commandments" (fifth point).[263]

Edwards then notes that the good man has an expectation of diligence (sixth point, taken from the key text), a desire to know his duty (seventh point, taken from the key text), and is sincere in his faith and not ashamed of his hope (eighth point, also taken from the key text before a citation of Rev 3:5 concerning Christ's confession of them before the Father). His ninth point is related to the eighth in noting that the good man sincerely desires to "glorify God."[264]

For the conclusion of the sermon, there is no section labeled application. The final two points are tied to application, however. The tenth states how good men will be strongly resolute to "keep all God's commands as long as they live" (taken from the key text). He compares this with resolution from the ungodly, which fail in their "defilement." The final point is how God "will never forsake" those who do not forsake God (relating back to the eighth point and Christ's confession of "good men" before His Father). The end of the sermon has a citation of the key text for the following sermon,

[261] R. Craig Woods, "A Good Man Walks in a Holy Way," 1.

[262] Edwards, "A Good Man Walks in a Holy Way," 2.

[263] Edwards, "A Good Man Walks in a Holy Way," 2–3.

[264] Ibid., 3–4.

Men Ought to Be Much in Thinking of Their Own Ways, again alluding to how it was to be an applicatory follow-up sermon to this one.[265]

Men Ought to Be Much in Thinking of Their Own Ways[266]

Date: March 1754
Key Text: Psalm 119:59–60 – "I thought on my ways, and turned my feet unto thy testimonies. I made haste, [and delayed not to keep thy commandments]."

As mentioned above, *Men Ought to Be Much in Thinking of Their Own Ways* is the briefest of the sermon manuscripts examined in this work. The sermon manuscript is written on two octavo-sized leaves and takes its key text from the verses cited at the end of *A Good Man Walks in a Holy Way* (Ps 119:59–60). The sermon has three short points of observation. The first is that men should think much of their own ways (with a blank space left to remind Edwards how he could extemporize this point).[267] The second observation is also taken from the key text: men should repent (turn their feet) to "the way of God's commandments."[268]

In giving instructions on how to repent, Edwards notes they should confess their sins, "take up resolutions" (likened to his own practice of writing his *Resolutions*), pray for better hearts, and "forsake" not only some sins but all of them. Edwards also charges they should pray for time to do God's will for them and that God would teach them to find help against the devil. His final point is that they should not delay (following the final point of the key text).[269]

Edwards's approach contrasts this duo of sermons with *Receiving the Blessed Fruits* (examined in the previous chapter). This duo of sermons focuses on entrance and heart regeneration for one unaware of their sins and need for regeneration. However, *Receiving the Blessed Fruits* focuses on deep examination for those entrenched in Congregational culture, challenging them to examine if their individual faith is genuine (in line with *Religious Affections*).

265 Edwards, "A Good Man Walks in a Holy Way," 3–4."

266 Edwards, "Men Ought to be Much in Thinking of Their Own Ways," ed. R. Craig Woods, *Jonathan Edwards Sermon Index* (Sermon 1113), (New Haven: Jonathan Edwards Center, Yale University), 1–3.

267 R. Craig Woods, "Men Ought To Be Much in Thinking of Their Own Ways," 1–2.

268 Edwards, "Men Ought To Be Much in Thinking of Their Own Ways," 2.

269 Ibid., 2.

There Are None So Happy as Those That Have God as Their Savior[270]

Date: November 1754
Key Text: Deuteronomy 33:29 – "Happy art thou, O Israel: who is like unto thee, O people saved by the Lord."

Another brief, outlined sermon by Edwards is *There Are None So Happy*, preached in November 1754.[271] The sermon begins with the key text and the doctrine: "They that have God to be their Savior are happy so that none is like 'em." His two doctrinal particulars are those who "have" God are "people and nations" and "particular persons."[272]

His first subpoint under those who "have" God is that they *are* happy. Second, their joy is *unique* beyond wealth, greatness, kingship, wisdom, bravery, long life, health, and even friendship. Edwards preaches that this joy is the "most excellent." It is the "best knowledge and wisdom." It is also the most valuable among ornaments, honor, food, clothing, and friends, and is a more certain happiness with the "longest continuance" of joy. Those who have Christ, Edwards adds, may be poorer, sicker, captive, and taken as slaves, but their happiness "can't be taken away." Instead, they shall "increase more and more" and "need not fear death."[273]

For his application, Edwards exhorts his audience to seek "this happiness" that "many of all sorts" have "obtained," noting his audience is "as capable as others" and that the Gospel is "free for all nations." They need, though, to forsake "all of this," "all sins," and "seek in the ways of God's appointment."[274] Of note (compared with *Honey from the Rock* examined in the last chapter) is the similar method of thematic sermons taken from a point in the key text. Honey is taken from the key text of *Honey from the Rock* about God's deliverance in desperate circumstances, and unique joy and happiness are taken from the key text in *There Are None So Happy*. This comparison demonstrates again Edwards's focus on re-engagement for those at Northampton and the necessity and benefit of entrance for the Mahican congregation at Stockbridge.

[270] Edwards, "There Are None So Happy as Those That Have God as Their Savior," ed. R. Craig Woods, *Jonathan Edwards Sermon Index* (Sermon 1130), (New Haven: Jonathan Edwards Center, Yale University), 1–5.

[271] R. Craig Woods, "There Are None So Happy," 1.

[272] Edwards, "There Are None So Happy," 3.

[273] Edwards, "There Are None So Happy," 3–4.

[274] Ibid., 4.

Christ the Resting Place of His People[275]

Date: July 1755
Key Text: Jeremiah 50:6 – "[My people hath been lost sheep: their shepherds have caused them to go astray, they have turned them away on the mountains: they have gone from mountain to hill,] they have forgotten their resting place."

In this sermon from July 1755, Edwards briefly outlined a sermon on Christ's place as the resting place for His people as the Great Shepherd. The manuscript has a curious horizontal note to mention "Mrs. Chamberlain." Mrs. Chamberlain had suffered tragedy the year before when two Schaghticoke Indians had broken into her house and killed two children and a servant, and later killed a Mr. Stevens on the road to Lenox. These killings were in response to the killing of Waumpaumcorse by English horse thieves the prior year. Finding Christ as a resting place would be a theme to use in light of such violence and tragedy.[276]

In view of this, the first particular is "they that are in Christ, may rest there, being safe from all that they were afraid of," including fear of God's anger, hell, enemies, death, and the "Day of Judgment." This rest, though, includes rest from the weariness of sin and from affliction (the second and third particulars). Affliction includes the "troubles of the world," wicked men, the devil, sickness, and the loss of friends. Edwards ends with the rest found through desires longed for and disappointments. Though there might be disappointments in the world, Edwards ends by stating, "Christ is strong and sure, and will never fail."[277] This sermon shows Edwards's role as a peacemaker in the midst of violence and conflict by offering the hope of the Gospel.

[275]Edwards, "Christ the Resting Place of His People," ed. R. Craig Woods, *Jonathan Edwards Sermon Index* (Sermon 1142), (New Haven: Jonathan Edwards Center, Yale University), 1–4.

[276]R. Craig Woods, "Christ the Resting Place of His People," 1.

[277]Edwards, "Christ the Resting Place of His People," 2–3.

Edwards's Farewell Sermons at Stockbridge

Farewell Sermon 1: *God's People Should Remember Them That Have Been Their Ministers*[278]

Date: January 8, 1758
Key Text: Hebrews 13:7–8 – "Remember them that have the rule over you, who have spoken to you the word of God: whose faith follow, considering the end of their conversation. Jesus Christ the same yesterday, and today, for forever."

The first of two final sermons Edwards would preach at Stockbridge, *God's People Should Remember*, is a short, outlined sermon titled "Farewell sermon to Indians at Stockbridge." Though it is titled the "Farewell sermon," Edwards would preach a second sermon on January 15, 1758, with the note "on departing from Stockbridge," though this second sermon could be to a mixed congregation.[279]

The sermon is briefly outlined with three propositions. The first is the charge that people who "lived under the gospel" should remember those ministers who preached the Bible faithfully to them. The reasons to do this, according to Edwards, are that those ministers have "been God's messengers" and will give an account of how they have "labored for their greatest good." The second proposition is that both minister and congregation will "come to an happy end at last," as the minister faithfully speaks the Word of God and the people "follow their instruction." Finally, an encouragement is given to the congregation that though they may have many ministers, "Jesus Christ, the great head of the church, is always the same." Edwards's application ends with a somber note to remember what he had instructed them, whether they had misused that instruction ("gone on in drinking" or "formerly have been of the church) or put it into practice ("that have made it your care to live agreeable to the gospel").[280]

Farewell Sermon 2: *Watch and Pray Always*[281]

Date: Jan. 15, 1758

[278]Edwards, "God's People Should Remember Them That Have Been Their Ministers," *Sermons and Discourses 1743–1758*, 713–716.

[279]Kimnach, "Farewell Sermons to the Indians," 711–713.

[280]Edwards, "God's People Should Remember," 713–714.

[281]Edwards, "Watch and Pray Always," *Sermons and Discourses 1743–1758*, 713–717.

Key Text: Luke 21:36 – “Watch ye, and pray always.”

Kimnach notes that *Watch and Pray Always* might be Edwards’s shortest sermon, written on a single octavo leaf. The sermon has five propositions with a short application. At the bottom of the sermon, written upside down, are the names of five Native American congregants Edwards had reminded himself “ought to be comforted.” These were “Chenequuge[?]/ Capt. Checksonkum[?]/ Roberts wife/ Siah’s wife/ Conokounts[?] wife.”[282]

The propositions are in response to the text. Why should the congregation “watch ye, and pray always”? They should do so because of the “dreadful things” coming upon the world; only the righteous can escape those things; all will be “called to appear before Christ,” and none other than the righteous “shall be thought worthy” to stand before Christ. To emphasize this fourth proposition further, he emphasizes that the righteous are worthy, and the wicked are not. His final proposition is for his audience to watch and pray so “we may be thought worthy [to stand before Christ].” Again, Edwards emphasizes they first watch, second pray, and third, always. His applications are two- to four-word reminders to emphasize what to watch against, how to be watchful, what needs watching, what to pray for, how to pray, and to pray always.[283]

Observations from Edwards’s Sermons at Stockbridge

Like in Edwards’s colonial preaching ministry, through observing Edwards’s sermons at Stockbridge among his Mahican and Mohawk audience, a recurrent theme is apparent: instruction and Gospel invitation. Like the quotes given above in his letter to William Pepperell, Edwards has instruction on his mind first and foremost when preaching to his new audience. He does not assume a high biblical literacy or focus on affectionate preaching. Edwards makes the conversive assumption of biblical illiteracy and ignorance of even basic biblical knowledge.

In *Days of Your Youth*, Edwards explains the basics of who God is, His role as Creator, and the Gospel invitation given. *Days of Your Youth* was a sermon on the same key text as *The Time of Youth*, though crafted for a mixed audience with a more explanatory exposition. Edwards’s explanation of the phrase “evil days” as days of old age in comparison to younger days, which he explains are the best days because they are the time at which youth

[282]Wilson H. Kimnach, “Watch and Pray Always,” 713–717.

[283]Edwards, “Watch and Pray Always,” 717.

are most able to respond to the Gospel, shows a focus on his whole audience (and not those with a higher biblical literacy). This focus is also seen in the ending invitation to an audience Edwards saw as in need of invitation as opposed to the audience of *The Time of Youth,* whom he saw as in need of applicatory exhortation.

Instruction on God as Creator and the creation and Fall narrative are given with another Gospel invitation in *Made in God's Image*. In the sacramental sermon, *Christ is to The Heart,* Edwards uses the same key text as *Christ the River* (preached nearly a decade earlier to a colonial audience), though it is composed afresh with more content. Edwards shows his ingenuity in using a river metaphor to illustrate God's love in the work of Christ.

To the Mohawks at the Treaty has another explanation of the Fall as well. As mentioned, instead of metaphysical language, Edwards uses the metaphor of a river in *Christ is to the Heart*. *To the Mohawks at the Treaty* had a similar theme of *Light in a Dark World,* though like *Christ is to The Heart, it* is a fresh sermon crafted for the occasion. In the sermon, Edwards focuses on his audience's need (Native Americans) to be illuminated with God's Word (the Bible). Those who had not instructed them previously in God's Word Edwards chastises.

When compared, *Christ Gave Himself for Us* shows Edwards's concern for his Native audience to attain the understanding of Christ's sacrifice and the Gospel invitation, as opposed to his focus on zeal for Christ in *Zeal an Essential Virtue* (preached earlier to a colonial audience). This is seen again in *In Remembrance of Christ* in comparison with *Self-Examination and the Lord's Supper* (both sacramental sermons with key texts taken from 1 Cor 11), where Edwards instructs on what the Lord's Supper is for an audience who were unfamiliar with it (as he further does in *The Lord's Supper is an Ordinance*).

When preaching *In Remembrance of Christ,* Edwards gives a basic introduction to the Lord's Supper, while *The Lord's Supper is an Ordinance* further explains the significance and establishment of the Lord's Supper as an ordinance by Christ. Edwards first instructs his audience on what the Lord's Supper is, then explains their participation in it and its significance.

The Poor in Spirit Are Happy, *They That Mourn Are Happy*, and *The Pure in Heart Are Happy* show Edwards's ability to build upon an instructive biblical theme from the text as they build on Jesus's instructions in the Beatitudes in Matthew 5. The *Poor in Spirit Are Happy* begins by instructing on what humility is (as seen by Christ's instruction in the Sermon on the Mount) and how it leads to repentance and salvation as God's children. Edwards then instructs his Native audience on what it means to mourn for sin in a holy way (based again on Jesus's teaching) and to be comforted in confession in *They That Mourn Are Happy*. Finally, purity is the theme of *The Pure in Heart Are Happy* (composed fresh though taken from the same key text as *The Pure in Heart Blessed*).

The contrast between the sermons was seen in the early metaphysical focus of *The Pure in Heart Blessed* on seeing God's glory with one's spiritual eyes instead of one's "bodily eyes." Edwards will briefly talk of spiritual and bodily sight at the end of *The Pure in Heart Are Happy*, but not until he has instructed his audience in what it means to be "pure in heart."

The next sermon series analyzed were Edwards's sermons on God's infinite attributes. These sermons show Edwards's thoughts on instructing his Native American audience on the infinitude of God. God's infinite mercy and grace are the first themes exposited by Edwards in *God is an Infinitely Merciful and Gracious God*. God's strength was next given in *God is Infinitely Strong*, and the final attribute given in the third sermon was God's holiness (in *God is Infinitely Holy*).

For *God is an Infinitely Merciful and Gracious God*, Edwards instructs on what God's mercy is, using a river metaphor, and then exhorts his audience to follow God's pattern of mercy and goodness. Next, in *God is Infinitely Strong*, Edwards shows strength beyond physical to instruct his audience on God's wisdom, foresight, and omniscience. This instruction is seen when Edwards tells his Native audience that all of the knowledge and wisdom of the earth and nature they have actually comes from God, and while their knowledge may be limited, God's is not.

His final image in *God is Infinitely Strong* is of a lamb taken out of the mouth of a bear, giving concrete thought to his audience for how they can escape the clutches of the enemy. Finally, in the third sermon of the series (*God is Infinitely Holy*), Edwards exposits thoroughly on God's holiness, but unlike *The Holiness of God*, Edwards takes more time in instructing his audience on what repentance is, their access to God through prayer, and the trust they can have in God's Word for truth.

The third sermon series on Luke 6:45 was examined next. Edwards sets up the series with *Persons' Speech*, generally showing how what is in a person (wickedness or holiness) will determine their outward actions and speech. This sets up the following two sermons where Edwards then expounds on the consequences for those who are good (*The Good Man's Treasure*) and those who are bad (*The Wicked Man's Treasure*). Again, we see instruction as the key to this trio of sermons. This is similar to Edwards's Acts series to his colonial congregation at Northampton though Edwards is far more concerned with visualizing the consequences of condemnation and subjugation to Satan in his *Turned* series.

Another set of sermons covered Revelation 22. *With God and the Lamb in Heaven* shows again how Edwards distinguishes his purpose in preaching to a different audience than when he preached *Serving God in Heaven*. For the colonials, it was about stirring affection for service. *With God and the Lamb in Heaven* is about inviting Natives into God's heavenly kingdom through the Gospel. *What Men Are When They Die*, the second sermon in the Revelation 22 series, shows a sharp contrast due to the mixed audience he preached to. Because of the issues caused by those such as the Williams clan, the sermon takes on more of a polemical exhortation to change one's bad ways before it is too late. This tone then sets up the third sermon, *Christ Will Come Quickly*, on Christ's second coming and the need to make haste in repentance.

In Edwards's sermons on Revelation 22, he again instructs and gives a rich picture of the goodness of eternity and fellowship with God. Even in giving a sermon with illustrative themes, Edwards takes the time to instruct his audience to help them attain understanding *before* affection.

A Good Man Walks in a Holy Way and *Men Ought to Be Much in Thinking of Their Own Ways* are inter-connected by Edwards as a sermon (*A Good Man Walks in a Holy Way*) with then a following applicatory sermon (*Men Ought to Be Much in Thinking of Their Own Ways*). Edwards's approach for these two sermons contrasts with *Receiving the Blessed Fruits* (examined in the previous chapter). This duo of sermons focuses on invitation and regeneration, whereas *Receiving the Blessed Fruits* focuses on examination for those apathetic as a challenge for them to examine if their faith is genuine.

There Are None So Happy demonstrates the method of sermonic themes taken from a point in the key text. As honey was taken from the key text of *Honey from the Rock*, joy and happiness are taken from the key text in *There Are None So Happy*. This demonstrates Edwards's focus on the need and reward of entrance into the Kingdom of God for Edwards's Native audience. The hope of the Gospel as a resting place was another theme in light of violence and conflict in *Christ the Resting Place of His People*, as Edwards preached after the tragedy which had befallen a Mrs. Chamberlain at the loss of two of her children to an attack by two Schaghticoke Indians.

Finally, in Edwards's farewell sermons, his heart is to have ministered faithfully to them, for them to have followed his instruction, and simply to watch and pray always. Edwards's focus was on imparting the remembrance of the Gospel he had preached to them and comforting those he would be leaving behind. A thread mentioned in the previous chapter on his farewell sermons at Northampton was in his leaving the Bible and prayer as the bedrock of what would sustain these congregations in his absence.

His ministry among the Native Americans at Stockbridge shows a change in homiletical style based on their biblical literacy, and a desire to implement the pedagogical principles Edwards was trained in himself through his preaching, and through the work of the school and its headmasters Woodbridge and Hawley.

The next chapter will assess the overall "success" or "failure" of Edwards's pedagogical preaching ministry and applications to be derived from his ministry among colonials and Native Americans at Stockbridge. But, through examining Native American ministry in colonial New England, the mission at Stockbridge, and Edwards's preaching therein, it becomes apparent the desire for, and the results from, faithful and earnest ministry apply in any context. As was seen through the testimonies from those at Martha's Vineyard and following, when given resources and care, the Gospel was responded to by those who saw the value in its guidance and hope.

CHAPTER 5: SUMMARY AND CONCLUSION

Seek that good treasure in your heart.

How much better than silver or gold.

How much more good will it do you.

[It is] better than all the silver and gold in the world.

You will be precious to God.

[You will be] one of God's precious things.

God's people are his treasure.

You shall have treasure in heaven.

God and Christ shall be your treasure.

You are taught how to get this treasure out of that excellent book, the Bible.[1]

Edwards is a complex figure to examine. His presuppositions coming into Stockbridge based on limited (and at times tragic) interactions with Native Americans had caused him at first to view them through a prejudiced light. His appointment as minister and interactions at Stockbridge, though, would cause his ignorant and divisive thoughts to be transformed into ecclesial union with both his colonial and Native congregants, leading him to stand as a powerful advocate in the face of the Williamses' schemes to exploit the Native community at Stockbridge. As seen through this book, however, the

[1]Jonathan Edwards, "The Good Man's Treasure," ed. R. Craig Woods, *Jonathan Edwards Sermon Index* (Sermon 1089), (New Haven: Jonathan Edwards Center, Yale University), 2–3.

greatest treasure Edwards sought to share with any of his congregations was the Word, "that excellent book, the Bible."[2]

An example Edwards observed and who gives context to his ministry is perhaps the young missionary David Brainerd, who endeared himself not only to Edwards's daughter Jerusha but to Edwards himself. This led to Edwards's posthumous printing of Brainerd's autobiography. David Brainerd would minister to Native Americans only a short distance from where Edwards settled in Stockbridge. Of his mission among the Natives, Brainerd would write in his journal:

> My People having now attained to a considerable Degree of Knowledge in the Principles of Christianity, I thought it proper to set up a catechetical Lecture among them; and this Evening attempted something in that Form; proposing Questions to them agreeable to the Reverend Assembly's *Shorter Catechism*, receiving their Answers, and then explaining and insisting as appear'd necessary and proper upon each Question. After which I endeavour'd to make some practical Improvement of the whole. This was the Method I enter'd upon.—They were able readily and rationally to answer many important Questions I proposed to them: So that, upon Trial, I found their Doctrinal Knowledge to exceed my own expectations.—In the Improvement of my Discourse, when I came to infer and open the Blessedness of those who have so great and glorious a God, as had before been spoken of, for their everlasting Friend and Portion, sundry were much affected; and especially when I exhorted, and endeavour'd to persuade them to be reconciled to God, thro' his dear Son, and thus to secure an Interest in his everlasting Favour. So that they appear'd to be not only enlightened and instructed, but affected and engaged in their Souls Concern by this Method of discoursing.[3]

This was written on December 21, 1745. Less than two years later, Brainerd would die at Edwards's parsonage, and six years later, Edwards

[2]Edwards, "The Good Man's Treasure," 3.

[3]David Brainerd, *"Mirabilia Dei inter Indicos, or The rise and progress of a remarkable work of grace amongst a number of the Indians in the provinces of New-Jersey and Pennsylvania, justly represented in a journal kept by order of the Honourable Society (in Scotland) for Propagating Christian Knowledge. : With some general remarks"* (1746; repr., Ann Arbor: *Evans Early American Imprint Collection Text Creation Partnership*, 2005), 90.

would himself take the call to minister in a similar fashion among the Mahicans at Stockbridge. In the quote above, there is an emphasis on catechism and instruction of the text, leading to affectation and engagement in piety among those ministered to. This dissertation has shown the emphasis on these cornerstones of ministry (catechesis, instruction of the text, and affectionate awakening) in Edwards's own upbringing and later throughout his ministry among both the colonial and Native congregations.

Through this work Edwards's teaching emphasis in preaching was seen as a new lens to study Edwards. While a wide breadth of works is written on Edwards's theology, biography, ministry, and even preaching, few covered his ministry and preaching at Stockbridge.

This work, though, is indebted to the great research and exploration of Edwards's time at Stockbridge and commends those who have diligently focused on the Native audience (Wheeler), Edwards's move to missional work (Paul), Edwards's missional preaching (Harder), and Edwards's complicated legacy as a slaveowner in light of his ministry at Stockbridge (Lowe). The present work has sought to fill in the foundational context of biblical literacy in the education and preaching ministry of Edwards among colonials and specifically at Stockbridge among his Native American congregation.

The foundation for Edwards's preaching ministry in general was seen through the Puritan influences on his preaching philosophy. Edwards's foundation of biblical literacy and his views of his congregations' biblical literacy were given to show how Edwards saw congregations with high biblical literacy but low biblical affection.

Edwards's own advancement of these homiletical methods was shown by analyzing his sermons throughout his colonial ministry. It was seen how Edwards's focus in preaching was to stir the hearts of his audience, to argue for doctrines and the applications of those doctrines logically, and to help awaken those who had slumbered to religious affection. This was done through illustrative sermons, dogged rhetoric, and individual application in later home study. In analyzing three sermon series from his ministry at Northampton, Edwards showed how he could juxtapose between God's wrath and blessing in the *Dreadful Fear and Desire of the Righteous*., how he could build on the theme of conversion and regeneration in the four-part series from Acts, and how he could leave his congregation at Northampton with the central foundation of the Bible and "lively exercises" of God's grace in his three-part series from Proverbs 6:22.

The testimonies of Native Congregations in Mayhews's works and Occom's own journal and testimonies demonstrated the encouraging response to earnest mission and the hurt and tragedy of exploitive interference. This section also showed the context in which Edwards would minister at Stockbridge through his proposals of catechism, education, sermonic instruction, and individual instruction at school and home. The results when this was put into practice in these Native accounts show the usefulness of Edwards's proposed method.

Next, an examination of the historical context at Stockbridge was given before looking at the evidence from primary documents for John Sergeant and Jonathan Edwards's evaluation of biblical literacy and methods for instruction. Again, this emphasis on literacy was in line with how Edwards was trained to attain biblical knowledge growing up and what he had practiced throughout his ministry among colonials.

Through this contextual lens, sermons preached by Edwards at Stockbridge to Native audiences were then analyzed to show the variation in method from Edwards between his sermons analyzed to colonials and sermons given over similar (if not the same) key texts at Stockbridge. The results demonstrated a greater emphasis on instruction and care in helping his audience apprehend the Word before he dove into theology and metaphysics. This was done through explaining biblical ideas and contexts in the introductions of his sermons. It was also seen in the short sermon series he preached at Stockbridge that were focused on instruction juxtaposed with the sermon series summarized above to colonials that were focused on themes and biblical visualization.

The teachings of Christ at the Sermon on the Mount were explained in Edwards's sermon series on the Beatitudes (highlighting humility, godly sorrow, and purity). Edwards's infinite sermon series explains God's attributes of mercy and grace, His power and omniscience, and His holiness. Instruction on being holy and the reward therein (and consequences for wickedness) were then shown in Edwards's sermon series on Luke 6:45. Finally, the joys of heaven, and the terror of sin, and Christ's second coming were given in his sermon series on Revelation 22.

It is fitting that Edwards's themes for his final two sermons at Stockbridge were on comfort and remembrance of doctrine, as his sermons at Stockbridge among Native Americans showed a focus on Gospel invitation and on teaching (and retaining) biblical knowledge. These show a preacher in Edwards who was aware of and focused on ministering to every congregation he preached to with the Word. The Bible was the foundation for every sermon he preached and became the focus on what he would impart to his congregations as his time closed with them. What then can be taken from his ministry is given in this final section.

Applications from Edwards's Ministry Among Native Americans

Brainerd, John Seargent, and Gideon Hawley had all endeared themselves to their Native congregants through their emphasis on the good of their congregants and the Gospel. But far too often, as seen in Edwards's ministry at Stockbridge, exploitation mingled with disease, war, and contention led to meager results during his time there. So, what takeaways are there for a ministry that seemed doomed to flounder under the weight of corruption, disease, and war?

A Watchman for Souls: Social Advocacy, The Great Commission, and Indigenous Mission

> In addition, Edwards fought against European exploitation of Native Americans throughout his time in Stockbridge. His letter to Joseph Paice in February 1751/2 ended up in the hands of the Archbishop of Canterbury. Edwards complained that English traders consistently cheated the Native Americans, and that money donated to aid in mission work actually ended up fueling the battle between Anglicans and dissenters in England. This had caused the Iroquois to distrust the English and to fear that, if they sent their children to English schools, the white men would enslave them. Closer to home, Edwards fought against the exploitation of his own congregation by his constant antagonists throughout his Stockbridge years, the Williams family. In letters to public officials, he detailed the Williams clan's misappropriation of funds donated for the education of Native American children for their own gain, in addition to the past unethical land deals in the Williams favor, all of which had contributed to the Stockbridge Indians' suspicion of whites. He hoped the officials would remedy the situation.[4]

[4]April C. Armstrong, "Last Were the Mahicans," *Southwestern Journal of Theology* 48:1, 26–27. Found in Edwards, *Letters and Personal Writings*, 435–436.

In looking at Moses Paul's choice of Samson Occom and Jonathan Edwards Jr., Banks (via Ava Chamberlain) notes the similitude of social and spiritual concern between Edwards Jr. and his father.[5] Banks brings out a statistic of note (via Paul) that during Edwards's time at Stockbridge, there were only seven exploitative transactions of Native land for colonial rum, whereas, in the decade following his tenure, there were eighty-seven.[6] Armstrong notes the benefit of Edwards Jr.'s childhood spent among the Mahicans at Stockbridge:

> Jonathan Edwards Jr. spent so much time with the Mahicans that his fluency in their language exceeded his fluency in English. Edwards encouraged his son to develop proficiency in Native American languages, hoping the boy would eventually become a missionary to them like his father.[7]

Because of his ties to the Edwards family, Gideon Hawley would seek out the nine-year-old Edwards Jr. to serve as his companion (because of his fluency in the Native language) while he served with the Oneida Indians in the wilderness of New York (Ouaquaga on the Susquehanna River) over 200 miles from where Edwards Sr. was serving in Stockbridge. Banks advises that this service came with dangers as Hawley and the younger Edwards would have to evade what Hawley described as "strange Indians" he supposed to be hostile.[8] Edwards Jr. would write:

> Out of my father's house, I seldom heard any language spoken, beside the Indian. By these means I acquired the knowledge of that language, and a great faculty in speaking it. It became more familiar to me than my mother tongue. I knew the names of some things in Indian, which I did not know in English; even all

[5] John S. Banks, *The Forgotten Edwards: A New Examination of the Life and Thought of Jonathan Edwards Junior*, (n.p: Jonathan Edwards Society, 2021), 40–41. Chamberlain's notes found in: Ava Chamberlain, "The Execution of Moses Paul: A Story of Crime and Contact in Eighteenth-Century Connecticut," *The New England Quarterly* 77, no. 3 (September 2004): 414–450.

[6] Banks, *The Forgotten Edwards*, 42. As Found also in: Roy M. Paul, *Jonathan Edwards and the Stockbridge Mohican Indians* (Peterborough, Canada: H&E Publishing, 2020), 93.

[7] Armstrong, "Last Were the Mahicans," 27.

[8] Banks, *The Forgotten Edwards*, 21–23. Also noted by Marsden as a "bright spot" from Edwards's time at Stockbridge due to Edwards Jr.'s fluency and connection with the Indians they ministered to. Marsden, *A Life*, 412.

> my thoughts ran in Indian: and though the true pronunciation of the language is extremely difficult to all but themselves.[9]

Banks examined in Edwards Jr.'s diary the phrase *machy anitauhau-wongkon wonk anannahkaun, which was* used three different times interchangeably with English. Through research from linguists Carl Masthay and Ives Goddard, Banks discovered the phrase means "evil thoughts and deeds."[10] Edwards Jr.'s convictions would be thought and written down in Mohican. His identity, if not whole, to a significant degree, would become Mohican. Later, he would advocate for the preservation of indigenous language and culture, here responded to by George Washington:

> I have long regretted that so many Tribes of the American Aborigines should have become almost or entirely extinct, without leaving such vestiges, as that the genius & idiom of their Languages might be traced. Perhaps, from such sources, the descent or kindred of nations, whose origins are lost in remote antiquity or illiterate darkness, might be more rationally investigated, than in any other mode. The task, you have imposed upon yourself, of preserving some materials for this purpose, is certainly to be commended.[11]

This shows a legacy passed on from Edwards Sr. to Edwards Jr. in advocacy and ministry to Native Americans. In two sermons given for Moses Paul, a Native American who was sentenced to execution for murder, Banks notes (in critique of Chamberlain) that Edwards Jr.'s sermons show the "Edwardsean principle of benevolence" through the purpose of applying true benevolence in his first sermon, and also dealing with "apparent injustice done by man in the first sermon":[12]

> Third. Let all be exhorted to receive Christ. God might have left [us] without a Saviour. [He was under] no obligation [to save

[9] Jonathan Edwards Jr., *Observations on the Language of the Muhhekaneew Indians* (New Haven: Josiah Meigs, 1788), 3. See also: *Observations on the Mahican Language*, American Language Reprints, ed. Claudio R. Salvucci, vol. 25 (Bristol, PA: Evolution, 2002), 9–10.

[10] Banks, *The Forgotten Edwards*, 28.

[11] George Washington, "From George Washington to Jonathan Edwards, 28 August 1788," *Founders Online*, National Archives. Original source: *1 January 1788–23 September 1788*, vol. 6, *The Papers of George Washington: Confederation Series*, ed. W. W. Abbot (Charlottesville: University Press of Virginia, 1997), 479–480.

[12] Banks, *The Forgotten Edwards*, 43–45.

> us]. So most [would] have perished [with] no possibility. But [God] removed the obstacles. Now [we] only repent and believe the gospel. [You do] not need to make an atonement. Christ has done [everything]. Acquiesce in [the atonement of Christ]. Certainly this [is] reasonable. [This is] necessary or we will] perish unless [we believe].[13]

This second sermon, given at the request of Paul by Jonathan Edwards Jr., shows Edwards Jr.'s focus on Gospel proclamation. There is no conflict for Edwards Jr. in advocacy and Gospel proclamation. For Edwards Jr., this is part and parcel with ministry.

Critics of Edwards Sr. at Stockbridge characterize him as a stoic theological writer secluded in his study. But from his letters to those such as Bellamy and Commissioners in Boston, it is clear he spent a significant portion of his time advocating for an end to the exploitation of his Mohawk and Mahican congregation at Stockbridge. While it is true that works such as *Freedom of the Will* were produced during his time at Stockbridge, he also produced letters of advocacy and fresh Gospel sermons while there. Hall notes self-sacrifice as a normative in the life of the "faithful shepherd." In advocating for Native Americans at Stockbridge, Edwards would give of himself in service to their protection and needs.[14]

Edwards's example provides a two-fold application for ministers today. Positively, one must see and advocate for the needs of those under his care in ministry. Negatively, one must not turn a blind eye to the injustices perpetuated on those in his congregation, especially ones that the minister could directly or indirectly be contributing to.

In the selection below, Edwards Jr. preaches on the hardness and obstacles to the Gospel created by an unjust society (referring in this case to the owning and trading of slaves):

> They are hurtful, as they deprave the morals of the people.—The incessant and inhuman cruelties practised in the trade, and in the subsequent slavery, necessarily tend to harden the human heart against the tender feelings of humanity in the masters of vessels, in the sailors, in the factors, in the proprietors of these slaves, in

[13] Jonathan Edwards Jr., "Volume 242," *The Forgotten Edwards: A New Examination of the Life and Thought of Jonathan Edwards Junior*, Appendix 3: ("Two Sermons For Moses Paul"), 181.

[14] David D. Hall, *The Faithful Shepherd: A History of the New England Ministry in the Seventeenth Century*, (Chapel Hill, NC: University of North Carolina Press, 1972), 174–175.

> their children, in the overseers, in the slaves themselves, and in all who habitually see those cruelties. Now the eradication or even the diminution of compassion, tenderness and humanity, is certainly a great depravation of heart, and must be followed with correspondent depravity of manners. And measures which lead to such depravity of heart and manners, cannot but be extremely hurtful to the state, and consequently are extremely impolitic.[15]

While Edwards Sr.'s mixed legacy of slave-owning and changing ignorance of Native Americans, Edwards Jr. carried on a legacy of advocacy and benevolence that was rooted in the theology and practice of his father (through his advocacy of Native Americans at Stockbridge). The tragedy is that it occurred a generation after Edwards Sr. and not with himself (with regards to abolitionism). In a world divided over race, politics, income, and culture, it is more important than ever to minister both in word and practice. As more negative attention is given to the past and present church, it is more important to harken and respond to the words of Paul to Titus to give to the young men in Titus 2:7–8, "Show yourself in all respects to be a model of good works, and in your teaching show integrity, dignity, and sound speech that cannot be condemned, so that an opponent may be put to shame, having nothing evil to say about us" (ESV).

Individualized Instruction in the Word

On August 6th, 1745, David Brainerd recorded the response to the individualized instruction he had given among the Crosweeksung in New Jersey. He shared of the morning attention given on a morning and how many were "much affected" and "surpizingly tender" with tears that freely were produced along with "sobs and groans." He advised there were fifty-five present for the morning and afternoon instruction, with forty capable of "attending diving service with understanding."[16]

At first, he notes many were eager to listen during the afternoon discourse, but there was not a remarkable amount of action. However, during the finish of his afternoon discourse, many were influenced and had a "great

[15]Jonathan Edwards Jr., "The Injustice and Impolicy of the Slave-Trade, and of the Slavery of the Africans: illustrated in a sermon preached before the Connecticut Society for the Promotion of Freedom, and for the Relief of Persons Unlawfully Holden in Bondage, at their annual meeting in New Haven, September 15, 1791," (1791; repr., Ann Arbor: *Evan Early American Imprint Collection Online Text Creation Partnership*, 2009).

[16]Brainerd, "*Mirabilia Dei inter Indicos*," 18–19.

concern." There were few present who "could refrain from tears and bitter cries." This individualized instruction by Brainerd would produce in this group a deep concern for not only the knowledge of godly interests but affection and agony "to obtain an interest in Christ." Brainerd adds that the more he discoursed with them on the love and compassion of Christ, the more they responded and were distressed at feeling "unable to come."[17] He adds:

> It was surprizing to see how their Hearts seem'd to be pierc'd with the tender and melting Invitations of the Gospel, when there was not a Word of Terror spoken to them. There were this Day two Persons that obtain'd Relief and Comfort, which (when I came to discourse with them particularly) appear'd solid, rational and scriptural. After I had enquir'd into the Grounds of their Comfort, and said many Things I thought proper to them, I asked them what they wanted God to do further for them? They replied, They wanted Christ should wipe their Hearts quite clean, &c. Surprizing were now the Doings of the Lord, that I can say no less of this Day (and I need say no more of it) than that the Arm of the Lord was powerfully and marvelously revealed in it.[18]

As mentioned in the last chapter, both Sergeant and Edwards would emphasize the need for instruction among the Mahicans at Stockbridge. Brainerd here shows the results from individualized attention and application of God's Word among those ministered to. In every place Edwards ministered, he carried forward the pedagogical practice he had inherited with its emphasis on biblical instruction in the pulpit, in the pastor's study, among the congregation in their homes, and each to their own families. This is important for the church today as it seeks to reach a culture that grows more biblically illiterate.

It was seen in the testimonies recorded by the Mayhews and Occom how this produced an indigenous religious movement among the Native congregations at places like Martha's Vineyard and New Stockbridge. It was the earnest desire of those like Sergeant, Woodbridge, Edwards, and Hawley to see this done at Stockbridge as well. While their results were lessened through exploitation and war, their desire and goal should be instructive to those desiring to see awakening and revival among their own congregations.

[17]Ibid., 19.

[18]Brainerd, "*Mirabilia Dei inter Indicos*," 19–20.

Be intentional in instruction. How does a great movement like the Great Awakening occur? It occurs through a biblical culture that emphasizes religious instruction and piety. What causes a youth like Jonathan Edwards to seek a private swamp hut for secret prayer? A culture so imbued with God's Word and pious identity that Edwards could not help but be instructed and personally respond to this movement of revival.

Someone who felt a similar culture was Mary Peckham, who experienced this during the "Hebrides Revival" of 1949. In *Saved in Revival*, an account of Peckham's testimony during the "Hebrides Revival," she recounts every home, whether saved or unsaved, conducting "family worship," which was more than reading a "few verses of Scripture" accompanied by a "little prayer" but included:

> If they are Christians, they will have a short prayer, read a Psalm, then sing the same Psalm and have a chapter of Scripture. They finish off with a long prayer that will embrace the whole community. If they are non-Christians, they will omit the singing part and possibly the first prayer. But they will read the Psalm, and they will read the chapter, and they will have a prayer.[19]

Peckham further comments on the atmosphere of religion and awakening she felt throughout her entire lifetime fueled by this emphasis on individual attention to piety and biblical literacy that imbued each household. But, just like in Edwards's day, it was not only in the household but in the schools as well. Peckham adds their curriculum included the Word of God, "not just in texts or in stories, but in chapters in our two languages – in English, which was our school language (only learned at school), and in Gaelic, which was our native tongue."[20]

They would also recount the 107 questions and answers from the Presbyterian *Shorter Catechism*. She adds that she did not understand the more technical terms of justification, sanctification, and redemption or what they meant, but they were seeds of the Gospel that would take shape later.[21]

Prayer and revival meetings would become, at first, a source of tension for Peckham when she could not escape the mention of and testimonies

[19]Mary Peckham, *Saved in Revival: Testimony of Mary Morrison, Convert of revival in the Hebrides*, ed. Juanita Snyder, Rosalind Masterson, Colin Peckham, and Norma Peckham (1966; repr., Cape Town, SA: Prairie Press, 2012), 7, eBook.

[20]Peckham, *Saved in Revival*, 7–9.

[21]Peckham, *Saved in Revival*, 9–10.

from them as an "unconverted sinner." But as she was drawn to Christ, and as the Word she had studied in her youth through reading the Bible in both English and Gaelic began to reoccur in her memory, it would pierce her hard heart and cause revival in her soul.[22]

Just like with Edwards and Peckham, any culture built around the Bible, prayer, instruction, and revival will produce awakening. God's Word is true, God's Word is powerful, and God's Word can produce revival in the hearts of His Church.

Earnest Intentional Preaching: Biblical Literacy and Exposition

> First, it is advantageous for a minister's preparation for preaching that he tie his reflections to its few but universal precepts and by their aid discover an abundance of things to say, from which he may later select those that are most useful for the church.... Second, it is advantageous for the hearers who, once acquainted with this method, can conveniently follow the thread of the sermon, commit it to memory, and review it at home with their families, without which, as Ames wisely admonishes, all the usefulness of the sermon dies.... Third, it is advantageous with respect to the very things that will be said, which will everywhere obtain their order and place.... But especially, fourth, it is advantageous for the practice of piety, which is the soul of a sermon, so that by its assistance, virtues and vices as well as other things are displayed from their very foundational principles throughout all their essentials.[23]

Both Edwards and his son Edwards Jr. would use van Mastricht as a guide in their theology and preaching practice. Edwards Jr. read through van Mastricht's *Theoretical-Practical Theology* seven times.[24] Here, van Mastricht gives the template for what would be the majority of Edwards's sermon preparation in selecting a few "universal precepts" to then exposit for understanding and retention.[25] Edwards Jr., like his father, would

[22]Ibid., 15–29.

[23]Petrus van Mastricht, *Theoretical-Practical Theology: Prolegomena*, vol. 1., ed. Joel R. Beeke, trans. Todd M. Rester (Grand Rapids: Reformation Heritage Books, 2018), location 2395, Kindle.

[24]Banks, *Forgotten Edwards*, 150.

[25]van Mastricht, *Theoretical-Practical Theology*, location 2395.

follow the three-stage progression of beginning with a text and providing its context and meaning, then a doctrine, and then giving an improvement or exhortation.[26] For Edwards Sr., though, as seen in this work, the context given would be in light of his audience's biblical literacy and what Edwards Sr. felt needed to be emphasized. John Broadus, in his guide to preaching, written in the 19th century, writes:

> There is in preaching very frequent need of Explanation. Numerous passages of Scripture are not understood, or are even misunderstood, by our hearers; and many have become so accustomed to passing over these, as to be no longer aware that they present any difficulty. Some of the most important doctrines of the Bible are in general very imperfectly understood; those who receive them need clearer views of what they profess to believe, and those who object to them are often in fact objecting to something very different from the real doctrine. The plan of salvation is seldom comprehended till one is really willing to conform to it, so that there is constantly arising new occasion for answering the great question, "What must I do to be saved?" And a thousand questions as to what is true and what is right in the practical conduct of life, perplex devout minds, and call for explanation. Preaching ought to be not merely convincing and persuasive, but eminently instructive.[27]

Edwards exampled preaching a style that was "eminently instructive" at Stockbridge. He would select "universal precepts" and then plan out how to illustrate them. He went to lengths to ensure his audience would understand the Scripture he used as his key texts. Only then would Edwards move on to stirring affections and giving the Gospel to his audience. For colonials, this might mean using illustrative language to give them a sense of the dreadfulness of God's wrath or the sweetness of God's love. For his native congregation, this might have meant giving metaphors of rivers and feasts to express the greatness of God or the bounty of the Gospel.

For those looking back at Edwards's preaching ministry today, it gives a guide to the importance and work of preaching for understanding. With a culture increasingly less biblically literate, it is more necessary than ever to

[26]Banks, *Forgotten Edwards*, 150–151.

[27]John A Broadus. *On the Preparation and Delivery of Sermons*, 4th ed, ed. Vernon L. Stanfield (New York: Harper & Row Publishers, 1979), 129.

instruct congregations on what the Bible says, what it means, and what they need to know and do because of it. Beyond instruction through, Edwards shows the need to stir the affections of the listener, or as Lloyd-Jones writes:

> What is the chief end of preaching? I like to think it is this. It is to give men and women a sense of God and His presence. As I have said already, during this last year I have been ill, and so have had the opportunity and privilege, of listening to others, instead of preaching myself. As I have listened in physical weakness this is the thing I have looked for and longed for and desired. I can forgive a man for a bad sermon. I can forgive the preacher almost anything if he gives me a sense of God, if he gives me something for my soul, if he gives me the sense that, though he is inadequate himself, he is handling something which is very great and very glorious, if he gives me some dim glimpse of the majesty and the glory of God, the love of Christ my Saviour, and the magnificence of the Gospel. If he does that I am his debtor, and I am profoundly grateful to him.[28]

Through his time as a Congregational colonial minister and as a Native American missionary, Edwards sought and showed in his preaching an intention to earnestly deliver the Word in a way that was of the greatest benefit to his audience. As Lloyd-Jones states, to "give them a sense of God and His presence."[29] Preaching was Edwards's primary avenue for ministry, and through a corpus of over 1,000 sermons, he showed great diligence in preparing fresh expositions of key texts.

This output stands in clear contrast to scholars who have claimed he spent his time at Stockbridge focused on theological treatises at the expense of his Native and colonial congregation. Even when he used the exact same key texts, as seen in this work, Edwards would expose them anew for his new audience. This is not to say that Edwards did not repreach sermons. As noted in the second chapter, Edwards had repreached *Sinners in the Hands of An Angry God* (his most famous sermon). But, as is seen in looking at the greater corpus, repreached sermons were the exception, not the rule.

Here is a quote from a lecture Lloyd-Jones gave on Edwards's preaching in 1976 at the Puritan and Westminster Conference of 1976:

[28]David Martyn Lloyd-Jones, *Preaching and Preachers: 40th Anniversary Edition*, ed. Kevin de Young (Grand Rapids: Zondervan, 2011), 110–111.

[29]Lloyd-Jones, *Preaching and Preachers*, 110–111..

> Let us now turn to Edwards' method of preaching. We note at once that he preached sermons, and that he did not deliver lectures. Edwards did not lecture about Christian truths. I am told frequently these days that many preachers seem to be lecturers rather than preachers. Preaching is not lecturing. Neither did Edwards just give a running commentary on a passage. That is not preaching either; though many today seem to think that it is. That was not Edwards' idea of preaching; and it has never been the classical idea of preaching. He started with a text. He was always Scriptural. He did not merely take a theme and speak on it, except when he was expounding some doctrine, but even then he chose a text. He was always expository. He was also invariably analytical. He had an analytical mind. He divides up his text, his statement; he wants to get at the essence of the message; so the critical, analytical element in his wonderful mind comes into play. He does this in order that he may arrive at the doctrine taught in the verse or section; and then he reasons about this doctrine, shows how it is to be found elsewhere in Scripture, and its relationship to other doctrines, and then establishes its truth. But he never stops at that. There is always the application. He was preaching to people and not giving a dissertation, not giving expression in public to his private thoughts in the study. He was always concerned to bring home the truth to the listeners, to show the relevance of it. But, above all, and I quote him, he believed that preaching should always be 'warm and earnest'. I remind you again that we are dealing here with a giant intellect and brilliant philosopher; and yet this is the man who places all this emphasis upon warmth and upon feeling.[30]

Through the sermons examined, Edwards's purpose in every sermon was more than a rote lecture, but a sermon intended to stir affections, persuade the excellency of doctrine, or preach for understanding among his later congregation. And, as examined, he was thoughtful in light of his audience. When he would preach on themes (as seen in the short sermon series at Stockbridge), biblical themes were always founded on Scripture.

[30]David Martyn Lloyd-Jones, *The Puritans: Their Origins and Successors: Addresses Delivered at the Puritan and Westminster Conferences 1959–1978* (Carlisle, PA: The Banner of Truth Trust, 2014), 358–359.

The application for ministers today is to be intentional in the exegesis, exposition, homiletic, and delivery of sermons. Follow Edwards's example of understanding the text, understanding himself (and his need of God's grace), understanding the audience (and their biblical needs in literacy, knowledge, and affection), and understanding the audience's need to know and respond to God's Word appropriately. Be earnest in preaching. Be intentional in preaching and give people a sense of the presence of the Almighty Savior!

Bibliography

Allen, John, Jonathan Burr, John Eliot, Richard Mather, John Phillips, Thomas Shepherd, Thomas Weld, and John Wilson. 1640. "Propositions Concerning Evidence of God's Love." Papers of the Winthrop Family Vol. 4. Massachusetts Historical Society. https://masshist.org/publications/winthop/index/.php/view/PWF04d264.

Ames, William. "The Marrow of Sacred Divinity Drawne Out of the Holy Scriptures." 1642. Reprint, Ann Arbor: *Early English Books Text Creation Partnership*, 2005.

Amory, Hugh, and David D. Hall, eds. *A History of the Book in America: The Colonial Book in the Atlantic World.* Chapel Hill, NC: University of North Carolina Press, 2007. Kindle.

Angoff, Charles. *Jonathan Edwards: His Life and Influence.* The Leverton Lecture Series. Cranbury, NJ: Associated University Presses, 1975.

Antracoli, Alexis A. "Mighty in the Scriptures: The Bible in Colonial Massachusetts, 1630–1776." PhD diss., Brandeis University, 2006.

Awbrey, Ben. *How Effective Sermons Advance.* Eugene, OR: Resource Publications, 2011.

_____. *How Effective Sermons Begin.* Fearn, Ross-shire, Scotland: Mentor, 2008.

Bailyn, Bernard. *Education in the Forming of American Society: Needs and Opportunities for Study.* Chapel Hill, NC: The University of North Carolina Press, 1960. Scribd.

Banks, John S. *The Forgotten Edwards: A New Examination of the Life and Thought of Jonathan Edwards Junior.* N.p.:Jonathan Edwards Society, 2021.

Barnes, Thomas G., ed. *The Book of the General Lawes and Libertyes Concerning the Inhabitants of the Massachusets*. 1648. Reprint, Pasadena, CA: Castle Press, 1975.

Baxter, Richard. *Gildas Salvianus, the reformed pastor shewing the nature of the pastoral work, especially in private instruction and catechizing*. 1656. Reprint, Ann Arbor: *Early English Texts Online Texts Creation Partnership,* 2005.

_____. *The Reformed Pastor*. Edited by Hugh Martin. London: SCM Press LTD, 1956.

_____."*Reliquiæ Baxterianæ*." 1696. Reprint, Ann Arbor: *Early English Texts Online Texts Creation Partnership*, 2003.

Bernard, Richard. "The Faithfull Shepheard: Or The Shepherds Faithfulnesse." 1648. Reprint, Ann Arbor: *Early English Texts Online Texts Creation Partnership,* 2014.

Blackwood, Andrew W. *Doctrinal Preaching for Today*. Nashville: Abingdon Press, 1956.

_____. *Expository Preaching for Today*. Nashville: Abingdon Press, 1953.

_____. *The Preparation of Sermons*. Nashville: Abingdon Press, 1948.

Boss, Robert L. *God-Haunted World: The Elemental Theology of Jonathan Edwards*. N.p.: Robert L. Boss, 2015.

Boss, Robert L., and Sarah B. Boss, eds. *The Miscellanies Companion*. N.p.: JE Society Press, 2018.

Bradstreet, Anne. "An Epitaph on My Dear and Ever Honoured Mother Mrs. Dorothy Dudley." *The Works of Anne Bradstreet: In Prose and Verse*. Charlestown: Abram E. Cutter, 1867.

Brainerd, David. "*Mirabilia Dei inter Indicos, or The rise and progress of a remarkable work of grace amongst a number of the Indians in the provinces of New-Jersey and Pennsylvania, justly represented in a journal kept by order of the Honourable Society (in Scotland) for Propagating Christian Knowledge. : With some general remarks*." 1746. Reprint, Ann Arbor: *Evans Early American Imprint Collection Text Creation Partnership*.

Bremer, Francis J. *The Puritan Experiment: New England Society from Bradford to Edwards*. Rev. ed. Lebanon, NH: University Press of New England, 1995.

_____. *Puritanism: Transatlantic Perspectives on a Seventeenth-Century Anglo-American Faith*. Boston: Massachusetts Historical Society, 1993.

Broadus, John A. *On the Preparation and Delivery of Sermons, 4th Ed.* Revised by Vernon L. Stanfield. New York: Harper & Row Publishers, 1979.

_____. *A Treatise On the Preparation and Delivery of Sermons, 17th Ed.* New York: A.C. Armstrong & Son, 1891.

Brown, Robert E. *Jonathan Edwards and the Bible*. Bloomington, IN: Indiana University Press, 2002.

Burr, Esther Edwards. *The Journal of Esther Edwards Burr, 1754–1757*. Edited by Carol F. Karlsen and Laurie Crumpacker. New Haven: Yale University Press, 1984.

Bushman, Richard L., ed. *The Great Awakening: Documents On the Revival of Religion, 1740–1745*. Chapel Hill, NC: University of North Carolina, 1989.

Carrick, John. *The Preaching of Jonathan Edwards*. Carlisle, PA: The Banner of Truth Trust, 2008.

Carse, James Pearce. "The Christology of Jonathan Edwards." PhD diss., Drew University, 1966.

Cartwright, Thomas. *Memoir of the Life and Writings of Thomas Cartwright, B.D.* Edited by Rev. B. Brook. London: W. Blackward and Sons, 1845.

Cherry, Conrad. *The Theology of Jonathan Edwards: A Reappraisal*. Garden City, NY: Anchor Books, 1966.

Child, Frank Samuel. *The Colonial Parson of New England: A Picture*. New York: Baker & Taylor, 1896.

Cho, Jaeyoung. "A Critical Examination of Jonathan Edwards's Theology of Preaching." PhD diss., New Orleans Baptist Theological Seminary, 2012.

Clark, Solomon. *Historical Catalogue of the Northampton First Church, 1661–1891*. Northampton, MA: Gazette Printing Company, 1891.

Cotton, John. "Gods Promise to His Plantation (1630)." In *The Kingdom, The Power, and the Glory: The Millenial Impulse in Early American Literature*, edited by Reiner Smolinski, 10–19. Dubuque, IA: Kendall-Hunt, 1998.

_____. "*A Practicall Commentary, Or an Exposition with Observations, Reasons, and Uses Upon the First Epistle Generall of John*. 1658. Reprint, Ann Arbor: *Early English Books Online Texts Creation Partnership*, 2011.

Cremin, Lawrence. *American Education: The Colonial Experience: 1607–1783*. New York: Harper and Row, 1970.

Crisp, Oliver, and Douglas A. Sweeney, eds. *After Jonathan Edwards: The Courses of the New England Theology*. New York: Oxford University Press, 2012.

Dexter, Franklin B., ed. *New Haven Town Records, 1649–1662*. New Haven: New Haven Historical Society, 1917.

Dwight, Sereno Edwards. *The Life of President Edwards*. New York: G & C & H Carvill, 1830.

Edwards, John. *The Preacher*. 2nd ed. London: J. Robinson, J. Lawrence, and J. Wyat, 1705.

Edwards, Jonathan. *The Blessing of God: Previously Unpublished Sermons of Jonathan Edwards*. Edited by Michael D. McMullen. Nashville, TN: Broadman & Holman, 2003.

_____. *Charity and Its Fruits: Living in the Light of God's Love*. Edited by Kyle Strobel. Wheaton, IL: Crossway, 2012.

_____. "Christ Gave Himself for Us." Edited by R. Craig Woods, *Jonathan Edwards Sermon Index* (Sermon 1018). New Haven: Jonathan Edwards Center, Yale University.

_____. "Christ's Light Accompanied with Life." Edited by R. Craig Woods, *Jonathan Edwards Sermon Index* (Sermon 650d). New Haven: Jonathan Edwards Center, Yale University.

_____. "Christ the Resting Place of His People." Edited by R. Craig Woods, *Jonathan Edwards Sermon Index* (Sermon 1142). New Haven: Jonathan Edwards Center, Yale University.

_____. "Christ Will Come Quickly to Judge All Men." Edited by R. Craig Woods, *Jonathan Edwards Sermon Index* (Sermon 1100). New Haven: Jonathan Edwards Center, Yale University.

_____. "The Desire of the Righteous Shall Be Granted." Edited by Kenneth P. Minkema, *Jonathan Edwards Sermon Index* (Sermon 871). New Haven: Jonathan Edwards Center, Yale University.

_____. "Dreadful Fear Will Seize the Hearts of the Wicked." Edited by Kenneth P. Minkema, *Jonathan Edwards Sermon Index* (Sermon 870). New Haven: Jonathan Edwards Center, Yale University.

_____. *Ethical Writings*. Edited by Paul Ramsey. Vol. 8, *The Works of Jonathan Edwards*. New Haven: Yale University Press, 1989.

_____. "The Foundation of a Good Hope of Heaven is Laid on a Rock." Edited by R. Craig Woods, *Jonathan Edwards Sermon Index* (Sermon 502). New Haven: Jonathan Edwards Center, Yale University.

_____. *The Glory and Honor of God: Volume 2 of the Previously Unpublished Sermons of Jonathan Edwards*. Edited by Michael D. McMullen. Nashville: Broadman & Holman, 2004.

_____. "God Invites Men to the Great Feast He Has Prepared." Edited by R. Craig Woods, *Jonathan Edwards Sermon Index* (Sermon 1057). New Haven: Jonathan Edwards Center, Yale University.

_____. "God is an Infinitely Merciful and Gracious God." Edited by R. Craig Woods, *Jonathan Edwards Sermon Index* (Sermon 1063). New Haven: Jonathan Edwards Center, Yale University.

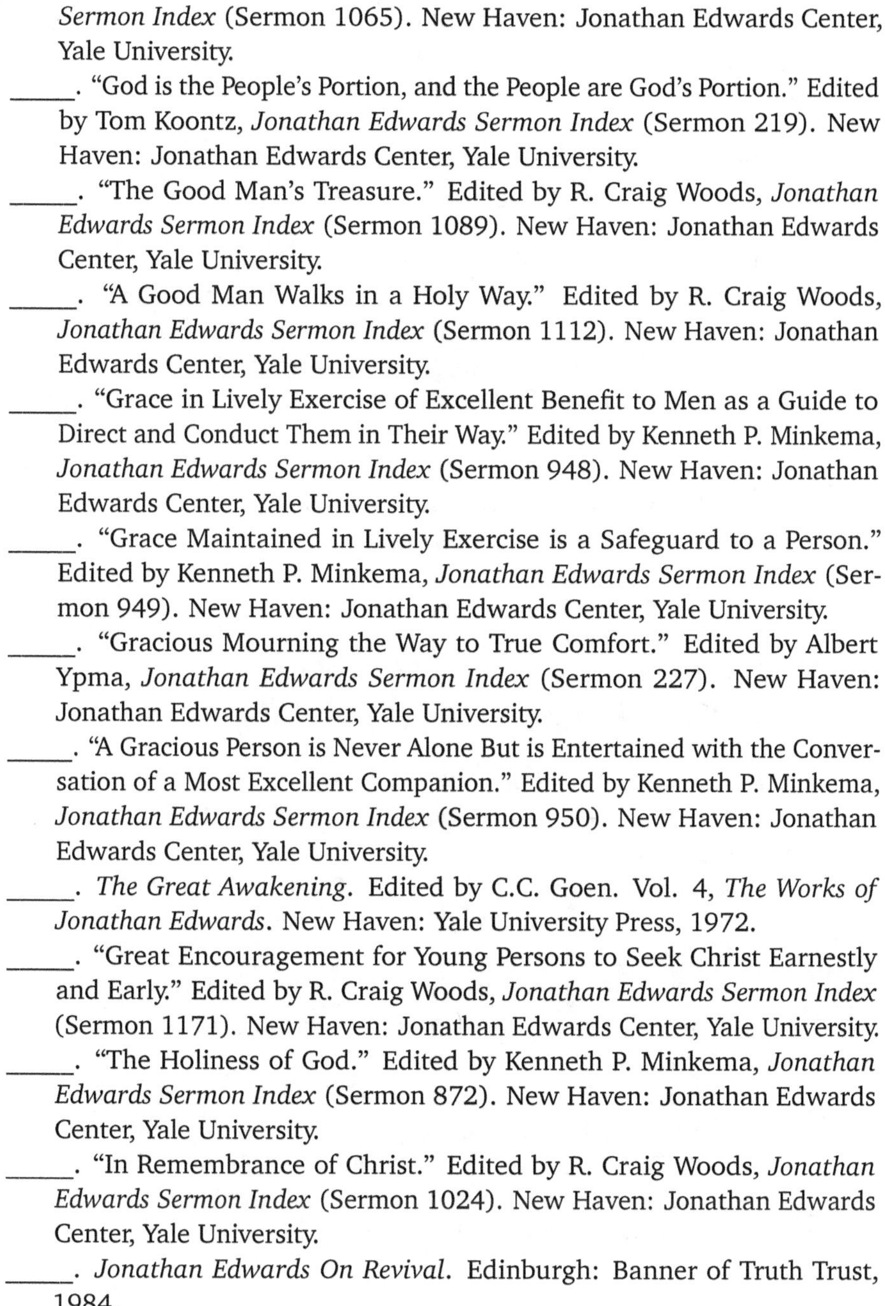

_____. "God is Infinitely Holy." Edited by R. Craig Woods, *Jonathan Edwards Sermon Index* (Sermon 1065). New Haven: Jonathan Edwards Center, Yale University.

_____. "God is the People's Portion, and the People are God's Portion." Edited by Tom Koontz, *Jonathan Edwards Sermon Index* (Sermon 219). New Haven: Jonathan Edwards Center, Yale University.

_____. "The Good Man's Treasure." Edited by R. Craig Woods, *Jonathan Edwards Sermon Index* (Sermon 1089). New Haven: Jonathan Edwards Center, Yale University.

_____. "A Good Man Walks in a Holy Way." Edited by R. Craig Woods, *Jonathan Edwards Sermon Index* (Sermon 1112). New Haven: Jonathan Edwards Center, Yale University.

_____. "Grace in Lively Exercise of Excellent Benefit to Men as a Guide to Direct and Conduct Them in Their Way." Edited by Kenneth P. Minkema, *Jonathan Edwards Sermon Index* (Sermon 948). New Haven: Jonathan Edwards Center, Yale University.

_____. "Grace Maintained in Lively Exercise is a Safeguard to a Person." Edited by Kenneth P. Minkema, *Jonathan Edwards Sermon Index* (Sermon 949). New Haven: Jonathan Edwards Center, Yale University.

_____. "Gracious Mourning the Way to True Comfort." Edited by Albert Ypma, *Jonathan Edwards Sermon Index* (Sermon 227). New Haven: Jonathan Edwards Center, Yale University.

_____. "A Gracious Person is Never Alone But is Entertained with the Conversation of a Most Excellent Companion." Edited by Kenneth P. Minkema, *Jonathan Edwards Sermon Index* (Sermon 950). New Haven: Jonathan Edwards Center, Yale University.

_____. *The Great Awakening*. Edited by C.C. Goen. Vol. 4, *The Works of Jonathan Edwards*. New Haven: Yale University Press, 1972.

_____. "Great Encouragement for Young Persons to Seek Christ Earnestly and Early." Edited by R. Craig Woods, *Jonathan Edwards Sermon Index* (Sermon 1171). New Haven: Jonathan Edwards Center, Yale University.

_____. "The Holiness of God." Edited by Kenneth P. Minkema, *Jonathan Edwards Sermon Index* (Sermon 872). New Haven: Jonathan Edwards Center, Yale University.

_____. "In Remembrance of Christ." Edited by R. Craig Woods, *Jonathan Edwards Sermon Index* (Sermon 1024). New Haven: Jonathan Edwards Center, Yale University.

_____. *Jonathan Edwards On Revival*. Edinburgh: Banner of Truth Trust, 1984.

_____. *A Jonathan Edwards Reader.* Edited by John E. Smith, Harry S. Stout, and Kenneth P. Minkema. New Haven: Yale University Press, 1995.

_____. *Letters and Personal Writings.* Edited by George S. Claghorn. Vol. 16, *The Works of Jonathan Edwards.* New Haven: Yale University Press, 1998.

_____. "The Lord's Supper is an Ordinance That Represents the Greatest Things." Edited by R. Craig Woods, *Jonathan Edwards Sermon Index* (Sermon 1026). New Haven: Jonathan Edwards Center, Yale University.

_____. "The Lord's Supper Ought to be Observed in Remembrance of Christ." Edited by R. Craig Woods, *Jonathan Edwards Sermon Index* (Sermon 328). New Haven: Jonathan Edwards Center, Yale University.

_____. "Made in God's Image." Edited by Kenneth P. Minkema, *Jonathan Edwards Sermon Index* (Sermon 998). New Haven: Jonathan Edwards Center, Yale University.

_____. "Men Ought to Be Much in Thinking of Their Own Ways." Edited by R. Craig Woods, *Jonathan Edwards Sermon Index* (Sermon 1113). New Haven: Jonathan Edwards Center, Yale University.

_____. *"Miscellanies," (Entry Nos. a-z, aa-zz, 1–500).* Edited by Harry S. Stout. Vol. 13, *The Works of Jonathan Edwards.* New Haven: Yale University Press, 1998.

_____. *"Miscellanies," (Entry Nos. 501–832).* Edited by Ava Chamberlain. Vol. 18, *The Works of Jonathan Edwards.* New Haven: Yale University Press, 2000.

_____. *"Miscellanies," (Entry Nos. 833–1152).* Edited by Amy Pantinga Pauw. Vol. 20, *The Works of Jonathan Edwards.* New Haven: Yale University Press, 2002.

_____. *"Miscellanies," (Entry Nos. 1153–1360).* Edited by Douglas A. Sweeney. Vol. 23, *The Works of Jonathan Edwards.* New Haven: Yale University Press, 2004.

_____. "Persons' Speech Shows What Fills Their Heart." Edited by R. Craig Woods, *Jonathan Edwards Sermon Index* (Sermon 1088). New Haven: Jonathan Edwards Center, Yale University.

_____. "The Poor in Spirit Are Happy Because the Kingdom of Heaven is Theirs." Edited by R. Craig Woods, *Jonathan Edwards Sermon Index* (Sermon 1049). New Haven: Jonathan Edwards Center, Yale University.

_____. "The Pure in Heart Are Happy Because They Shall See God." Edited by R. Craig Woods, *Jonathan Edwards Sermon Index* (Sermon 1051). New Haven: Jonathan Edwards Center, Yale University.

_____. "Receiving the Blessed Fruits of Religion by Practicing It with Our Whole Hearts." Edited by Justin Hawkins, *Jonathan Edwards Sermon Index* (Sermon 146). New Haven: Jonathan Edwards Center, Yale University.

_____. *Religious Affections*. Edited by Paul Ramsey. Vol. 2, *The Works of Jonathan Edwards*. New Haven: Yale University Press, 1993.

_____. *The Religious Affections*. 7th ed. Edinburgh: Banner of Truth Trust, 2007.

_____. "Seek God in the Days of Your Youth." Edited by R. Craig Woods, *Jonathan Edwards Sermon Index* (Sermon 982). New Haven: Jonathan Edwards Center, Yale University.

_____. *Sermons and Discourses, 1720–1723.* Edited by Wilson H. Kimnach. Vol. 10, *The Works of Jonathan Edwards*. New Haven: Yale University Press, 1992.

_____. *Sermons and Discourses, 1723–1729.* Edited by Kenneth P. Minkema. Vol. 14, *The Works of Jonathan Edwards*. New Haven: Yale University Press, 1997.

_____. *Sermons and Discourses, 1730–1733.* Edited by Mark Valeri. Vol. 17, *The Works of Jonathan Edwards*. New Haven: Yale University Press, 1999.

_____. *Sermons and Discourses, 1734–1738.* Edited by M.X. Lesser. Vol. 19, *The Works of Jonathan Edwards*. New Haven: Yale University Press, 2001.

_____. *Sermons and Discourses, 1739–1742.* Edited by Harry S. Stout, Nathan O. Hatch, and Kyle P. Farley. Vol. 22, *The Works of Jonathan Edwards*. New Haven: Yale University Press, 2003.

_____. *Sermons and Discourses, 1743–1758.* Edited by Wilson H. Kimnach. Vol. 25, *The Works of Jonathan Edwards*. New Haven: Yale University Press, 2006.

_____. *The Sermons of Jonathan Edwards: A Reader*. Edited by Wilson H. Kimnach, Kenneth P. Minkema, and Douglas A. Sweeney. New Haven: Yale University Press, 1999.

_____. "The Sins of Youth Abide to the Grave." Edited by Carol King, *Jonathan Edwards Sermon Index* (Sermon 274). New Haven: Jonathan Edwards Center, Yale University.

_____. "The Sovereignty of God's Mercy." Edited by Kenneth P. Minkema, *Jonathan Edwards Sermon Index* (Sermon 833). New Haven: Jonathan Edwards Center, Yale University.

_____. "There Are None So Happy as Those That Have God as Their Savior." Edited by R. Craig Woods, *Jonathan Edwards Sermon Index* (Sermon 1130). New Haven: Jonathan Edwards Center, Yale University.

_____. "They That Mourn Are Happy Because They Shall Be Comforted." Edited by R. Craig Woods, *Jonathan Edwards Sermon Index* (Sermon 1050). New Haven: Jonathan Edwards Center, Yale University.

_____. "The Time of Youth the Best Time to Be Improved To Religious Purposes." Edited by Charles T. Thaluri, *Jonathan Edwards Sermon Index* (Sermon 214). New Haven: Jonathan Edwards Center, Yale University.

_____. "Tis Not Inconsistent with God's Attributes to Punish Ungodly Men with Eternal Misery." Edited by Kenneth P. Minkema, *Jonathan Edwards Sermon Index* (Sermon 265). New Haven: Jonathan Edwards Center, Yale University.

_____. "Turned From An Alien to An Heir." Edited by Kenneth P. Minkema, *Jonathan Edwards Sermon Index* (Sermon 886). New Haven: Jonathan Edwards Center, Yale University.

_____. "Turned From Darkness to Light." Edited by Kenneth P. Minkema, *Jonathan Edwards Sermon Index* (Sermon 883). New Haven: Jonathan Edwards Center, Yale University.

_____. "Turned From Satan to God." Edited by Kenneth P. Minkema, *Jonathan Edwards Sermon Index* (Sermon 884). New Haven: Jonathan Edwards Center, Yale University.

_____. "Turned From Wrath to Forgiveness." Edited by Kenneth P. Minkema, *Jonathan Edwards Sermon Index* (Sermon 885). New Haven: Jonathan Edwards Center, Yale University.

_____. "What Men Are When They Die, They Will Be to All Eternity." Edited by R. Craig Woods, *Jonathan Edwards Sermon Index* (Sermon 1099). New Haven: Jonathan Edwards Center, Yale University.

_____. "The Wicked Man's Treasure." Edited by R. Craig Woods, *Jonathan Edwards Sermon Index* (Sermon 1090). New Haven: Jonathan Edwards Center, Yale University.

_____. "With God and the Lamb in Heaven." Edited by R. Craig Woods, *Jonathan Edwards Sermon Index* (Sermon 1098). New Haven: Jonathan Edwards Center, Yale University.

Edwards, Jonathan, Jr. "Volume 242." *The Forgotten Edwards: A New Examination of the Life and Thought of Jonathan Edwards Junior*, Appendix 3: ("Two Sermons For Moses Paul"). Edited by John S. Banks. N.p.: Jonathan Edwards Society, 2021.

_____. *Observations on the Language of the Muhhekaneew Indians.* New Haven:

Josiah Meigs, 1788.

_____. *Observations on the Mahican Language.* American Language Reprints 25.

Edited by Claudio R. Salvucci. Bristol, PA: Evolution, 2002.

_____. "The Injustice and Impolicy of the Slave-Trade, and of the Slavery of the Africans: illustrated in a sermon preached before the Connecticut Society for the Promotion of Freedom, and for the Relief of Persons Unlawfully Holden in Bondage, at their annual meeting in New Haven, September 15, 1791." 1791. Reprint, Ann Arbor: *Evan Early American Imprint Collection Online Text Creation Partnership*, 2009.

Edwards, Sarah Pierpont. *Family Writings and Related Documents.* Edited by the Jonathan Edwards Center. Vol. 41, *The Works of Jonathan Edwards Online*. Jonathan Edwards Center.

Eliot, John, and Thomas Mayhew. "Tears of Repentance: or, a further Narrative of the Progress of the Gospel Amongst the Indians in New England." 1653. Reprint, Ann Arbor: *Early English Texts Online Creation Partnership*, 2008.

Everhard, Matthew V. *A Theology of Joy: Jonathan Edwards and Eternal Happiness in the Holy Trinity*. N.p.: JE Society Press, 2018.

Everts, Louis H. *History of the Connecticut Valley in Massachusetts*. Philadelphia: J.B. Lippincott & Co., 1879.

Fairbairn, A.M. "Jonathan Edwards." In *The Prophets of the Christian Faith*, edited by Lyman Abbot, 145–166. New York: The Macmillan Company, 1896.

Finn, Nathan A., and Jeremy M. Kimble, eds. *A Reader's Guide to the Major Writings of Jonathan Edwards*. Wheaton, IL: Crossway, 2017.

Foxcroft, Thomas. "Cleansing Our Way in Youth Press'd, as of the Highest Importance: and Observing the Word of God Recommended, as the Only Sufficient Means." 1719. Reprint, Ann Arbor: *Evans Early American Imprint Collection Online Texts Creation Partnership*, 2008.

Ford, Paul Leicester, ed. *The New-England Primer: A History of Its Origin and Development with a Reprint of the Unique Copy of the Earliest Known Edition and Many Fac-Simile Illustrations and Reproductions*. New York: Dodd, Mead, and Company, 1897.

Foxe, John. *The Unabridged Acts and Monuments Online (TAMO)*. Sheffield: The Digital Humanities Institute, 2011. https://www.dhi.ac.uk/foxe/.

Frazier, Patrick. *The Mohicans of Stockbridge*. Lincoln, NE: University of Nebraska Press, 1992.

Gambrell, Mary Latimer. *Ministerial Training in Eighteenth-Century New England*. London: Columbia University Press, 1937.

Gardiner, H. Norman, ed. *Jonathan Edwards: A Retrospect*. New York: Houghton, Mifflin and Company, 1901.

Gaustad, Edwin S. *The Great Awakening in New England*. Chicago: Quadrangle Books, 1968.

Gerstner, John H. *Jonathan Edwards On Heaven and Hell*. Morgan, PA: Soli Deo Gloria, 1998.

Graves, Dan, ed. *The Schleitheim Confession*. Worcester, PA: Christian History Institute, 2023.

Gura, Philip F. *Jonathan Edwards: America's Evangelical*. New York: Hill and Wang, 2006. Kindle.

Hall, David D. *The Faithful Shepherd: A History of the New England Ministry in the Seventeenth Century*. Chapel Hill, NC: University of North Carolina Press, 1972.

Hambrick-Stowe, Charles E. *The Practice of Piety: Puritan Devotional Disciplines in Seventeenth-Century New England*. Chapel Hill, NC: University of North Carolina Press, 1982. Scribd.

Hamilton, S. Mark. *A Treatise On Jonathan Edwards: Continuous Creation and Christology*. San Bernardino, CA: JE Society Press, 2017.

Harder, Michael. "True Excellency: The Missionary Preaching of Jonathan Edwards." PhD diss., Southeastern Baptist Theological Seminary, 2022.

Heisler, Greg. *Spirit-Led Preaching: The Holy Spirit's Role in Sermon Preparation and Delivery*. Nashville: B & H Academic, 2007.

Hopkins, Samuel. *The Life and Character of the Late Reverend Jonathan Edwards*. Boston: S. Kneeland, 1765.

Hopkins, A.M., Samuel. *Historical Memoirs Relating to the Housatonic Indians*. 1753 Reprint. New York: William Abatt, 1911.

Hoyt, Arthur S. *The Pulpit and American Life*. New York: The Macmillan Company, 1921.

International Mission Board. *Foundations*, Version 4. International Mission Board, 2002.

Johnson, Barbara A. *Reading Piers Plowman and The Pilgrim's Progress: Reception and the Protestant Reader*. Carbondale, IL: Southern Illinois University Press, 1992.

Kellaway, William. *The New England Company 1649–1776: Missionary Society to the American Indians*. London: Longmans, 1961.

Kidd, Thomas S. *America's Colonial History: Clashing Cultures and Faiths*. New Haven: Yale University Press, 2016.

_____. *George Whitefield: America's Spiritual Founding Father*. New Haven: Yale University Press, 2014.

_____. *The Great Awakening: The Roots of Evangelical Christianity in Colonial America*. New Haven: Yale University Press, 2007.

Klassen, Ernest Eugene. *Revival Preaching: Twelve Lessons from Jonathan Edwards*.

Eugene, OR: Resource Publications, 2021.

Lee, Joseph W. "Jonathan Edwards, Samuel Hopkins, and Theological Ethics of Social Concern." PhD diss., Dallas Theological Seminary, 2018.

Lee, Sang Hyun, ed. *The Princeton Companion to Jonathan Edwards*. Princeton: Princeton University Press, 2005.

Lloyd-Jones, David Martyn. *Preaching and Preachers: 40th Anniversary Edition*. Edited by Kevin de Young. Grand Rapids: Zondervan, 2011.

_____. *The Puritans: Their Origins and Successors: Addresses Delivered at the Puritan and Westminster Conferences 1959–1978*. Carlisle, PA: The Banner of Truth Trust, 2014.

Lockridge, Kenneth A. *A New England Town: The First Hundred Years. Dedham, Massachusetts, 1636–1736*. New York: Norton, 1970.

_____. *Literacy in Colonial New England: An Enquiry into the Social Context of Literacy in the Early Modern West*. New York: W.W. Norton and Company, 1974.

Locke, John. *The Educational Writings of John Locke: A Critical Edition with Introduction and Notes*. Edited by James L. Axtell. New York: Cambridge at the University Press, 1968.

Lowe, John Thomas. "'The Practice that Prevails': Jonathan Edwards, Slavery, and Race." PhD diss., Vrije Universiteit Amsterdam, 2022.

MacArthur, John. "Moving from Exegesis to Exposition." In *Preaching: How to Preach Biblically*, edited by John MacArthur, 236–248. Nashville: Thomas Nelson, 2005.

MacFarlane, Gertrude E. "The Educational History of Northampton, Massachusetts 1663–1940." MS Thesis, Massachusetts State College, 1940.

Marsden, George M. *Jonathan Edwards: A Life*. New Haven: Yale University Press, 2003.

_____. *Fundamentalism and American Culture*. 2nd ed. Oxford: Oxford University Press, 2006.

_____. *Religion and American Culture*. San Diego: Harcourt Brace Jovanovich, 1990.

Mather, Cotton. "*The Young Man Spoken to: Another Essay, to Recommend and Inculcate the Maxims of Early Religion, Unto Young Persons; and Especially the Religion of the Closet*." 1712. Reprint, Ann Arbor: *Evan Early American Imprint Collection Online Text Creation Partnership*, 2009.

Mather, Richard. *A Farewell Exhortation to the Church and People of Dorchester in New-England*. 1657. Reprint, Ann Arbor: *Early English Books Online Text Creation Partnership*, 2005.

Mayhew, Experience. *Indian converts: or, Some account of the lives and dying speeches of a considerable number of the Christianized Indians of Martha's Vineyard, in New-England.* London: Samuel Gerrish, 1727.

_____. *Experience Mayhew's Indian Converts: A Cultural Edition*. Amherst, MA: University of Massachusetts Press, 2008.

McClymond, Michael James, and Gerald R. McDermott. *The Theology of Jonathan Edwards*. New York: Oxford University Press, 2012.

McDermott, Gerald R., ed. *Understanding Jonathan Edwards: An Introduction to America's Theologian*. Oxford: Oxford University Press, 2009.

McMullen, Michael, Douglas Sweeney, John Mark Yeats. "Edwards and Pastoral Challenges" (Spotify). This Week in Church History. Midwestern Baptist Theological Seminary. June, 21, 2020. https://open.spotify.com/episode/09qAAgc09J5CpOIELVQpzH.

Medefind, Jedd, and Erik Lokkesmoe. *The Revolutionary Communicator: Seven Principles Jesus Lived to Impact, Connect, and Lead.* Lake Mary, FL: Relevant Books, 2004.

Merkle, Benjamin, and Thomas R. Schreiner. *Shepherding God's Flock: Biblical Leadership in the New Testament and Beyond.* Grand Rapids: Kregel Publications, 2014.

Middlekauff, Robert. *The Mathers: Three Generations of Puritan Intellectuals 1596–1728*. Berkely: University of California Press, 1999.

Miller, Perry. *Jonathan Edwards*. The American Men of Letters Series. Westport, CT: Greenwood Press Publishers, 1973.

_____. *The New England Mind*. Third Printing of Reissue. Hartford, MA: Harvard University Press, 1967.

Miller, Perry; and Thomas H. Johnson. *The Puritans*, Vol. 2. New York: Harper & Row Publishers, 1963.

Minkema, Kenneth Pieter. "The Edwardses: A Ministerial Family in Eighteenth Century New England." PhD diss., University of Connecticut, 1988.

Moody, Josh, ed. *Jonathan Edwards and Justification*. Wheaton, IL: Crossway, 2012.

Morgan, Edmund S., ed. *The Founding of Massachusetts: Historians and the Sources*. New York: The Bobbs-Merrill Company, 1964.

_____. *The Puritan Family: Religion & Domestic Relations in Seventeenth-Century New England*. New ed. New York: Harper & Row Publishers, 1966.

Morris, William Sparkes. *The Young Jonathan Edwards: A Reconstruction*. Brooklyn, NY: Carlson, 1991.

Murray, Iain H. *Jonathan Edwards: A New Biography*. 1987. Reprint, Edinburgh: Banner of Truth, 2008.

Nichols, Stephen J. *Heaven on Earth: Capturing Jonathan Edwards's Vision of Living in Between*. Wheaton, IL: Crossway Books, 2006.

Noll, Mark A. *In the Beginning Was the Word: The Bible in American Public Life, 1492–1783*. Oxford: Oxford University Press, 2016. Kindle.

Occom, Samson. *The Collected Writings of Samson Occom, Mohegan*. Edited by Joanna Brooks. Leadership and Literature in Eighteenth-Century Native America. New York: Oxford University Press, 2006.

Paul, Roy M. *Jonathan Edwards and the Stockbridge Mohican Indians: His Mission and Sermons*. Peterborough, ON: H & E Publishing, 2020. Kindle.

Peckham, Mary. *Saved in Revival: Testimony of Mary Morrison, Convert of revival in the Hebrides*. Edited by Juanita Snyder, Rosalind Masterson, Colin Peckham, and Norma Peckham. 1966. Reprint, Cape Town, SA: Prairie Press, 2012. eBook.

Peel, Albert, ed. *The Savoy Declaration of Faith and Order, 1658*. London: Independent Press, 1939.

Perkins, William. "The Arte of Prophesying." In *The Works of William Perkins, Vol. 10*, edited by J. Stephen Yuille. Grand Rapids: Reformation Heritage Books, 2020. Scribd.

Prime, Derek J., and Alistair Begg. *On Being a Pastor: Understanding Our Calling and Work*. Chicago: Moody Publishers, 2004.

Rivett, Sarah. *Unscripted America: Indigenous Languages and the Origins of a Literary Nation*. Oxford Studies in American Literary History. New York: Oxford University Press, 2017.

Robinson, Haddon W., ed. *Biblical Sermons: How Twelve Preachers Apply the Principles of Biblical Preaching*. Grand Rapids: Baker Book House, 1989.

_____. *Biblical Preaching: The Development and Delivery of Expository Messages*.

Grand Rapids: Baker Book House, 1980.

Schaff, Philip. *The Creeds of Christendom: With a History and Critical Notes*. New York: Harper and Brothers, 1919.

Scheick, William J. *Critical Essays on Jonathan Edwards*. Boston: G.K. Hall, 1980.

Selement, George. "The Means to Grace: A Study of Conversion in Early New England." PhD diss., Calvin College, 1970.

Sergeant, John. *A Letter From the Rev. Mr. Sergeant of Stockbridge, to Dr. Coleman of Boston*. Boston: Rogers and Fowle, 1743.

Shurtleff, Nathaniel B., ed. *Records of the Governor and Company of the Massachusetts Bay in New England, Vol. II*. Boston: William White, 1853.

Silverman, David J. *Red Brethren: The Brothertown and Stockbridge Indians and the Problem of Race in Early America*. Ithaca, NY: Cornell University Press, 2010. Kindle.

Simonson, Harold Peter. *Jonathan Edwards, Theologian of the Heart*. Macon, GA: Mercer University Press, 1982.

Simpson, Alan. *Puritanism in Old and New England*. Chicago: University of Chicago Press, 1955.

Stein, Stephen J., ed. *The Cambridge Companion to Jonathan Edwards*. New York: Cambridge University Press, 2007.

Stievermann, Jan, and Douglas A. Sweeney, eds. *The Oxford Handbook of Jonathan Edwards*. Oxford: Oxford University Press, 2021.

Stoddard, Solomon. *"The Doctrine of Instituted Churches Explained and Proved from the Word of God."* 1700. Reprint, Ann Arbor: *Early English Books Online Texts Creation Partnership*, 2012.

Stout, Harry S. *The New England Soul: Preaching and Religious Culture in Colonial New England*. New York: Oxford University Press, 1986.

Stout, Harry S., Kenneth P. Minkema, and Adriaan C. Neele, eds. *The Jonathan Edwards Encyclopedia*. Grand Rapids: Eerdmans, 2017.

Strachan, Owen, and Doug Sweeney. *The Essential Jonathan Edwards*. Chicago: Moody Publishers, 2018.

Strobel, Kyle C. *Jonathan Edwards's Theology: A Reinterpretation*. T&T Clark Studies in Systematic Theology 19. London: Bloomsbury, 2014. Kindle.

Sweeney, Douglas A. *Edwards the Exegete: Biblical Interpretation and Anglo-Protestant Culture on the Edge of the Enlightenment*. New York: Oxford University Press, 2016. Kindle.

_____. *Jonathan Edwards and the Ministry of the Word: A Model of Faith and Thought*. Downers Grove, IL: IVP Academic, 2009. Kindle.

Sweeney, Douglas A., and Allen C. Guelzo, eds. *The New England Theology: From Jonathan Edwards to Edwards Amasa Park*. Grand Rapids: Baker Academic, 2006.

Thomas, Robert. "Exegesis and Expository Preaching." In *Preaching: How to Preach Biblically*, edited by John MacArthur, 107–119. Nashville: Thomas Nelson, 2005.

Tracy, Joseph. *The Great Awakening*. New York: Arno Press & The New York Times, 1969.

Trumbull, Benjamin D.D. *A Complete History of Connecticut: Civil and Ecclesiastical*. New Haven: Maltby, Goldsmith, 1818.

Trumbull, James Russell. *History of Northampton Massachusetts: From Its Settlement in 1654*. Northampton: Press of Gazette, 1898.

Turnbull, Ralph G. *Jonathan Edwards the Preacher*. Grand Rapids: Baker Book House, 1958.

Van Dixhoorn, Chad B., ed. *Creeds, Confessions, and Catechisms: A Reader's Edition*. Wheaton, IL: Crossway, 2022. Scribd.

_____. *God's Ambassadors: The Westminster Assembly and the Reformation of the English Pulpit, 1643–1653*. Grand Rapids: Reformation Heritage Books, 2017. Scribd.

Van Engen, Abram. "A City on a Hill: The Bible and "Christian America." *Christian History Magazine* Issue 138. *America's Book: How the Bible Helped Shape a Nation*. 2021.

van Mastricht, Petrus. *Theoretical-Practical Theology: Prolegomena, vol. 1*. Edited by Joel R. Beeke. Translated by Todd M. Rester. Grand Rapids: Reformation Heritage Books, 2018. Kindle.

van Vliet, Jan. "William Ames: Marrow of the Theology and Piety of the Reformed Tradition." PhD diss., Westminster Theological Seminary, 2002.

Van Wyk, John Ray. "To Understand Things As Well As Words": An Examination of Jonathan Edwards As An Educator and His Pedagogical Methodology." PhD diss., Trinity Evangelical Divinity School, 2016.

Vaughan, Alden T., and Francis J. Bremer, Eds. *Puritan New England: Essays on Religion, Society, and Culture*. New York: St. Martin's Press, 1977.

Washington, George. "From George Washington to Jonathan Edwards, 28 August 1788." *Founders Online*, National Archives. Original source: *1 January 1788–23 September 1788*. Vol. 6, *The Papers of George Washington: Confederation Series*. Edited by W. W. Abbot. Charlottesville: University Press of Virginia, 1997.

Watkins, Owen C. *The Puritan Experience: Studies in Spiritual Autobiography*. New York: Schocken Books, 1972.

Weber, Donald. *Rhetoric and History in Revolutionary New England*. New York: Oxford University Press, 1988.

Wheeler, Rachel M. "Living Upon Hope: Mahicans and Missionaries, 1730–1760." PhD diss., Yale University, 1999.

_____. *To Live Upon Hope: Mohicans and Missionaries in the Eighteenth-Century Northeast*. Ithaca, NY: Cornell University Press, 2008. Kindle.

White, John. *A Way Unto the Tree of Life Discovered in Sundry Directions for the Profitable Reading of the Scriptures.* 1647. Reprint, Ann Arbor: *Early English Books Online Text Creation Partnership*, 2014.

Whitefield, George. *George Whitefield's Journals*. New ed. Edinburgh: Banner of Truth Trust, 1960.

Wilson, Patricia Anne. "The Theology of Grace in Jonathan Edwards." PhD diss., The University of Iowa, 1973.

Winship, George Parker. *The Cambridge Press 1638–1692: A Re-examination of the Evidence Concerning the Bay Psalm Book and the Eliot Indian Bible*. Freeport, NY: Book for Libraries Press, 1968.

Winslow, Ola Elizabeth. *Jonathan Edwards, 1703–1750: A Biography*. New York: Macmillan, 1940.

Wright, Thomas Goddard. *Literary Culture in Early New England: 1620–1730*. New Haven: Yale University Press, 1920.

Articles

Armstrong, April C. "Last Were the Mahicans," *Southwestern Journal of Theology* 48, no. 1, (Fall 2005): 26–27.

Burrus, Daniel W. "The Confessional Journey of John Owen." *The Westminster Theological Journal* 84, no. 1 (Spring 2022): 82–101.

Chamberlain, Ava. "The Grand Sower of the Seed: Jonathan Edwards's Critique of George Whitefield." *The New England Quarterly* 70, no. 3 (September 1997): 368–385.

_____. "The Execution of Moses Paul: A Story of Crime and Contact in Eighteenth-Century Connecticut," *The New England Quarterly* 77, no. 3 (September 2004): 414–450.

Cohen, Matt. "The History of the Book in New England: The State of the Discipline." *Book History* 11 (2008): 301–323.

Ehrhard, Jim. "A Critical Analysis of the Tradition of Jonathan Edwards as a Manuscript Preacher." *The Westminster Theological Journal* 60, no. 1 (Spring 1998): 71–84.

Fiering, Norman S. "Will and Intellect in the New England Mind." *The William and Mary Quarterly* 29, no. 4 (October 1972): 515–558.

Filson, David Owen. "Fit preaching: 'Fitness' in the Preaching of Jonathan Edwards." *Presbyterian* 31, no. 2 (Fall 2005): 89–100.

Fisher, George P. "The Elements of Puritanism." *The North American Review* 133, no. 299 (October 1881): 326–337.

Grimes, Mary Cochran. "Saving Grace Among Puritans and Quakers: A Study of 17th and 18th Century Conversion Experiences." *Quaker History* 72, no. 1 (Spring 1983): 3–26.

Gura, Philip F. "Notes on Edward Taylor from the Diaries of Stephen Williams." *American Literature* 34, no. 2 (May 1962): 270–274.

Hannah, John D. "The Homiletical Skill of Jonathan Edwards." *Bibliotheca Sacra* 159, no. 633 (January 2002): 96–107.

Heacock, Clint. "Rhetorical Influences Upon the Preaching of Jonathan Edwards." *The Journal of the Evangelical Homiletics Society* 12, no. 2 (September 2012): 11–30.

Jeon, Heejoon. "Jonathan Edwards and the Anti-Slavery Movement." *The Journal of the Evangelical Theological Society* 63, no. 4 (Dec. 2020): 773–788.

Kretzoi, Charlotte. "Attitude and Form: Puritan Style in 17th Century American Prose." *Hungarian Studies in English* 14 (1981): 57–68.

Laud. Leslie E. "Moral Education in America: 1600s-1800s." *The Journal of Education* 179, no. 2 (1997): 1–10.

Lim, Paul C.H. "A Pen in God's Hand." *Christian History* 89, Winter 2006. https://christianhistoryinstitute.org/magazine/article/pen-in-gods-hand.

Logan Jr., Samuel T. "The Hermeneutics of Jonathan Edwards." *The Westminster Theological Journal* 43, no. 1 (Fall 1980): 79–96.

Main, Gloria L. "An Inquiry into When and Why Women Learned to Write in Colonial New England." *Journal of Social History* 24, no. 3 (Spring 1991): 579–589.

Martin, Jan J. "William Tyndale, John Foxe, and the 'Boy That Driveth the Plough.'" *Religious Educator* 17, no. 2 (2016): 86–105.

McDermott, Gerald R. "Jonathan Edwards and American Indians: The Devil Sucks Their Blood." *The New England Quarterly* 72, no. 4 (December 1999): 539–557.

McKim, Donald K. "The Functions of Ramism in William Perkins' Theology." *The Sixteenth Century Journal* 16, no. 4 (Winter 1985): 503–517.

Minkema, Kenneth P., Catherine A. Brekus, and Harry S. Stout. "Agitations, Convulsions, Leaping, and Loud Talking: The 'Experiences' of Sarah

Pierpont Edwards." *The William and Mary Quarterly* 78, no. 3 (July 2021): 491–536.

_____. "A Chronology of Edwards' Life and Writings." Jonathan Edwards Center at Yale University.

Minkema, Kenneth P., and Harry S. Stout. "The Edwardsean Tradition and the Antislavery Debate, 1740–1756." *The Journal of American History* 92, no. 1 (June 2005): 47–74.

Minkema, Kenneth P. "Jonathan Edwards on Slavery and the Slave Trade." *The William and Mary Quarterly* 54, no. 4 (Oct. 1991): 823–834.

_____. "Jonathan Edwards' Defense of Slavery," *Massachusetts Historical Review* 4 (January 2002): 23–59.

Monaghan, E. Jennifer. "Family Literacy in early 18th-century Boston: Cotton Mather and His Children." *Reading Research Quarterly* 26, no. 4 (Autumn 1991): 342–370.

_____. "Literacy Instruction and Gender in Colonial New England." In "Reading in America," edited by Cathy M. Davidson. Special issue, *American Quarterly* 40, no. 1 (1988): 18–41.

_____. "She Loved to Read in Good Books." *History of Education Quarterly* 30, no. 4 (Winter 1990): 492–521.

Paul, Robert S. "The Accidence and the Essence of Puritan Piety." *Austin Seminary Bulletin*, XCIII, no. 8 (May 1978): 5–45.

Perlmann, Joel, and Dennis Shirley. "When Did New England Women Acquire Literacy?" *The William and Mary Quarterly* 48, no. 1 (January 1991): 50–67.

Perlmann, Joel, Silvana R. Siddali, and Keith Whitescarver. "Literacy, Schooling, and Teaching among New England Women, 1730–1820." *History of Education Quarterly* 37, no. 2, Special Issue on Education in Early America (Summer 1997): 117–139.

Renihan, James M. "God Freely Justifieth... By Imputing Christ's Active... And Passive Obedience." *The Master's Journal* 32, no. 1 (Spring 2021): 61–75.

Silverman, David J. "Indians, Missionaries, and Religious Translation: Creating Wampanoag Christianity in Seventeenth-Century Martha's Vineyard." *The William and Mary Quarterly* 62, no. 2 (April 2005): 141–174.

Sprunger, Keith L. "Ames, Ramus, and the Method of Puritan Theology." *The Harvard Theological Review* 59, no. 2 (April 1966): 133–151.

Sweeney, Douglas A. "Jonathan Edwards, The Harmony of Scripture, and Canonical Exegesis." *Trinity Journal* 34, no. 2 (Fall 2013): 171–207.

Vinovskis, Maris A. "Introduction: Explorations in Early American Education." In "On Education in Early America." Special Issue, *History of Education Quarterly* 37, no. 2 (Summer 1997): 111–116.

Wheeler, Rachel M. "Lessons from Stockbridge: Jonathan Edwards and the Stockbridge Indians." In *Jonathan Edwards at 300: Essays on the Tercentenary of His Birth*, edited by Harry S. Stout, Kenneth P. Minkema, and Caleb J.D. Maskell, 131–40. Lanham, MD: University Press of America, 2005.

Winiarski, Douglas L. "Jonathan Edwards, Enthusiast? Radical Revivalism and the Great Awakening in the Connecticut Valley." *Church History* 74, no. 4 (December 2005): 683–739.

Index

Below is a brief index of significant names and topics.

www.ingramcontent.com/pod-product-compliance
Lightning Source LLC
LaVergne TN
LVHW020707110826
845149LV00012B/2150

* 9 7 9 8 9 9 4 5 9 3 3 1 8 *